Pro TypeScript

Application-Scale JavaScript Development

Second Edition

Steve Fenton

Apress®

Pro TypeScript: Application-Scale JavaScript Development

Steve Fenton
Basingstoke, United Kingdom

ISBN-13 (pbk): 978-1-4842-3248-4   ISBN-13 (electronic): 978-1-4842-3249-1
https://doi.org/10.1007/978-1-4842-3249-1

Library of Congress Control Number: 2017961729

Cover image designed by Freepik

Managing Director: Welmoed Spahr
Editorial Director: Todd Green
Acquisitions Editor: Gwenan Spearing
Development Editor: Laura Berendson
Technical Reviewer: Rich O'Kelly, Martin Milsom, Dan Horrocks-Burgess, Jamie Wright
Coordinating Editor: Nancy Chen
Copy Editor: Karen Jameson
Compositor: SPi Global
Indexer: SPi Global
Artist: SPi Global

Distributed to the book trade worldwide by Springer Science+Business Media New York, 233 Spring Street, 6th Floor, New York, NY 10013. Phone 1-800-SPRINGER, fax (201) 348-4505, e-mail orders-ny@springer-sbm.com, or visit www.springeronline.com. Apress Media, LLC is a California LLC and the sole member (owner) is Springer Science + Business Media Finance Inc (SSBM Finance Inc). SSBM Finance Inc is a **Delaware** corporation.

For information on translations, please e-mail rights@apress.com, or visit http://www.apress.com/rights-permissions.

Apress titles may be purchased in bulk for academic, corporate, or promotional use. eBook versions and licenses are also available for most titles. For more information, reference our Print and eBook Bulk Sales web page at http://www.apress.com/bulk-sales.

Any source code or other supplementary material referenced by the author in this book is available to readers on GitHub via the book's product page, located at www.apress.com/9781484232484. For more detailed information, please visit http://www.apress.com/source-code.

Printed on acid-free paper

For Rebecca, Lily, Deborah, Victoria, and Mum

Contents

About the Author

Steve Fenton is the Principal Developer at Profound Works. He has been sharing his passion for TypeScript since October 2012, presenting at developer meet-ups, running training sessions, and answering questions on Stack Overflow. He has worked on large-scale JavaScript applications for over 14 years, and with TypeScript for over 5 years. In his spare time, he writes unit-testing frameworks, behavior-driven development frameworks, and web crawlers. He lives in Basingstoke, United Kingdom, with his wife Rebecca and daughter Lily, and enjoys studying psychology and philosophy.

Acknowledgments

A book is enjoyable when you work with the right people, and those people are Gwenan Spearing at Apress and my smart technical reviewers Rich O'Kelly, Martin Milsom, Dan Horrocks-Burgess, and Jamie Wright. I am incredibly grateful to Nancy Chen for being so patient with my sporadic writing habits, last-minute changes, and vague estimates.

This second edition would not have been possible without the contributions of all the smart people that helped create the first book; Mark Jones, Mark Rendle, Basarat Ali Syed, Christine Ricketts, Boris Yankov, Diullei Gomes, Masahiro Wakame, Jason Jarrett, Bart van der Schoor, John Reilly, Igor Oleinikov, Luke Hoban, Jonathan Turner, and of course - Ryan Cavanaugh.

I am also grateful to all of my amazing colleagues, past and present, who inspire me to keep learning and growing.

Introduction

Atwood's Law: any application that can be written in JavaScript will eventually be written in JavaScript.

—Jeff Atwood

TypeScript is a language created and maintained by Microsoft, and released under an open-source Apache 2.0 License (2004). The language is focused on making the development of JavaScript programs scale to many thousands of lines of code. In fact, Microsoft has written both the Azure Management Portal (1.2 million lines of code) and the Visual Studio Code editor (300,000 lines of code) in TypeScript. The language attacks the large-scale JavaScript programming problem by offering better design-time tooling, compile-time checking, and dynamic module loading at runtime.

As you might expect from a language created by Microsoft, there is excellent support for TypeScript within Visual Studio, but plenty of other development tools have also added support for the language, including VS Code, WebStorm, Eclipse, Sublime Text, Vi, Atom, IntelliJ, and Emacs among others. The widespread support from these tools as well as the permissive open-source license makes TypeScript a viable option outside of the traditional Microsoft ecosystem.

The TypeScript language is a typed superset of JavaScript, which is compiled to plain JavaScript in the flavor of your choosing. This makes programs written in TypeScript highly portable as they can run on almost any machine — in web browsers, on web servers, and even in native applications on operating systems that expose a JavaScript API, such as WinJS.

The language features found in TypeScript can be divided into three categories based on their relationship to JavaScript (see Figure 1). The first two sets are related to versions of the ECMA-262 ECMAScript Language Specification, which is the official specification for JavaScript. The ECMAScript 5 specification forms the basis of TypeScript and supplies the largest number of features in the language. Subsequent versions of the ECMAScript specification are rolled into TypeScript releases, often as early previews that feature down-level compilation to older versions of the specication. The third and final set of language features includes items that are not planned to become part of the ECMAScript standard, such as generics and type annotations. All the additional features of TypeScript can be output to a number of widely supported versions of JavaScript.

TypeScript has several native frameworks, including Angular, Ionic, RxJs 5, and Dojo 2. Additionally, because TypeScript is such a close relative of JavaScript, you can consume the myriad of existing libraries and frameworks written in JavaScript; Aurelia, Backbone, Bootstrap, Durandal, jQuery, Knockout, Modernizr, PhoneGap, Prototype, Raphael, React, Underscore, Vue, and many more are all usable in TypeScript programs. Correspondingly, once your TypeScript program has been compiled it can be consumed from any JavaScript program too.

TypeScript's similarity to JavaScript is beneficial if you already have experience with JavaScript or other C-like languages. The similarity also aids the debugging process as the generated JavaScript correlates closely to the original TypeScript code. Source maps can also be generated to aid debugging, with browser developer tools displaying your TypeScript code during in-browser debugging.

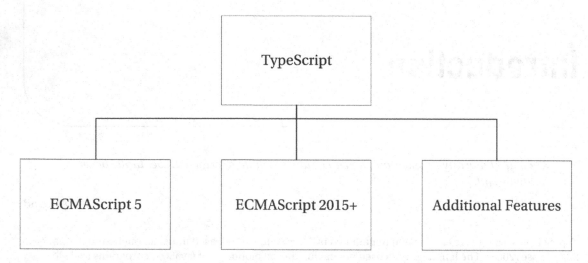

Figure 1. *TypeScript language feature sources*

If you still need to be convinced about using TypeScript or need help convincing others, I summarize the benefits of the language as well as the problems it can solve in the following sections. I also include an introduction to the components of TypeScript and some of the alternatives. If you would rather get started with the language straight away, you can skip straight to Chapter 1.

Who This Book Is For

This book is for programmers and architects working on large-scale JavaScript programs, either running in a browser, on a server, or on an operating system that exposes a JavaScript API. Previous experience with JavaScript or another C-like language is useful when reading this book, as well as a working knowledge of object orientation and design patterns, although I'll cover some aspects of this in detail later.

Structure

This book is organized into ten chapters and four appendices.

Chapter 1: TypeScript Language Features: describes the language features in detail, from simple type annotations to important structural elements, with stand-alone examples of how to use each one.

Chapter 2: Code Organization: clarifies how code can be organized, loaded, and packaged with a view to growing your program to millions of lines of code.

Chapter 3: The Type System: explains the details of working within TypeScript's structural type system and describes the details on type erasure, type inference, and ambient declarations.

Chapter 4: Object Orientation in TypeScript: introduces the important elements of object orientation and contains examples of design patterns and SOLID principles in TypeScript. This chapter also introduces the concept of mixins with practical examples.

Chapter 5: Understanding the Runtime: describes the impact of scope, callbacks, events, and extensions on your program.

Chapter 6: Running TypeScript in a Browser: a thorough walkthrough including working with the Document Object Model, AJAX, session and local storage, IndexedDB, geolocation, hardware sensors, and web workers as well as information on packaging your program for the Web.

Chapter 7: Running TypeScript on a Server: an explanation of running programs on a JavaScript server with examples for Node and a basic end-to-end example application written in Express and Mongoose.

Chapter 8: Exceptions, Memory, and Performance: describes exceptions and exception handling with information on memory management and garbage collection. It includes a simple performance testing utility to exercise and measure your program.

Chapter 9: Using JavaScript Libraries: explains how to consume any of the millions of JavaScript libraries from within your TypeScript program, including information on how to create your own type definitions and how to migrate your JavaScript program to TypeScript.

Chapter 10: Automated Testing: a walkthrough of automated testing in your TypeScript program with examples written using the Jest framework.

Appendix 1: JavaScript Quick Reference: an introduction to the essential JavaScript features for anyone who needs to brush up on their JavaScript before diving into TypeScript.

Appendix 2: TypeScript Compiler: explains how to use the compiler on the command line and describes many of the flags you can pass to customize your build.

Appendix 3: Bitwise Flags: dives into the details of bitwise flags including the low-level details of how they work as well as examples using TypeScript enumerations.

Appendix 4: Coding Katas: introduces the concept of coding katas and provides an example for you to try, along with techniques you can use to make katas more effective.

The TypeScript Components

TypeScript is made up of three distinct but complementary parts, which are shown in Figure 2.

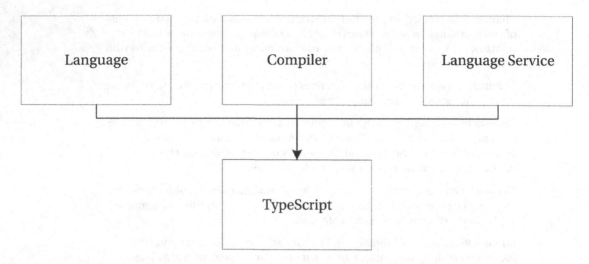

Figure 2. *The TypeScript components*

The language consists of the new syntax, keywords, and type annotations. As a programmer, the language will be the component you will become most familiar with. Understanding how to supply type information is an important foundation for the other components because the compiler and language service are most effective when they understand the complex structures you use within your program.

The compiler performs the type erasure and code transformations that convert your TypeScript code into JavaScript. It will emit warnings and errors if it detects problems and can perform additional tasks such as combining the output into a single file, generating source maps, and more.

The language service provides type information that can be used by development tools to supply autocompletion, type hinting, refactoring options, and other creative features based on the type information that has been gathered from your program.

Compile or Transpile?

The term *transpiling* has been around since the last century, but there is some confusion about its meaning. In particular, there has been some confusion between the terms compilation and transpilation. Compilation describes the process of taking source code written in one language and converting it into another language. Transpilation is a specific kind of compilation and describes the process of taking source code written in one language and transforming it into another language *with a similar level of abstraction*. So, you might compile a high-level language into an assembly language, but you would transpile TypeScript to JavaScript as they are similarly abstracted.

Other common examples of transpilation include C++ to C, CoffeeScript to JavaScript, Dart to JavaScript, and PHP to C++.

Which Problems Does TypeScript Solve?

Since its first beta release in 1995, JavaScript (or LiveScript as it was known at the time it was released) has spread like wildfire. Nearly every computer in the world has a JavaScript interpreter installed. Although it is perceived as a browser-based scripting language, JavaScript has been running on web servers since its inception, supported on Netscape Enterprise Server, IIS (since 1996), and on Node since 2011. JavaScript can even be used to write native applications on operating systems such as Windows.

Despite its popularity, it hasn't received much respect from developers — possibly because it contains many snares and traps that can entangle a large program much like the tar pit pulling the mammoth to its death, as described by Fred Brooks (1975). If you are a professional programmer working with large applications written in JavaScript, you will almost certainly have rubbed up against problems once your program chalked up a few thousand lines. You may have experienced naming conflicts, substandard programming tools, complex modularization, unfamiliar prototypal inheritance that makes it hard to reuse common design patterns easily, and difficulty keeping a readable and maintainable code base. TypeScript solves problems such as these.

Because JavaScript has a C-like syntax, it looks familiar to most programmers. This is one of JavaScript's key strengths, but it is also the cause of many surprises, especially in the following areas:

- Prototypal inheritance

- Equality and type juggling

- Management of modules

- Scope

- Lack of types

Typescript solves or eases these problems in several ways. Each of these topics is discussed in this introduction.

Prototypal Inheritance

Prototype-based programming is a style of object-oriented programming that is mainly found in interpreted dynamic languages. It was first used in a language called Self, created by David Ungar and Randall Smith in 1986, but it has been used in a selection of languages since then. Of these prototypal languages, JavaScript is by far the most widely known, although this has done little to bring prototypal inheritance into the mainstream. Despite its validity, prototype-based programming is somewhat esoteric; class-based object orientation is far more commonplace and will be familiar to most programmers.

TypeScript solves this problem by adding classes, namespaces, modules, and interfaces. This allows programmers to transfer their existing knowledge of objects and code structure from other languages, including implementing interfaces, inheritance, and code organization. Classes and modules are an early preview of JavaScript proposals and because TypeScript can compile to earlier versions of JavaScript, it allows you to use these features independent of support for the newer ECMAScript specifications. All these features are described in detail in Chapter 1.

Equality and Type Juggling

JavaScript has always supported dynamically typed variables, and as a result it expends effort at runtime working out types and coercing them into other types on the fly to make statements work that in a statically typed language would cause an error.

The most common type coercions involve strings, numbers, and Boolean target types. Whenever you attempt to concatenate a value with a string, the value will be converted to a string, if you perform a mathematical operation an attempt will be made to turn the value into a number, and if you use any value in a logical operation there are special rules that determine whether the result will be true or false. When an automatic type conversion occurs, it is commonly referred to as *type juggling*.

In some cases, type juggling can be a useful feature, in particular in creating shorthand logical expressions. In other cases, type juggling hides an accidental use of different types and causes unintended behavior as discussed in Chapter 1. A common JavaScript example is shown in Listing 1.

Listing 1. Type juggling

```
const num = 1;
const str = '0';

// result is '10' not 1
const strTen = num + str;

// result is 20
const result = strTen * 2;
```

TypeScript gracefully solves this problem by introducing type checking, which can provide warnings at design and compile time to pick up potential unintended juggling. Even in cases where it allows implicit type coercion, the result will be assigned the correct type. This prevents dangerous assumptions from going undetected. This feature is covered in detail in Chapter 3.

The introduction of types in TypeScript does not preclude the use of dynamic types. You can choose when to use types, and when to go without them. TypeScript does not force you to do anything, it is just there to help.

Management of Modules

If you have worked with JavaScript, it is likely that you will have come across a dependency problem. Some of the common problems include the following:

- Forgetting to add a script tag to a web page

- Adding scripts to a web page in the wrong order

- Finding out you have added scripts that aren't used

There is also a series of issues you may have come across if you are using tools to combine your scripts into a single file to reduce network requests or if you minify your scripts to lower bandwidth usage.

- Combining scripts into a single script in the wrong order

- Finding out that your chosen minification tool doesn't understand single-line comments

- Trying to debug combined and minified scripts

You may have already solved some of these issues using module loading, as the pattern is gaining traction in the JavaScript community. However, TypeScript makes module loaders the default way of working and allows your modules to be compiled to suit the most prevalent module loading styles without requiring changes to your code. The details of module loading in web browsers are covered in Chapter 6 and on the server in Chapter 7.

Scope

In most modern C-like languages, the curly braces create a new context for scope. A variable declared inside a set of curly braces cannot be seen outside of that block. JavaScript has bucked this trend traditionally by being functionally scoped, which means blocks defined by curly braces have no effect on scope. Instead, variables are scoped to the function they are declared in, or the global scope if they are not declared within a function. There can be further complications caused by the accidental omission of the var keyword within a function, thus promoting the variable into the global scope. More complications are caused by *variable hoisting*, resulting in all variables within a function behaving as if they were declared at the top of the function.

The introduction of the const and let variable declarations have gone some way to solving this problem, and if you are starting from a clean sheet you can avoid the older var variable declaration altogether.

Despite some tricky surprises with scope, JavaScript does provide a powerful mechanism that wraps the current lexical scope around a function declaration to keep values to hand when the function is later executed. These closures are one of the most powerful features in JavaScript.

TypeScript eases scope problems by warning you about implicit global variables, provided you avoid adding variables to the global scope. This safety net is demonstrated in Listing 2.

Listing 2. Accidental global scope error

```
function process() {
    // Error! Cannot find name 'accidentalGlobal;
    accidentalGlobal = 5;
}
```

Lack of Types

The problem with JavaScript isn't that it has no types, because each variable does have a type; it is just that the type can be changed by each assignment. A variable may start off as a string, but an assignment can change it to a number, an object, or even a function. The real problem here is that the development tools cannot be improved beyond a reasonable guess about the type of a variable. If the development tools don't know the types, the autocompletion and type hinting is often too general to be useful.

By formalizing type information, TypeScript allows development tools to supply specific contextual help that otherwise would not be possible.

Which Problems Are Not Solved?

> *TypeScript is not a crutch any more than JSLint is a crutch. It doesn't hide JavaScript (as CoffeeScript tends to do).*

—Ward Bell

TypeScript remains largely faithful to JavaScript. The TypeScript specification adds many language features, but it doesn't attempt to change the ultimate style and behavior of the JavaScript language. It is just as important for TypeScript programmers to embrace the idiosyncrasies of the runtime as it is for JavaScript programmers. The aim of the TypeScript language is to make large-scale JavaScript programs manageable and maintainable. No attempt has been made to twist JavaScript development into the style of C#, Java, Ruby, Python, or any other language (although it has taken inspiration from many languages).

Prerequisites

To benefit from the features of TypeScript, you'll need access to an integrated development environment that supports the syntax and compiler. The examples in this book were written using Visual Studio 2017, but you can use VS Code, WebStorm/PHPStorm, Eclipse, Sublime Text, Vi, Emacs, or any other development tools that support the language; you can even try many of the simpler examples on the TypeScript Playground provided by Microsoft. I often use the TypeScript Playground when answering questions on the language.

From the Visual Studio 2013 Spring Update (Update 2), TypeScript is a first-class language in Visual Studio. Prior to this, an additional extension needed to be installed. Although the examples in this book are shown in Visual Studio, you can use any of the development tools that were listed above. In particular, Visual Studio Code is a free cross-platform editor with native TypeScript support - so you can write your TypeScript code on any machine you have on hand, regardless of the operating system.

It is also worth downloading and installing Node (which is required to follow many of the examples) as it will allow you to access the Node Package Manager and the thousands of modules and utilities available through it. For example, you can use task runners such as Grunt and Gulp to watch your TypeScript files and compile them automatically each time you change them if your development tools don't do this for you.

Node is free and can be downloaded for multiple platforms from the official Node website.

```
https://nodejs.org/
```

To avoid being greatly sidetracked, I have avoided using any task runners to perform additional operations outside of Visual Studio, but once you have mastered TypeScript you will almost certainly want to add a task runner, such as Gulp or Grunt, to your development workflow. I have referenced some web dependencies from the node_modules folder in the examples in this book; but on a real-world project I would use a task runner to lift and shift the website dependencies into a different folder that I would be happy to deploy to a web server. The node_modules folder often contains a great deal of files that I would not deploy to a web server.

TypeScript Alternatives

TypeScript is not the only alternative to writing to plain JavaScript.

The strongest TypeScript alternative is Babel, a compiler that exposes the latest ECMAScript features with plugins for down-level compilation and polyfills to make your program work in current browsers. The aim of the Babel project is to make the latest features available much sooner than they otherwise would be, but Babel doesn't introduce compile-time type checking. Babel also features in many TypeScript workflows, where Babel is executed after the TypeScript compiler, rather than using TypeScript to perform the down-level compilation. You can read about Babel on the official website:

```
https://babeljs.io/
```

For a number of years, CoffeeScript was a popular alternative with a terse syntax that compiles to sensible JavaScript code. CoffeeScript doesn't offer many of the additional features that TypeScript offers, such as static type checking. It is also a very different language to JavaScript, which means you need to translate snippets of code you find online into CoffeeScript to use them. In 2017, however, CoffeeScript reached the top three "most dreaded languages" in the Stack Overflow developer survey (next to VBA, and Visual Basic 6). In the same survey, TypeScript landed in the top three most loved languages. You can find out more about CoffeeScript on the official website:

```
http://coffeescript.org/
```

Another alternative is Google's Dart language. Dart has much in common with TypeScript. It is class-based, object oriented, and offers optional types that can be checked by a static checker. Dart was originally conceived as a replacement for JavaScript, and was only intended to be compiled to JavaScript to provide wide support in the short term while native support for Dart was added to browsers.

It seems unlikely at this stage that Dart will get the kind of browser support that JavaScript has won, so the compile-to-JavaScript mechanism will likely remain core to Dart's future in the web browser. The decision by Google to adopt TypeScript for the Angular project may be indicative of their commitment to Dart, although it is still described as a long-term project. You can read about Dart on the official website for the language:

```
https://www.dartlang.org/
```

There are also converters that will compile from most languages to JavaScript, including C#, Ruby, Java, and Haskell. These may appeal to programmers who are uncomfortable stepping outside of their primary programming language.

It is also worth bearing in mind that for small applications and web page widgets, you can defer the decision and write the code in plain JavaScript. With TypeScript in particular, there is no penalty for starting in JavaScript as you can simply paste your JavaScript code into a TypeScript file later on to make the switch. Equally, there is little penalty for writing small programs in TypeScript, especially if you already have a workflow in place to generate combined or minified files each time you save your application.

Summary

TypeScript is an application-scale programming language that provides early access to proposed new JavaScript features and powerful additional features like static type checking. You can write TypeScript programs to run in web browsers or on servers and you can reuse code between browser and server applications.

TypeScript solves many problems in JavaScript, but it respects the patterns and implementation of the underlying JavaScript language, for example, the ability to have dynamic types.

You can use many integrated development environments with TypeScript, with several providing first-class support including type checking and autocompletion that will improve your productivity and help eliminate mistakes at design time.

Key Points

- TypeScript is a language, a compiler, and a language service.

- You can paste existing JavaScript into your TypeScript program.

- Compiling from TypeScript to JavaScript is known specifically as transpiling.

- TypeScript is not the only alternative way of writing JavaScript, but it has gained incredible traction in its first five years.

CHAPTER 1

■ ■ ■

TypeScript Language Features

What if we could strengthen JavaScript with the things that are missing for large scale application development, like static typing, classes [and] modules... that's what TypeScript is about.

—Anders Hejlsberg

TypeScript is a superset of JavaScript. That means that the TypeScript language includes the entire JavaScript language plus a collection of useful additional features. This contrasts with the various subsets of JavaScript and the various linting tools that seek to reduce the available features to create a smaller language with fewer surprises. This chapter will introduce you to the extra language features, starting with simple type annotations and progressing to more advanced features and structural elements of TypeScript. This chapter doesn't cover every feature included in the ECMAScript language specification, so if you need a refresher on JavaScript, take a look at Appendix 1.

One important thing to remember is that all the standard control structures found in JavaScript are immediately available within a TypeScript program. This includes the following:

- Control flows

- Data types

- Operators

- Subroutines

The basic building blocks of your program will come from JavaScript, including if statements, switch statements, loops, arithmetic, logical tests, and functions. This is one of the key strengths of TypeScript — it is based on a language (and a family of languages) that is already familiar to a vast and varied collection of programmers. JavaScript is thoroughly documented not only in the ECMA-262 specification, but also in books, on developer network portals, forums, and question-and-answer websites. When features are added to JavaScript, they will also appear in TypeScript.

The TypeScript compiler is typically updated with new JavaScript features early in their specification. Most of the features are available before browsers support them. In many cases, you can use the features in your TypeScript program as the compiler will convert them into code that targets the older versions of the ECMAScript standard.

Each of the language features discussed in this chapter has short, self-contained code examples that put the feature in context. For the purposes of introducing and explaining features, the examples are short and to the point; this allows the chapter to be read end to end. However, this also means you can refer back to the chapter as a reference later on. Once you have read this chapter, you should know everything you will need to understand the more complex examples described throughout the rest of the book.

© Steve Fenton 2018
S. Fenton, *Pro TypeScript*, https://doi.org/10.1007/978-1-4842-3249-1_1

JavaScript Is Valid TypeScript

Before we find out more about the TypeScript syntax, it is worth stressing one important fact: All JavaScript is valid TypeScript. You don't need to discard any of your JavaScript know-how as it can all be transferred directly to your TypeScript code. You can take existing JavaScript code, add it to a TypeScript file, and all the statements will be valid. There is a subtle difference between valid code and error-free code in TypeScript; because, although your code may work, the TypeScript compiler will warn you about any potential problems it has detected. Finding subtle and previously undetected bugs is a common story shared by programmers making the transition to TypeScript.

If you transfer a JavaScript listing into a TypeScript file, you may receive errors or warnings even though the code is considered valid. A common example comes from the dynamic type system in JavaScript wherein it is perfectly acceptable to assign values of different types to the same variable during its lifetime. TypeScript detects these assignments and generates errors to warn you that the type of the variable has been changed by the assignment. Because this is a common cause of errors in a program, you can correct the error by creating separate variables, by performing a type assertion, or by making the variable dynamic. There is further information on type annotations later in this chapter, and the type system is discussed in detail in Chapter 3.

Unlike some compilers that will only create output where no compilation errors are detected, the TypeScript compiler will still attempt to generate sensible JavaScript code. The TypeScript code shown in Listing 1-1 generates an error, but the JavaScript output is still produced. This is an admirable feature, but as always with compiler warnings and errors, you should correct the problem in your source code and get a clean compilation. If you routinely ignore these messages, your program will eventually exhibit unexpected behavior. In some cases, your listing may contain errors that are so severe that the TypeScript compiler won't be able to generate the JavaScript output.

■ **Caution**   The only exceptions to the "all JavaScript is valid TypeScript" rule are the `with` statement and vendor-specific extensions, until they are formally added to the ECMAScript specification. You could technically still use the `with` statement, but all statements within the block would be unchecked.

The JavaScript `with` statement in Listing 1-1 shows two examples of the same routine. Although the first calls `Math.PI` explicitly, the second uses a `with` statement, which adds the properties and functions of `Math` to the current scope. Statements nested inside the `with` statement can omit the `Math` prefix and call properties and functions directly, for example, the `PI` property or the `floor` function.

At the end of the `with` statement, the original lexical scope is restored, so subsequent calls outside of the `with` block must use the `Math` prefix.

Listing 1-1. Using JavaScript's "with" statement

```
// Not using with
const radius1 = 4;
const area1 = Math.PI * radius1 * radius1;

// Using with
const radius2 = 4;
with (Math) {
    const area2 = PI * radius2 * radius2;
}
```

The with statement was not allowed in strict mode in ECMAScript 5 and later versions of ECMAScript use strict mode by default for classes and modules. TypeScript treats with statements as an error and will treat all types within the with statement as dynamic types. This is due to the following:

- The fact it is disallowed in strict mode.

- The general opinion that the with statement is dangerous.

- The practical issues of determining the identifiers that are in scope at compile time.

So, with these minor exceptions to the rule in mind, you can place any valid JavaScript into a TypeScript file and it will be valid TypeScript. As an example, here is the area calculation script transferred to a TypeScript file.

■ **Note** The ECMAScript 6 specification, also known as "ES6 Harmony," represented a substantial change to the JavaScript language. The specification has been divided into annual chunks, released as ECMAScript 2015, ECMAScript 2016, and so on.

Listing 1-2. Transferring JavaScript in to a TypeScript file

```
const radius = 4;
const area = Math.PI * radius * radius;
```

In Listing 1-2, the statements are just plain JavaScript, but in TypeScript the variables radius and area will both benefit from type inference. Because radius is initialized with the value 4, it can be inferred that the type of radius is number. With just a slight increase in effort, the result of multiplying Math.PI, which is known to be a number, with the radius variable that has been inferred to be a number, it is possible to infer the type of area is also a number.

With type inference at work, assignments can be checked for type safety. Figure 1-1 shows how an unsafe assignment is detected when a string is assigned to the radius variable. There is a more detailed explanation of type inference in Chapter 3. For now, rest assured that type inference is a good thing, and it will save you a lot of effort.

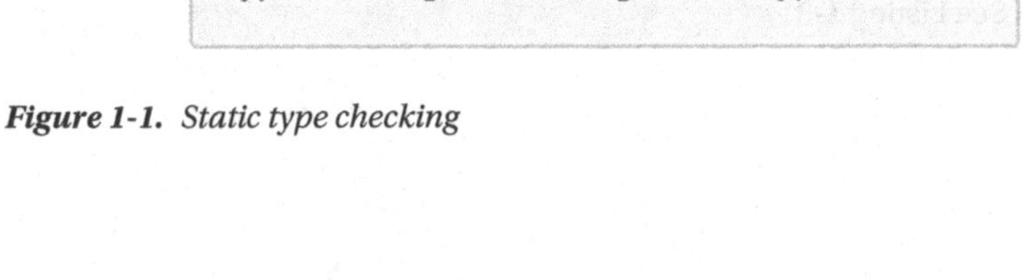

```
1    let radius = 4;
2    const area = Math.PI * radius * radius;
3
4    radius = 'A string'
```

[●] let radius: number

Type '"A string"' is not assignable to type 'number'.

Figure 1-1. *Static type checking*

Variables

TypeScript variables must follow the JavaScript naming rules. The identifier used to name a variable must satisfy the following conditions.

The first character must be one of the following:

- an uppercase letter

- a lowercase letter

- an underscore

- a dollar sign

- a Unicode character from categories—*Uppercase letter* (Lu), *Lowercase letter* (Ll), *Title case letter* (Lt), *Modifier letter* (Lm), *Other letter* (Lo), or *Letter number* (Nl)

Subsequent characters follow the same rule and additionally allow the following:

- numeric digits

- a Unicode character from categories—*Non-spacing mark* (Mn), *Spacing combining mark* (Mc), *Decimal digit number* (Nd), or *Connector punctuation* (Pc)

- the Unicode characters U+200C (Zero Width Non-Joiner) and U+200D (Zero Width Joiner)

You can test a variable identifier for conformance to the naming rules using the JavaScript variable name validator by Mathias Bynens.

```
http://mothereff.in/js-variables
```

■ **Note**   The availability of some of the more exotic characters can allow some interesting identifiers. You should consider whether this kind of variable name causes more problems than it solves. For example, this is valid JavaScript: `const ʘ_ʘ = 'Dignified';`

Variables declared with `const` or `let` are block scoped, whereas variables declared with the older `var` keyword are function scoped. If you omit these keywords, you are implicitly (and perhaps accidentally) declaring the variable in the global scope. It is advisable to reduce the number of variables you add to the global scope, as they are at risk of name collisions. You can avoid the global scope by declaring variables local to their use, such as within functions, modules, namespaces, classes, or a simple set of curly braces if you are using the block-scoped keywords.

When you limit the scope of a variable, it means it cannot be manipulated from outside of the scope of which it was created. The scope follows a nesting rule that allows a variable to be used in the current scope, and in inner nested scopes – but not outside. In other words, you can use variables declared in the current scope and variables from wider scopes. See Listing 1-3.

Listing 1-3. Block scope

```
let globalScope = 1;

{
    let blockScope = 2;

    // OK. This is from a wider scope
    globalScope = 100;

    // Error! This is outside of the scope the variable is declared in
    nestedBlockScope = 300;

    {
        let nestedBlockScope = 3;

        // OK. This is from a wider scope
        globalScope = 1000;

        // OK. This is from a wider scope
        blockScope = 2000;
    }
}
```

TypeScript catches scope violations and will warn you when you attempt to access a variable that is declared in a narrower scope. You can help the compiler to help you by avoiding a valid, but often accidental coding style of reusing a name in a different scope. In Listing 1-4, the logging statements work correctly, with both firstName variables being preserved separately. This means the original variable is not overwritten by the nested variable with the same name.

Listing 1-4. Name reuse with let

```
let firstName = 'Chris';

{
    let firstName = 'Tudor';

    console.log('Name 1: ' + firstName);
}

console.log('Name 2: ' + firstName);
// Output:
// Name 1: Tudor
// Name 2: Chris
```

If in place of the let keyword the var keyword had been used, both logging statements would show the name "Tudor," as shown in Listing 1-5. Despite both variables appearing to be a separate declaration, only one variable named firstName exists, and it is overwritten by the nested scope.

Listing 1-5. Name reuse with var

```
var firstName = 'Chris';

{
    var firstName = 'Tudor';

    console.log('Name 1: ' + firstName);
}

console.log('Name 2: ' + firstName);

// Output:
// Name 1: Tudor
// Name 2: Tudor
```

Based on this example, you could decide whether you want let-flavored scope, or var-flavored scope for the variable whose name you reuse; or you can use better variable names to avoid relying on either behavior.

Constants

Constants are variables that follow the scope rules of the let keyword, but that cannot be reassigned. When you declare a variable with the const keyword, you can't later assign a new value to the variable. It is important to note that this doesn't make the variable immutable, as you can see in Listing 1-6. Direct assignments after a constant is declared are not allowed, but the value within the constant can be mutated, for example, by calling methods on the value already assigned, or by adding items in the case of an array

Listing 1-6. Constants

```
const name = 'Lily';

// Error! Cannot assign to name because it is a constant
name = 'Princess Sparkles';

const digits = [1, 2, 3];

// Mutable - this changes the value of digits without using an assignment
digits.push(4, 5, 6);
```

The recommended coding style is to start by using the const keyword for all variables, and open a variable to reassignment with the let keyword if you decide to allow it. Constants reduce code complexity by following the principle of least privilege as you don't need to continue scanning the program to see whether a later assignment will change the value; but be aware that the variable is not immutable and can be changed in other ways.

Types

TypeScript is optionally statically typed; this means that types are checked automatically to prevent accidental assignments of invalid values. It is possible to opt out of this by declaring dynamic variables. Static type checking reduces errors caused by accidental misuse of types. You can also create types to replace primitive types to prevent parameter ordering errors, as described in Chapter 3. Most important, static typing allows development tools to provide intelligent autocompletion.

Figure 1-2 shows autocompletion that is aware of the variable type, and supplies a relevant list of options. It also shows the extended information known about the properties and methods in the autocompletion list. Contextual autocompletion is useful enough for primitive types — but most reasonable integrated development environments can replicate simple inference even in a JavaScript file. However, in a program with many custom types, modules, and classes, the deep type knowledge of the TypeScript Language Service means you will have sensible autocompletion throughout your entire program.

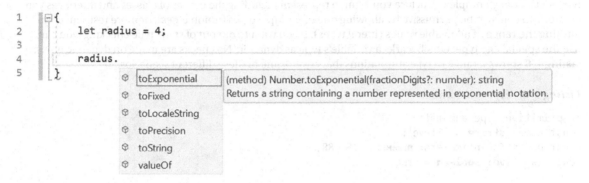

Figure 1-2. *TypeScript autocompletion*

Type Annotations

Although the TypeScript language service is expert at inferring types automatically, there are times when it can't fathom your intentions. There will also be times where you will wish to make a type explicit for safety or to narrow the type. In these cases, you can use a type annotation to specify the type.

For a variable, the type annotation comes after the identifier and is preceded by a colon. Figure 1-3 shows the combinations that result in a typed variable. The combinations are shown in order of preference with the first being most desirable. The least preferable is the most verbose style of both adding a type annotation and assigning the value. Although this is the style shown in many examples in this chapter, in practice this is the one you will use the least.

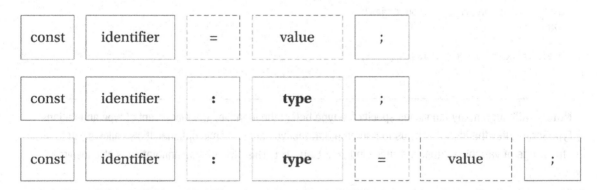

Figure 1-3. *Typed variable combinations*

To demonstrate type annotations in code, Listing 1-7 shows an example of a variable that has an explicit type annotation that marks the variable as a string. Primitive types are the simplest form of type annotation, but you are not restricted to such simple types.

Listing 1-7. Explicit type annotation

```
const name: string = 'Steve';
```

The type used to specify an annotation can be a primitive type, an array type, a function signature, a type alias, or any complex structure you want to represent including the names of classes and interfaces you create. You can also be permissive by allowing one of multiple types (union types), or more restrictive by limiting the range of allowable values (literal types). If you want to opt out of static type checking, you can use the special any type, which marks a variable's type as dynamic. No checks are made on dynamic types. Listing 1-8 shows a range of type annotations that cover some of these different scenarios.

Listing 1-8. Type annotations

```
// primitive type annotation
const name: string = 'Steve';
const heightInCentimeters: number = 182.88;
const isActive: boolean = true;

// array type annotation
const names: string[] = ['James', 'Nick', 'Rebecca', 'Lily'];

// function annotation with parameter type annotation and return type annotation
let sayHello: (name: string) => string;

// implementation of sayHello function
sayHello = function (name) {
    return 'Hello ' + name;
};

// object type annotation
let person: { name: string; heightInCentimeters: number; };

// Implementation of a person object
person = {
    name: 'Mark',
    heightInCentimeters: 183
};
```

■ **Note**   Although many languages specify the type before the identifier, the placement of type annotations in TypeScript after the identifier helps to reinforce that the type annotation is optional. It also allows you to use the full range of variable statements, including `const` and `let`. This style of type annotation is also inspired by *type theory*.

If a type annotation becomes too complex, you can create an interface, or a type alias to represent the type to simplify annotations. Listing 1-9 demonstrates how to simplify the type annotation for the person object, which was shown at the end of previous example in Listing 1-8. This technique is especially useful if you intend to reuse the type as it provides a reusable definition. Interfaces and type aliases are not limited to describing object types; they are flexible enough to describe any structure you are likely to encounter. Interfaces are discussed in more detail later in this chapter.

When choosing whether to use an interface or a type alias, it is worth understanding the things an interface can do that a type alias cannot do. An interface can be used in an extends or implements clause, which means you can explicitly use them when defining other interfaces and classes. An interface can also accept type arguments, making the interface generic. A type alias can do neither of these.

Listing 1-9. Interface and type alias

```
// Interface
interface PersonInterface {
    name: string;
    heightInCentimeters: number;
}

const sherlock: PersonInterface = {
    name: 'Bendict',
    heightInCentimeters: 183
}

// Type Alias
type PersonType = {
    name: string;
    heightInCentimeters: number;
};

const john: PersonType = {
    name: 'Martin',
    heightInCentimeters: 169
}
```

Primitive Types

The primitive types in TypeScript are incredibly basic, but through the tools of the type system you can combine them, widen them, and narrow them to represent the concepts in your program. These types directly represent the underlying JavaScript types and follow the standards set for those types:

- string – a sequence of UTF-16 code units

- boolean – true or false

- number – a double-precision 64-bit floating point value

- symbol – a unique, immutable symbol, substitutable for a string as an object key

There are no special types to represent integers or other specific variations on the numeric type as it wouldn't be practical to perform static analysis to ensure all possible values assigned are valid.

The type system also contains several types that represent special values:

- The undefined type is the value of a variable that has not been assigned a value.

- The null type can be used to represent an intentional absence of an object value. For example, if you had a method that searched an array of objects to find a match, it could return null to indicate that no match was found.

- The void type is used to represent cases where there is no value, for example, to show that a function doesn't return anything.

- The never type represents an unreachable section of code, for example a function that throws an exception has the return type of never.

Object and Dynamic Types

Everything that isn't a primitive type in TypeScript is a subclass of the object type. Most of the types in your program are likely to fall within this definition.

The final item in our types is the dynamic any type, which can be used to represent literally any type. When using dynamic types, there is no compiler type checking for the type.

The any type is also used by the compiler in situations where it cannot infer the type automatically, although you can disallow these implicit any types using a complier flag (please refer to Appendix 2 for a full list of options you can specify for compilation). You can also use it in cases where you don't want the type to be checked by the compiler, which gives you access to all of the dynamic features of the JavaScript language.

Now that the fundamental types are all described, the next section covers some special mechanisms for combining the types in ways that either narrow or widen the range of allowable values.

Enumerations

Enumerations are one of the simplest narrowing types. Enumerations represent a collection of named elements that you can use to avoid littering your program with hard-coded values. By default, enumerations are zero based although you can change this by specifying the first value, in which case numbers will increment from value you set. You can opt to specify values for all identifiers if you wish to.

In Listing 1-10 the VehicleType enumeration can be used to describe vehicle types using well-named identifiers throughout your program. The value passed when an identifier name is specified is the number that represents the identifier, for example, in Listing 1-10 the use of the VehicleType.Lorry identifier results in the number 5 being stored in the type variable. It is also possible to get the identifier name from the enumeration by treating the enumeration like an array.

Listing 1-10. Enumerations

```
enum VehicleType {
    PedalCycle,
    MotorCycle,
    Car,
    Van,
    Bus,
    Lorry
}

const type = VehicleType.Lorry;

const typeName = VehicleType[type]; // 'Lorry'
```

In TypeScript enumerations are open ended. This means all declarations with the same name inside a common root will contribute toward a single type. When defining an enumeration across multiple blocks, subsequent blocks after the first declaration must specify the numeric value to be used to continue the sequence, as shown in Listing 1-11. This is a useful technique for extending code from third parties, in ambient declarations, and from the standard library.

Listing 1-11. Enumeration split across multiple blocks

```
enum BoxSize {
    Small,
    Medium
}

//...

enum BoxSize {
    Large = 2,
    XLarge,
    XXLarge
}
```

Consumers of enumerations declared in multiple blocks can tell no difference with an enumeration declared in one block, as shown in Figure 1-4.

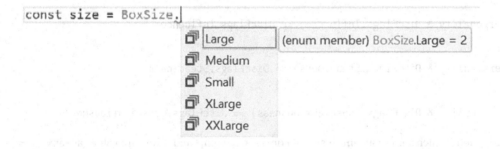

Figure 1-4. Using a multi-block enumeration

■ **Note** The term *common root* comes from graph theory. In TypeScript, this term relates to a particular location in the tree of modules within your program. Whenever declarations are considered for merging, they must have the same fully qualified name, which means the same name at the same level in the tree.

Bit Flags

You can use an enumeration to define bit flags. Bit flags allow a series of items to be selected or deselected by switching individual bits in a sequence on and off. To ensure that each value in an enumeration relates to a single bit, the numbering must follow the binary sequence whereby each value is a power of two, for example:

```
1, 2, 4, 8, 16, 32, 64, 128, 256, 512, 1,024, 2,048, 4,096, and so on
```

Listing 1-12 shows an example of using an enumeration for bit flags. By default, when you create a variable to store the state, all items are switched off. To switch on an option, it can simply be assigned to the variable. To switch on multiple items, items can be combined with the bitwise OR operator (|). Items remain switched on if you happen to include them multiple times using the bitwise OR operator. Bitwise Flags are explained in detail in Appendix 3.

Listing 1-12. Flags

```
enum DiscFlags {
    None = 0,
    Drive = 1,
    Influence = 2,
    Steadiness = 4,
    Conscientiousness = 8
}

// Using flags
var personality = DiscFlags.Drive | DiscFlags.Conscientiousness;

// Testing flags

// true
var hasD = (personality & DiscFlags.Drive) == DiscFlags.Drive;

// false
var hasI = (personality & DiscFlags.Influence) == DiscFlags.Influence;

// false
var hasS = (personality & DiscFlags.Steadiness) == DiscFlags.Steadiness;

// true
var hasC = (personality & DiscFlags.Conscientiousness) == DiscFlags.Conscientiousness;
```

The value assigned to each item in an enum can be constant, or computed. Constant values are any expression that can be interpreted by the type system, such as literal values, calculations, and binary operators. Computed values are expressions that could not be efficiently interpreted by the compiler, such as assigning a string length, or calling out to a method. The terminology here is dangerously overloaded; the term "constant" when considering "constant vs computed" should not be confused with the const keyword, which can be used with variables and with a special kind of enumeration, called a constant enumeration.

Constant Enumerations

A constant enumeration can be created using the const keyword, as shown in Listing 1-13. Unlike a normal enumeration, a constant enumeration is erased during compilation and all code referring to it is replaced with hard-coded values.

Listing 1-13. Constant enumeration

```
const enum VehicleType {
    PedalCycle,
    MotorCycle,
    Car,
```

```
    Van,
    Bus,
    Lorry
}

const type = VehicleType.Lorry;
```

The compiled JavaScript output for this example is shown in Listing 1-14. The entire enumeration is gone, and the code referencing the lorry vehicle type has been replaced with the value 5. To aid comprehension, comments are inserted to describe the literal values.

Listing 1-14. JavaScript output of a constant enumeration

```
var type = 5 /* Lorry */;
```

To make the inlining of values possible, constant enumerations are not allowed to have computed members.

Union Types

A union type widens the allowable values by specifying that the value can be of more than a single type. Libraries such as jQuery commonly expose functions that allow you to pass either a jQuery object, or a string selector, for example; and union types allow you to limit the possible values to just these two types (rather than resorting to a completely dynamic type).

As Listing 1-15 demonstrates, it is possible to create a type that is either a Boolean or a number. Union types use the pipe-delimeter to separate each of the possible types, which you can read as an "OR." Attempting to supply a value that doesn't match one of the types in the union results in an error.

Listing 1-15. Union Types

```
// Type annotation for a union type
let union: boolean | number;

// OK: number
union = 5;

// OK: boolean
union = true;

// Error: Type "string" is not assignable to type 'number | boolean'
union = 'string';

// Type alias for a union type
type StringOrError = string | Error;

// Type alias for union of many types
type SeriesOfTypes = string | number | boolean | Error;
```

When creating a union type, consider using a type alias to reduce the repetition of the definition in your program and to give the concept a name. A union can be created using any types available in your program, not just primitive types.

Literal Types

Literal types can be used to narrow the range of allowable values to a subset of the type, such as reducing a string, to a set of specific values. Listing 1-16 shows a type of Kingdom, which has the six taxonomic divisions of living organisms as possible values. Variables with the Kingdom type may only use the specific values included in the literal type.

Listing 1-16. String literal type

```
type Kingdom = 'Bacteria' | 'Protozoa' | 'Chromista' | 'Plantae' | 'Fungi' | 'Animalia';

let kingdom: Kingdom;

// OK
kingdom = 'Bacteria';

// Error: Type 'Protista' is not assignable to type 'Kingdom'
kingdom = 'Protista';
```

Literal types are really just union types made up of specific values, so you can also create a number literal type, or a union/literal hybrid type using the same syntax.

Listing 1-17. Number literal types and hybrid union/literal types

```
// Number literal type
type Fibonacci = 1 | 2 | 3 | 5 | 8 | 13;

let num: Fibonacci;

// OK
num = 8;

// Error: Type '9' is not assignable to type 'Fibonacci'
num = 9;

// Hybrid union/literal type
type Randoms = 'Text' | 10 | false;

let random: Randoms;

// OK
random = 'Text';
random = 10;
random = false;

// Error: Not assignable.
random = 'Other String';
random = 12;
random = true;
```

The behavior of literal types is similar to the behavior of enumerations, so if you are using only numbers in your literal type, consider whether an enumeration would be more expressive in your program.

Intersection Types

An intersection type combines several different types into a single supertype that includes the members from all participating types. Where a union type is "either type A or B," an intersection type is "both type A and B." Listing 1-18 shows two interfaces for Skier and Shooter, which are combined into the biathelete intersection type. Intersection types use the ampersand character, which you can read as "AND."

Listing 1-18. Intersection Types

```
interface Skier {
    slide(): void;
}

interface Shooter {
    shoot(): void;
}

type Biathelete = Skier & Shooter;
```

To see the result of an intersection type, Figure 1-5 shows the autocompletion displayed for the biathelete type, with both the shoot and slide methods present. The autocompletion also shows the originating type of the members.

```
let biathelete: Biathelete = null;

biathelete.
            ⊕ shoot    (method) Shooter.shoot(): void
            ⊕ slide
```

Figure 1-5. *Intersection type members*

Intersection types are useful for working with mixins, which you'll read about in Chapter 4.

Arrays

TypeScript arrays have precise typing for their contents. To specify an array type, you simply add square brackets after the type name. This works for all types whether they are primitive or custom types. When you add an item to the array, its type will be checked to ensure it is compatible. When you access elements in the array, you will get quality autocompletion because the type of each item is known. Listing 1-19 demonstrates each of these type checks.

There are some interesting observations to be made in Listing 1-19. When the monuments variable is declared, the type annotation for an array of Monument objects can either be the shorthand: Monument[ ] or the longhand: Array<Monument>—there is no difference in meaning between these two styles. Therefore, you should opt for whichever you feel is more readable. Note that the array is instantiated after the equals sign using the empty array literal ([ ]). You can also instantiate it with values, by adding them within the brackets, separated by commas.

The objects being added to the array using monuments.push(...) are not explicitly Monument objects. This is allowed because they are compatible with the Monument interface. If you miss a property you will be warned that the type is not compatible; and if you add an additional member you will receive a warning too, which helps to catch misspelled member names.

The array is sorted using monuments.sort(...), which takes in a function to compare values. When the comparison is numeric, the comparer function can simply return a - b, in other cases you can write custom code to perform the comparison and return a positive or negative number to be used for sorting (or a zero if the values are the same).

Listing 1-19. Typed arrays

```typescript
interface Monument {
    name: string;
    heightInMeters: number;
}

// The array is typed using the Monument interface
const monuments: Monument[] = [];

// Each item added to the array is checked for type compatibility
monuments.push({
    name: 'Statue of Liberty',
    heightInMeters: 46
});

monuments.push({
    name: 'Peter the Great',
    heightInMeters: 96
});

monuments.push({
    name: 'Angel of the North',
    heightInMeters: 20
});

function compareMonumentHeights(a: Monument, b: Monument) {
    if (a.heightInMeters > b.heightInMeters) {
        return -1;
    }
    if (a.heightInMeters < b.heightInMeters) {
        return 1;
    }
    return 0;
}

// The array.sort method expects a comparer that accepts two Monuments
const monumentsOrderedByHeight = monuments.sort(compareMonumentHeights);

// Get the first element from the array, which is the tallest
const tallestMonument = monumentsOrderedByHeight[0];

// Peter the Great
console.log(tallestMonument.name);
```

The elements in an array are accessed using an index. The index is zero based, so the first element in the monumentsOrderedByHeight array is monumentsOrderedByHeight[0]. When an element is accessed from the array, autocompletion is supplied for the name and heightInMeters properties.

To find out more about using arrays and loops, refer to Appendix 1.

Tuple Types

A tuple type uses an array, and specifies the type of elements based on their position. Listing 1-20 shows a tuple type where three items in the array are typed.

Listing 1-20. Tuple types

```
let poem: [number , boolean , string];

// OK
poem = [1, true, 'love'];

// Error: 'string' is not assignable to 'number'
poem = ['my', true, 'love'];
```

When accessing the types by index, the type is known and will be checked by the compiler. The autocompletion list will also be type specific as shown in Figure 1-6, where the third item (at index 2) is known to be a string.

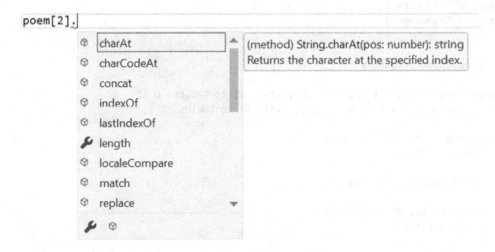

Figure 1-6. *Autocompletion members for tuple types*

Tuples are named after the number of items they define (and tuples larger than seven items are named *n-tuples*).

- Pair: 2 items

- Triple: 3 items

- Quadruple: 4 items

- Quintuple: 5 items

- Sextuple: 6 items

- Septuble: 7 items

The common use case for tuples is the ability to return multiple values from a method without having to define a more complex structure. Conceptually, tuples are useful as long as the data is related and its lifetime is short.

Dictionary Types

You can represent dictionaries in TypeScript using an index type, as shown in Listing 1-21. The index type specifies the key and its type in square brackets, and the type of the value afterwards as a type annotation. The cephalopod dictionary is an object with dynamic keys, but TypeScript will ensure the types of the keys and values are correct.

Listing 1-21. Indexed types

```
interface Cephalopod {
    hasInk: boolean;
    arms: number;
    tentacles: number;
}

interface CephalopodDictionary {
    [index: string]: Cephalopod;
}

let dictionary: CephalopodDictionary = {};

dictionary['octopus vulgaris'] = { hasInk: true, arms: 8, tentacles: 0 };
dictionary['loligo vulgaris'] = { hasInk: true, arms: 8, tentacles: 2 };

// Error. Not assignable to type 'Cephalopod'
dictionary[0] = { hasInk: true };

const octopus = dictionary['octopus vulgaris'];

// 0 (The common octopus has no tentacles)
console.log(octopus.tentacles);

// Remove item
delete dictionary['octopus vulgaris'];
```

Dictionaries can be used to map language translations, or anywhere you need to look up items against a unique key.

Mapped Types

To reduce the amount of effort required to create similar types that differ only in optionality, or readability, mapped types allow you to create variations of an existing type in a single expression. Mapped types use the keyof keyword, which is an index type query that gathers a list of permitted property names for a type in your program.

In Listing 1-22, the options type is manually repeated into the readonly type, the optional type, and the nullable type. There are only two members on the options interface, but already this is verbose code.

Listing 1-22. Manual type variations

```
interface Options {
    material: string;
    backlight: boolean;
}

// Manually created readonly interface
interface ManualReadonlyOptions {
    readonly material: string;
    readonly backlight: boolean;
}

// Manually created optional interface
interface ManualOptionalOptions {
    material?: string;
    backlight?: string;
}

// Manually created nullable interface
interface ManualNullableOptions {
    material: string | null;
    backlight: string | null;
}
```

The alternative to all this repetition is shown in Listing 1-23. Three reusable types are created that can be used to generate read-only, optional, or nullable type variations with a single line of code. The three named types create these variations of the options interface.

Listing 1-23. Mapped types

```
interface Options {
    material: string;
    backlight: boolean;
}

// Mapped types
type ReadOnly<T> = { readonly [k in keyof T]: T[k]; }
type Optional<T> = {[k in keyof T]?: T[k]; }
type Nullable<T> = {[k in keyof T]: T[k] | null; }
```

```
// Creating new types from mapped types
type ReadonlyOptions = Readonly<Options>;
type OptionalOptions = Optional<Options>;
type NullableOptions = Nullable<Options>;
```

The types you create with a mapped type can be used in type annotations in place of the original interface as shown in Listing 1-24, with the behavior of each one being updated accordingly.

Listing 1-24. Using mapped types

```
// Read-only type
const options1: ReadonlyOptions = {
    backlight: true,
    material: 'plastic'
};

// Error. Property is read-only
options1.backlight = false;

// Optional type
const options2: OptionalOptions = {
    // All members are optional
};

// Nullable type
const options3: NullableOptions = {
    backlight: null,
    material: null
};
```

The three mapped types in Listing 1-23 can be directly transferred to your program to allow you to quickly create your own type variations whenever you need them.

Type Assertions

In cases in which TypeScript determines that an assignment is invalid, but you know that you are dealing with a special case, you can override the type using a type assertion. When you use a type assertion, you are taking responsibility from the compiler and must ensure that the assignment is valid. Your program may not work correctly if you make a mistake. The type assertion precedes a statement, as shown in Listing 1-25. The property variable could be a house or a mansion, so a subsequent assignment to a variable declared as Mansion would fail. Because we know that the variable is compatible with the Mansion interface (it has all three properties required to satisfy the interface), the type assertion <Mansion> confirms this to the compiler.

Listing 1-25. Type assertions

```
interface House {
    bedrooms: number;
    bathrooms: number;
}
```

```
interface Mansion {
    bedrooms: number;
    bathrooms: number;
    butlers: number;
}

function getProperty() : House | Mansion {
    // ...
}

const property = getProperty();

// OK as the property is on both House and Mansion
const bedroomCount = property.bedrooms;

// Errors: Property 'butlers' does not exist on type 'House | Mansion'
const butlerCount = property.butlers;

// OK with type assertion
const workingButlerCount = (<Mansion>property).butlers;
```

Although a type assertion overrides the type as far as the compiler is concerned, there are still checks performed when you assert a type. It is possible to force a type assertion, as shown in Listing 1-26, by adding an additional <any> type assertion between the actual type you want to use and the identifier of the variable. When you force a type assertion, you are taking on additional responsibility as the compiler doesn't think your code will work.

Listing 1-26. Forced type assertions

```
const name: string = 'Avenue Road';

// Error: Type 'string' cannot be converted to type 'number'
const bedroomCount: number = <number>name;

// Works
const workingBedroomCount: number = <number><any>name;
```

Type Guards

When dealing with a wide type definition, you may find you need to narrow it in order to use a member that would otherwise be unavailable. Listing 1-27 shows a function with an argument that is either a string or a number. Attempting to use the length member from a string or the toFixed method on numbers will result in error unless a type guard is used. A type guard is a statement that results in the type becoming narrower, for example the if-statement in the example checks that the type of the variable is a string, which means the compiler knows the type in both the if-branch, and the else-branch (because if it isn't a string, it must be a number).

Listing 1-27. Type Guard

```typescript
function typeGuardExample(stringNumber: string | number) {
    // Error: Property does not exist
    const a = stringNumber.length;
    const b = stringNumber.toFixed();

    // Type guard
    if (typeof stringNumber === 'string') {
        // OK
        return stringNumber.length;
    } else {
        // OK
        return stringNumber.toFixed();
    }
}
```

The standard type guards include typeof and instanceof; but if that doesn't cover your situation, you can write your own custom type guard. Listing 1-28 shows a custom type guard that determines if a supplied object meets the requirements of the SpeedControllable interface. The custom type guard function uses the special type annotation treadmill is SpeedControllable, this tells the compiler that the function can be used to narrow types as part of a type guard. The custom type guard function returns a Boolean indicating whether the type is SpeedControllable.

Listing 1-28. Custom Type Guard

```typescript
interface SpeedControllable {
    increaseSpeed(): void;
    decreaseSpeed(): void;
    stop(): void;
}

interface InclineControllable {
    lift(): void;
    drop(): void;
}

function isSpeedControllable(treadmill: SpeedControllable | any)
    : treadmill is SpeedControllable {
    if (treadmill.increaseSpeed
        && treadmill.decreaseSpeed
        && treadmill.stop) {
        return true;
    }

    return false;
}

function customTypeGuardExample(treadmill: SpeedControllable | InclineControllable) {
    // Error: Property does not exist
    const a = treadmill.increaseSpeed();
    const b = treadmill.lift();
```

```
// Type guard
if (isSpeedControllable(treadmill)) {
    // OK
    treadmill.increaseSpeed();
} else {
    // OK
    treadmill.lift();
}
}
```

The result is identical to the standard type guard and the type of the treadmill parameter is known in the if-branch and the else-branch. When you use a type guard against a union of many types (rather than just two), you may need to use additional type guards to further narrow the leftover type.

Discriminated Unions

A discriminated union, or tagged union, allows you to combine union types, type aliases, and type guards to get full autocompletion and checking for types with a common string literal property. The components that make up a discriminated union are the following:

1.   Several types that share a common string literal property, called a discriminant.

2.   A type alias for a union of these types, called a union.

3.   A type guard that checks the discriminant.

In Listing 1-29 the cube and cuboid types both share the discriminant "kind." The types are added to the prism union, which results in full autocompletion in the switch statement in the volume function. The switch statement acts as a type guard, meaning the type of prism in each case is the correct narrowed type.

The default case is used like a safety net to ensure there are no types that are part of the discriminated union that have been left out of the switch statement. For example, if you were to add a triangular prism to the discriminated union, you would receive a warning "Argument of type 'TriangularPrism' is not assignable to parameter of type 'never'," which tells you that it was not handled by the volume method.

Listing 1-29. Discriminated union

```
interface Cube {
    kind: 'cube'; // Discriminant
    size: number;
}

interface Cuboid {
    kind: 'cuboid'; // Discriminant
    width: number;
    depth: number;
    height: number;
}

// Union
type Prism = Cube | Cuboid;
```

```
function volume(prism: Prism): number {
    // Type Guard
    switch (prism.kind) {
        case 'cube':
            return prism.size * prism.size * prism.size;
        case 'cuboid':
            return prism.width * prism.depth * prism.height;
        default:
            assertNever(prism);
            break;
    }
}

function assertNever(arg: never): never {
    throw new Error("Possible new tagged type: " + arg);
}
```

If you are following an object-oriented approach, you might not get much mileage from this feature, but it is a common use case for functional programming.

Operators

All the standard JavaScript operators are available within your TypeScript program. The JavaScript operators are described in Appendix 1. This section describes operators that have special significance within TypeScript because of type restrictions or because they affect types.

Increment and Decrement

The increment (++) and decrement (--) operators can only be applied to variables of type any, number, or enum. This is mainly used to increase index variables in a loop or to update counting variables in your program, as shown in Listing 1-30. In these cases, you will typically be working with a number type. The operator works on variables with the any type, as no type checking is performed on these variables.

Listing 1-30. Increment and decrement

```
let counter = 0;

do {
    ++counter;
} while (counter < 10);

// 10
alert(counter);
```

When incrementing or decrementing an enumeration, the number representation is updated. Listing 1-31 shows how incrementing the size variable results in the next element in the enumeration and decrementing the size variable results in the previous element in the enumeration. Beware when you use this method as you can increase and decrease the value beyond the bounds of the enumeration.

Listing 1-31. Increment and decrement of enumerations

```
enum Size {
    S,
    M,
    L,
    XL
}

var size = Size.S;
++size;
console.log(Size[size]); // M

var size = Size.XL;
--size;
console.log(Size[size]); // L

var size = Size.XL;
++size;
console.log(Size[size]); // undefined
```

Binary Operators

The operators in the following list are designed to work with two numbers. In TypeScript, it is valid to use the operators with variables of type number or any. Where you are using a variable with the any type, you should ensure it contains a number. The result of an operation in this list is always a number.

Binary operators: - * / % << >> >>> & ^ |

The plus (+) operator is absent from this list because it is a special case: a mathematical addition operator as well as a concatenation operator. Whether the addition or concatenation is chosen depends on the type of the variables on either side of the operator. As Listing 1-32 shows, this is a common problem in JavaScript programs in which an intended addition results in the concatenation of the two values, resulting in an unexpected value. This will be caught in a TypeScript program if you try to assign a string to a variable of the number type, or try to return a string for a function that is annotated to return a number.

The rules for determining the type resulting from a plus operation are the following:

- If the type of either of the arguments is a string, the result is always a string.

- If the type of both arguments is either number or enum, the result is a number.

- If the type of either of the arguments is any, and the other argument is not a string, the result is any.

- In any other case, the operator is not allowed.

Listing 1-32. Binary plus operator

```
// 6: number
const num = 5 + 1;

// '51': string
const str = 5 + '1';
```

When the plus operator is used with only a single argument, it acts as a shorthand conversion to a number. This unary use of the plus operator is illustrated in Listing 1-33. The unary minus operator also converts the type to number and changes its sign.

Listing 1-33. Unary plus and minus operators

```
const str: string = '5';

// 5: number
const num = +str;

// -5: number
const negative = -str;
```

Bitwise Operators

Bitwise operators in TypeScript accept values of all types. The operator treats each value in the expression as a sequence of 32 bits and returns a number. Bitwise operators are useful for working with Flags, as discussed in the earlier section on Enumerations and in Appendix 3.

The full list of bitwise operators is shown in Table 1-1.

Table 1-1. *Bitwise Operators*

Operator	Name	Description
&	AND	Returns a result with a 1 in each position that both inputs have a 1.
|	OR	Returns a result with a 1 in each position where either input has a 1.
^	XOR	Returns a result with a 1 in each position where exactly one input has a 1.
<<	Left Shift	Bits in the left-hand argument are moved to the left by the number of bits specified in the right-hand argument. Bits moved off the left side are discarded and zeroes are added on the right side.
>>	Right Shift	Bits in the left-hand argument are moved to the right by the number of bits specified in the right-hand argument. Bits moved off the right side are discarded and digits matching the left most bit are added on the left side.
>>>	Zero-fill Right Shift	Bits in the left-hand argument are moved to the right by the number of bits specified in the right-hand argument. Bits moved off the right side are discarded and zeroes are added on the left side.
~	NOT	Accepts a single argument and inverts each bit.

Logical Operators

Logical operators are usually used to test Boolean variables or to convert an expression into a Boolean value. This section explains how logical operators are used in TypeScript for this purpose, and how logical AND and logical OR operators can be used outside of the context of Boolean types.

NOT Operator

The common use of the NOT (!) operator is to invert a Boolean value: for example, `if (!isValid)` conditionally runs code if the isValid variable is `false`. Using the operator in this way does not affect the type system.

The NOT operator can be used in TypeScript in ways that affect types. In the same way the unary plus operator can be used as a shorthand method for converting a variable of any type to a number, the NOT operator can convert any variable to a `Boolean` type. This can be done without inverting the truth of the variable by using a sequence of two unary NOT operators (!!). Both are illustrated in Listing 1-34. Traditionally, a single ! is used to invert a statement to reduce nesting in your code, whereas the double !! converts a type to a Boolean.

Listing 1-34. NOT operator

```
const truthyString = 'Truthy string';
let falseyString: string;

// False, it checks the string but inverts the truth
const invertedTest = !truthyString;

// True, the string is not undefined or empty
const truthyTest = !!truthyString;

// False, the string is empty
const falseyTest = !!falseyString;
```

When converting to a Boolean using this technique, the JavaScript type juggling rules apply. For this reason, it is worth familiarizing yourself with the concepts of "truthy" and "falsey" that apply to this operation. The term *falsey* applies to certain values that are equivalent to `false` when used in a logical operation. Everything else is "truthy" and is equivalent to `true`. The following values are "falsey" and are evaluated as `false`

- `undefined`
- `null`
- `false: boolean`
- `'': string` (empty string)
- `0: number`
- NaN (the JavaScript Not a Number value)

All other values are evaluated as `true`. Surprising examples of this include:

- `'0': string`
- `'False': string`

This style of checking differs from other languages, but allows a rather powerful shorthand test of a variable as shown in Listing 1-35. Given that a variable can be `undefined` or `null`, and you probably don't want to check for both, this is a useful feature. If you want to perform a type-safe check with no juggling, you can use the three-character operators `===` or `!==`; for example, `if (myProperty === false)` tests that the type on both sides of the comparison are the same and their values are the same.

Listing 1-35. Shorthand Boolean test

```
var myProperty;

if (myProperty) {
    // Reaching this location means that...
    // myProperty is not null
    // myProperty is not undefined
    // myProperty is not boolean false
    // myProperty is not an empty string
    // myProperty is not the number 0
    // myProperty is not NaN
}
```

AND Operator

The common use of the logical AND operator (&&) is to assert that both sides of a logical expression are true, for example, if (isValid && isRequired). If the left-hand side of the expression is false (or is falsey, meaning it can be converted to false), the evaluation ends. Otherwise, the right-hand side of the expression is evaluated.

The AND operator can also be used outside of a logical context because the right-hand side of the expression is only evaluated if the left-hand side is truthy. In Listing 1-36, the console.log function is only called if the console object is defined. In the second example, the player2 variable is only set if there is already a player1 value. Where the result of the expression is assigned to a variable, the variable will always have the type of the right-hand expression.

Listing 1-36. AND operator

```
// longhand
if (console) {
    console.log('Console Available');
}

// shorthand
console && console.log('Console Available');

const player1 = 'Martin';

// player2 is only defined if player1 is defined
const player2 = player1 && 'Dan';

// 'Dan'
alert(player2);
```

OR Operator

The common use of the logical OR (||) operator is to test that one of two sides to an expression are true. The left-hand side is evaluated first and the evaluation ends if the left-hand side is true. If the left-hand side is not true, the right-hand side of the expression is evaluated.

The less common use of the OR operator is to coalesce two values, substituting a value on the left with one on the right in cases where the left-hand value is falsey. Listing 1-37 illustrates this usage. The result has the best common type between the two types in the expression. Best common types are explained in more detail in Chapter 3.

Listing 1-37. OR operator

```typescript
// Empty strings are falsey
let errorMessages = '';

// result is 'Saved OK'
let result = errorMessages || 'Saved OK';

// Filled strings are truthy
errorMessages = 'Error Detected';

// result is 'Error Detected'
result = errorMessages || 'Saved OK';

let undefinedLogger;

// if the logger isn't initialized, substitute it for the result of the right-hand
expression
const logger = undefinedLogger || { log: function (msg: string) { alert(msg); } };

// alerts 'Message'
logger.log('Message');
```

Short-Circuit Evaluation

Both the logical AND operator and the logical OR operator benefit from short-circuit evaluation. This means that as soon as the statement can be logically answered, evaluation stops. While this saves the processing of the second statement, the real benefit is that it means you can ensure a value is defined before you use it.

In Listing 1-38, the if-statement would fail in a language that didn't support short-circuit evaluation because a property is being accessed on the caravan variable, which is undefined. Because an undefined variable is falsey, only the left hand of the expression needs to be evaluated to know that the whole expression is false, so the caravan.rooms property is never accessed.

Listing 1-38. Short-circuit evaluation

```typescript
interface Caravan {
    rooms: number;
}

let caravan: Caravan;

if (caravan && caravan.rooms > 5) {
    //...
}
```

Conditional Operator

When you write an if-else statement that results in different values being assigned to the same variable (as shown in Listing 1-39), you can shorten your code using a conditional operator, although there are some benefits to consistently using symmetrical if-else statements; one of which is that it makes code duplication easier to spot.

Listing 1-39. The If-statement

```
const isValid = true;
let message: string;

// Long-hand equivalent
if (isValid) {
    message = 'Okay';
} else {
    message = 'Failed';
}
```

The conditional operator is a shorthand way to assign one of two values based on a logical test, as illustrated in Listing 1-40. When a conditional operator is used in TypeScript, the result has the best common type between the two possible values. Best common types are described in Chapter 3.

Listing 1-40. Conditional operator

```
const isValid = true;

// Conditional operator
const message = isValid ? 'Okay' : 'Failed';
```

Type Operators

There is a collection of operators available that can assist you when working with objects in JavaScript. Operators such as `typeof`, `instanceof`, `in`, and `delete` are particularly relevant to working with classes; you will find more information on these operators in the section dedicated to classes later in this chapter.

Destructuring

Destructuring allows you to unpack an array or object into named variables. Listing 1-41 shows an array of triangle numbers being unpacked into two variables that capture the first and second items in the array. Once the array has been destructured, the named variables contain the values. The original array is not affected by the destructuring.

Listing 1-41. Array destructuring

```
const triangles = [1, 3, 6, 10, 15, 21];

// Destructuring
const [first, second] = triangles;
```

```
// 1
console.log(first);

// 3
console.log(second);
```

You can also use rest parameters when destructuring. Rest parameters are preceded by the three-dot (...) prefix and crop up in other areas too, such as functions. The rest parameter must appear last in the list, and it will receive all the values left after the named arguments have been unpacked. Listing 1-42 adds a rest parameter to the triangle number example.

Listing 1-42. Array destructuring with a rest parameter

```
const triangles = [1, 3, 6, 10, 15, 21];

// Destructuring with a rest argument
const [first, second, ...remaining] = triangles;

// 1
console.log(first);

// 3
console.log(second);

// [6, 10, 15, 21]
console.log(remaining);
```

You can skip items in the array by leaving blank spaces between commas, as shown in Listing 1-43 where the third item is skipped. You can skip as many items as you wish, by simply not specifying a variable name.

Listing 1-43. Skipping items

```
const triangles = [1, 3, 6, 10, 15, 21];

// Skipping third item
const [first, second, , fourth] = triangles;

// 1
console.log(first);

// 3
console.log(second);

// [10]
console.log(fourth);
```

One creative use of destructing is to swap the values of variables without introducing intermediate variables. Listing 1-44 transfers the values in one go using a destructuring assignment.

Listing 1-44. Variable swapping

```
let a = 3;

let b = 5;

// Swapping
[a, b] = [b, a];

// 5
console.log(a);

// 3
console.log(b);
```

You can also use destructuring to unpack objects. The syntax for object destructuring is slightly different, as shown in Listing 1-45. The left-hand side of the expression looks like an object literal, but where the values are actually the new variables that will be assigned the values that appear on their left. You can think of destructuring as array literals that extract data, and object literals that extract data.

Listing 1-45. Object destructuring

```
const highSchool = { school: 'Central High', team: 'Centaurs' };

// Object destructuring
const { school: s, team: t } = highSchool;

// 'Central High'
console.log(s);

// 'Centaurs'
console.log(t);
```

You can also auto-unpack objects if you use variable names that match the property names. In Listing 1-46 the variables use the same names as the members of the high school object: school and team.

Listing 1-46. Auto-unpacking

```
const highSchool = { school: 'Central High', team: 'Centaurs' };

// Auto-unpacking
const { school, team } = highSchool;

// 'Central High'
console.log(school);

// 'Centaurs'
console.log(team);
```

When you use a rest parameter in object destructuring, it will result in an object containing all the properties that you didn't explicitly unpack. Listing 1-47 demonstrates object destructuring rest parameters.

Listing 1-47. Object destructuring with rest parameter

```
const pets = { cat: 'Pickle', dog: 'Berkeley', hamster: 'Hammy'}

// Object destructuring
const { dog, ...others } = pets;

// 'Berkeley'
console.log(dog);

// Object { cat: 'Pickle', hamster: 'Hammy'}
console.log(others);
```

If you destructure past the available values, the result will be undefined, as shown in Listing 1-48, where the fourth variable will be undefined because the array only has three items.

Listing 1-48. Undefined result

```
const triangles = [1, 3, 6];

// Destructuring past available values
const [first, second, third, fourth] = triangles;

// undefined
console.log(fourth);
```

To mitigate against undefined values, you can supply default values as part of the destructuring expression. Listing 1-49 shows default values for the third and fourth variables. Because there are three items in the array, the third variable has the value 6, but the fourth variable gets the default value of -1, instead of being undefined.

Listing 1-49. Default values

```
const triangles = [1, 3, 6];

// Destructuring past available values
const [first, second, third = -1, fourth = -1] = triangles;

// 6
console.log(third);

// -1
console.log(fourth);
```

Tuples and destructuring are a powerful combination. If you have a method that returns a tuple, you can immediately destructure it into named variables. This keeps the lifespan of the tuple type as short as possible and expresses the return value better by making each variable explicit. Listing 1-50 shows the tuple/destructuring combination in action.

Listing 1-50. Tuples and Destructuring

```
// Returning a tuple
function getThreeLandmarks(): [string, string, string] {
    return ['Golden Gate Bridge', 'Palace of Westminster', 'Colosseum '];
}

// Destructuring the tuple into named variables
const [sanFrancisco, london, rome] = getThreeLandmarks();
```

Destructuring is valuable when it makes your code more readable. Although you could do some clever stuff with destructuring, the smart move is to judge whether it results in code that expresses the intent better, or whether it just makes the code confusing. The examples in this section are all very conservative uses of the feature and are concise, but readable.

Spread Operator

The spread operator does the opposite of destructuring and can be used to pack arrays and objects using a shallow copy. The spread operator works with properties, but sadly not methods. Listing 1-51 shows array spreading, resulting in the values being packed into the new array. The spread operator reuses the rest parameter syntax once again.

Listing 1-51. Array spreading

```
const squares = [1, 4, 9, 16, 25];
const powers = [2, 4, 8, 16, 32];

// Array spreading
const squaresAndPowers = [...squares, ...powers];

// [1, 4, 9, 16, 25, 2, 4, 8, 16, 32]
console.log(squaresAndPowers);
```

The syntax is almost identical for object spreading, as shown in Listing 1-52, resulting in an object with all the members of both input objects. If the same member appears on both objects, the last assignment wins and overwrites any previous value.

Listing 1-52. Object spreading

```
const emergencyService = {
    police: 'Chase',
    fire: 'Marshall',
};

const utilityService = {
    recycling: 'Rocky',
    construction: 'Rubble'
};
```

```
// Object spreading
const patrol = { ...emergencyService, ...utilityService };

// { police: 'Chase', fire: 'Marshall', recycling: 'Rocky', construction: 'Rubble' }
console.log(patrol);
```

You can even use the spread operator for function arguments; the code in Listing 1-53 causes the function to be called with the individual numbers supplied in the hexagon array.

Listing 1-53. Spread operator in function call

```
function add(a: number, b: number, c: number) {
    return a + b + c;
}

const hexagons = [1, 6, 15];

// Spread operator in function call
const result = add(...hexagons);

// 22
console.log(result);
```

One of the primary benefits of the spread operator is that it removes the need for loop syntax in many scenarios, which makes your code more readable and more expressive.

Functions

Now you understand the detailed minutia of types, you are ready to apply that knowledge to a subject that is right at the heart of a TypeScript program: functions. Although there are some interesting code organization options using classes, namespaces, and modules - functions are the building blocks of readable, maintainable, and reusable code.

In TypeScript, you are likely to find that most functions are written as methods that belong to a class. It makes sense to use modules and classes to organize your code into logical units. Whether you choose to use these structural elements, functions are improved by several TypeScript language features.

With variables, there is just a single location for a type annotation, which is directly after the identifier. With functions, there are several places that can be annotated with type information. In Listing 1-54 you will see that each parameter can be given a type annotation. In the example in Listing 1-54, the getAverage function accepts three parameters and each one can have a different type. When the function is called, the type of each argument passed to the function is checked. The types are also known within the function, which allows sensible autocompletion suggestions and type checking inside the function body.

There is an additional type annotation outside of the parentheses that indicates the return type. In Listing 1-54 the function returns a string. Each return statement is checked against this annotation to ensure the return value is compatible with the return type. You can use the void type to indicate that the function does not return a value. This will prevent code inside the function from returning a value and stop calling code from assigning the result of the function to a variable.

Listing 1-54. Function type annotations

```
function getAverage(a: number, b: number, c: number): string {
    const total = a + b + c;
    const average = total / 3;
    return 'The average is ' + average;
}

const result = getAverage(4, 3, 8); // 'The average is 5'
```

The type annotations on a function are one of the few places where explicitly adding annotations pays dividends. If you don't annotate the return type, TypeScript may infer a union type in cases where different branches return different types. The annotations for the parameters keep calling code inline and ensure the types are enforced within the function.

Optional Parameters

In JavaScript, it is possible to call a function without supplying any arguments, even where the function specifies parameters. It is even possible in JavaScript to pass more arguments than the function requires. In TypeScript, the compiler checks each call and warns you if the arguments fail to match the required parameters in number or type.

Because arguments are thoroughly checked, you will need to annotate optional parameters to inform the compiler that it is acceptable for an argument to be omitted by the calling code. To make a parameter optional, suffix the identifier with a question mark, as shown in Listing 1-55, which is an updated version of the getAverage function, which accepts either two or three arguments.

Optional parameters must be located after any required parameters in the parameter list. For example, the second parameter cannot be optional if the third parameter is required.

Listing 1-55. Optional paramters

```
function getAverage(a: number, b: number, c?: number): string {
    let total = a;
    let count = 1;

    total += b;
    count++;

    if (typeof c !== 'undefined') {
        total += c;
        count++;
    }

    const average = total / count;
    return 'The average is ' + average;
}

// 'The average is 5'
const result = getAverage(4, 6);
```

When you use an optional parameter, you must check the value to see if it has been initialized. The typeof check is the common pattern for this check. If you used the shorthand check of (b), you would find that empty string and numeric zeroes would be treated as if the variable was undefined. The longer expression if (typeof b === 'undefined') avoids this by thoroughly checking the type and value.

Default Parameters

Default parameters are complementary to optional parameters. Wherever you consider using an optional parameter you should also consider the use of a default parameter as an alternative design. When you specify a default parameter, it allows the argument to be omitted by calling code and in cases where the argument is not passed the default value will be used instead.

To supply a default value for a parameter, assign a value in the function declaration as shown in Listing 1-56.

Listing 1-56. Default parameters

```typescript
function concatenate(items: string[], separator = ',', beginAt = 0, endAt = items.length) {
    let result = '';

    for (let i = beginAt; i < endAt; i++) {
        result += items[i];
        if (i < (endAt - 1)) {
            result += separator;
        }
    }

    return result;
}

const items = ['A', 'B', 'C'];

// 'A,B,C'
const result = concatenate(items);

// 'B-C'
const partialResult = concatenate(items, '-', 1);
```

The JavaScript code generated by default parameters includes a type of check just as the one manually written for optional parameters in Listing 1-55. This means that the default parameters result in a check inside the function body that assigns the default value if no argument is passed. In the case of default parameters, though, these checks only appear in the output, which keeps the TypeScript code listing short and succinct. Because the checks are moved inside the function body, you can use a wide range of runtime values as default values — you aren't restricted to compile-time constants as you are in other languages. The default value could be calculated, or even obtained from one of the parameters (as is the case for parameter endAt in Listing 1-56), or refer to any property, variable, constant, or other value that can be accessed from within the function body.

Rest Parameters

Rest parameters allow calling code to specify zero or more arguments of the specified type. For the arguments to be correctly passed, rest parameters must follow these rules

- Only one rest parameter is allowed.

- The rest parameter must appear last in the parameter list.

- The type of a rest parameter must be an array type.

To declare a rest parameter, prefix the identifier with three periods and ensure that the type annotation is an array type, as shown in Listing 1-57.

Listing 1-57. Rest Parameters

```
function getAverage(...a: number[]): string {
    let total = 0;
    let count = 0;

    for (let i = 0; i < a.length; i++) {
        total += a[i];
        count++;
    }

    const average = total / count;
    return 'The average is ' + average;
}

// 'The average is 6'
const result = getAverage(2, 4, 6, 8, 10);
```

Your function should expect to receive any number of arguments, including none. In your compiled JavaScript code, you will see that the compiler has added code to map the arguments list to your array variable within the method body.

■ **Note**   If you require that at least one argument is passed, you would need to add a required parameter before the rest parameter to enforce this minimum requirement. This would be the correct signature for the getAverage function in Listing 1-57 to avoid a potential divide-by-zero error.

Overloads

I have deliberately covered union types, as well as optional, default, and rest parameters before introducing function overloads; in most cases you can write a method using these language features and avoid writing an overload. Where this isn't possible, you should consider writing separate, well-named functions that make their different intentions explicit. That isn't to say that there are no valid uses for function overloads and if you have considered the other options and chosen to use overloads that is a perfectly reasonable selection.

In many languages, each overload has its own implementation but in TypeScript the overloads all decorate a single implementation, as highlighted in Listing 1-58. The actual signature of the function appears last and is hidden by the overloads. This final signature is called an *implementation signature*. The implementation signature must define parameters and a return value that are compatible with all preceding signatures. As this implies, the return types for each overload can be different and the parameter lists can differ not only in types, but also in number of arguments. If an overload specifies fewer parameters than the implementation signature, the implementation signature would have to make the extra parameters optional, default, or rest parameters.

When you call a function that has overloads defined, the compiler constructs a list of signatures and attempts to determine the signature that matches the function call. If there are no matching signatures, the call results in an error. If one or more signature matches, the earliest of the matching signatures (in the order they appear in the file) determines the return type.

Listing 1-58. Overloads

```
function getAverage(a: string, b: string, c: string): string;
function getAverage(a: number, b: number, c: number): string;
// implementation signature
function getAverage(a: any, b: any, c: any): string {
    const total = parseInt(a, 10) + parseInt(b, 10) + parseInt(c, 10);
    const average = total / 3;
    return 'The average is ' + average;
}

// The average is 5
const result = getAverage(4, 3, 8);
```

Overloads introduce a burden to the function as types may need to be tested or converted, and they may cause multiple logical branches within the function. In cases where the types are compatible and no additional code needs to be written within the function, overloads allow a single function to be used in multiple cases.

For Listing 1-58, a simpler solution would be to use union types of string | number with a single function signature. Union types can probably eliminate most cases for function overloads, and the remaining cases can typically be replaced with optional or default parameters. If you have more than a handful of overloads in your program, you may be missing an opportunity to use these language features.

■ **Note** When you use overloads, the implementation signature cannot be called directly, so all calls must be compatible with one of the overloads.

Specialized Overload Signatures

Specialized overload signatures refer to the ability in TypeScript to create overloads based on string constants. Rather than the overloads being based on different parameters, they are based on the string value of an argument as shown in Listing 1-59. This allows a single implementation of a function to be reused in many cases without requiring the calling code to convert the types.

There are some rules to follow when using specialized overload signatures

- There must be at least one nonspecialized signature.

- Each specialized signature must return a subtype of a nonspecialized signature.

- The implementation signature must be compatible with all signatures.

Listing 1-59. Specialized overload signatures

```
class HandlerFactory {
    getHandler(type: 'Random'): RandomHandler;
    getHandler(type: 'Reversed'): ReversedHandler;
    getHandler(type: string): Handler; // non-specialized signature
    getHandler(type: string): Handler { // implementation signature
        switch (type) {
            case 'Random':
                return new RandomHandler();
            case 'Reversed':
                return new ReversedHandler();
            default:
                return new Handler();
        }
    }
}
```

The most common case for specialized signatures is that the nonspecialized signature returns a superclass, with each overload returning a more specialized subclass that inherits (or is structurally compatible with) the superclass. This is how the classic definition for the Document Object Model (DOM) method getElementsByTagName was declared in the early versions of the TypeScript standard library, which means you get back an appropriately typed NodeList depending on the HTML tag name you pass to the function. An extract of this method signature is shown in Listing 1-60 (the current version of the standard library uses a slightly different mechanism).

When you write signatures that satisfy these rules, you may find that your implementation signature is identical to your nonspecialized signature. Remember that the implementation signature is hidden from calling code, so although it looks like duplication, it is necessary. This was illustrated in Listing 1-59, which shows how specialized subclasses are annotated as the return type where a specific value is passed in the type parameter.

Listing 1-60. getElementsByTagName

```
// This example does not list all variations...
getElementsByTagName(name: "a"): NodeListOf<HTMLAnchorElement>;
getElementsByTagName(name: "blockquote"): NodeListOf<HTMLQuoteElement>;
getElementsByTagName(name: "body"): NodeListOf<HTMLBodyElement>;
getElementsByTagName(name: "button"): NodeListOf<HTMLButtonElement>;
getElementsByTagName(name: "form"): NodeListOf<HTMLFormElement>;
getElementsByTagName(name: "h1"): NodeListOf<HTMLHeadingElement>;
getElementsByTagName(name: string): NodeList; // Non-specialized signature
getElementsByTagName(name: string): NodeList { // implementation signature
    return document.getElementsByTagName(name);
}
```

This is an unusual technique, but is necessary for the purposes of defining the behavior you would expect from web browsers. The specialized overloads inspect the value being passed and select the overload based on that value, for example, if you pass a name argument with the value "blockquote", the second signature in Listing 1-60 will be matched and the return type is NodeListOf<HTMLQuoteElement>.

Arrow Functions

TypeScript provides shorthand syntax for defining a function. The arrow function is inspired by proposed additions to the ECMAScript standard. Arrow functions allow you to leave out the function keyword and define your functions in an ultracompact way. All the functions in Listing 1-61 result in identical JavaScript functions in the output when you target ECMAScript 3 or 5.

■ **Note**   The TypeScript compiler has options to target version 3 and version 5 of the ECMAScript specification and has support for the new annual versions such as ECMA2015 onward. Version 4 of the ECMAScript specification was abandoned, so technically it doesn't exist.

Listing 1-61. Arrow functions

```
const shortAddNumbers = (a: number, b: number) => a + b;

const mediumAddNumbers = (a: number, b: number) => {
    return a + b;
}

const longAddNumbers = function (a: number, b: number) {
    return a + b;
}
```

Each of the function variations in Listing 1-61 defines a function that accepts two numbers and returns the sum of those numbers. In the shortest example, although there is no return keyword, the compiler will return the result of the single expression. If you want to write multiple expressions, you will need to wrap the function in braces and use the return keyword.

Sometimes the single expression to be returned by an arrow function will be an object, for example, { firstName: 'Mark', lastName: 'Rendle' }. The braces around the object declaration confuse the TypeScript compiler, so you need to mark it as an expression by surrounding it with parentheses, as shown in Listing 1-62.

Listing 1-62. Wrapping an object in parentheses

```
const makeName = (f: string, l: string) => ({ first: f, last: l });
```

You can also use an arrow syntax to preserve the lexical scope of the this keyword. This is particularly useful when working with callbacks, promises, or events as these represent situations where you are likely to lose the current scope. This is discussed in more detail in the section on classes later in this chapter, but it is also useful outside of classes as shown in Listing 1-63.

The ScopeLosingExample object uses the standard syntax to create the function that is called when the timer expires. The scope of this is lost when the function is invoked by the timer, so the value of this.text is undefined, as we are no longer in the object context. In the ScopePreservingExample the only change is the use of the arrow syntax, which fixes the scope problem and allows the correct value to be obtained.

Listing 1-63. Preserving scope with arrow syntax

```
const scopeLosingExample = {
    text: "Property from lexical scope",
    run: function () {
        setTimeout(function () {
            alert(this.text);
        }, 1000);
    }
};

// alerts undefined
scopeLosingExample.run();

const scopePreservingExample = {
    text: "Property from lexical scope",
    run: function () {
        setTimeout(() => {
            alert(this.text);
        }, 1000);
    }
};

// alerts "Property from lexical scope"
scopePreservingExample.run();
```

Behind the scenes, the TypeScript compiler creates a variable named _this just before the arrow function is defined and sets its value to the current value of this. It also substitutes any usages of this within the function with the newly introduced _this variable, so the statement now reads _this.text in the JavaScript output. The use of the _this variable inside the function creates a closure around the variable, which preserves its context along with the function. You can follow this pattern yourself, which is useful if you ever need both the original meaning of this as well as the functionally scoped meaning of this, such as when you are handling events.

Function Currying

Currying is a process whereby a function with multiple parameters is decomposed into multiple functions that each take a single parameter. The resulting chain of functions can be called in stages, with the partly applied stage becoming a reusable implementation of the combined function and value.

You can use arrow functions for function currying, as shown in Listing 1-64. The first function takes a single parameter named a, and returns another function that has captured the value of the original argument. The function that is returned accepts a single parameter named b, and when called returns the product of a and b. You can hold onto the result of the first function call and use it many times, which is one of the key points of currying.

Listing 1-64. Currying with arrow functions

```
// Currying
const multiply = (a: number) => (b: number) => a * b;

// Pass both arguments in sequence: 30
const numA = multiply(5)(6);
```

```
// Pass just the first argument and re-use
const orderOfMagnitude = multiply(10);

// 10
const deca = orderOfMagnitude(1);

// 100
const hecta = orderOfMagnitude(deca);

// 1,000
const kilo = orderOfMagnitude(hecta);
```

If you find the first function call chain strange, you can implement a function that can be called with one or two arguments, as shown in Listing 1-65. This example uses an overload to allow the single argument, or two argument variations – and a guard clause that branches the code to either return a function, or a number. This enables the "normal" call to multiply with two arguments, as well as supporting function currying.

Listing 1-65. Currying with function overloads

```
function multiply(a: number): (b: number) => number;
function multiply(a: number, b: number): number;
function multiply(a: number, b: number = null) {
    if (b === null) {
        return (b: number) => a * b;
    }

    return a * b;
}

// Pass both arguments "normally": 30
const numA = multiply(5, 6);

// Pass just the first argument and re-use
const orderOfMagnitude = multiply(10);

// 10
const deca = orderOfMagnitude(1);

// 100
const hecta = orderOfMagnitude(deca);

// 1,000
const kilo = orderOfMagnitude(hecta);
```

If you are struggling to come up with a real application of this feature, a practical example is shown in Listing 1-66, where instead of repeating the first argument of a logging function, it can be specified a single time and applied each time the logging function is called. This reduces repetition and improves readability.

Listing 1-66. Practical currying

```typescript
const log = (source: string) => (message: string) => console.log(source, message);

const customLog = log('Custom Log:');

// Custom Log: Message One
customLog('Message One');

// Custom Log: Message Two
customLog('Message Two');
```

If you find yourself calling out to a function several times with similar arguments, you may be able to apply currying to clean up the function calls.

Interfaces

TypeScript interfaces can be used for several purposes. As you would expect, an interface can be used as an abstract type that can be implemented by concrete classes, but they can also be used to define any structure in your TypeScript program. Interfaces are also the building blocks for defining the contracts made available by third-party libraries and frameworks that are not written in TypeScript. There is more detail on writing ambient declarations to define external code in Chapter 9.

Interfaces are declared with the `interface` keyword and contain a series of annotations to describe the contract that they represent. The annotations describe properties and functions, as you might expect, and constructors and indexers, which are not as common in other languages. When writing interfaces to describe classes you intend to implement in your program, you won't need to define constructors or indexers. These features are included to help you describe external code with structures that may not be analogous to classes. This is discussed in Chapter 4.

Listing 1-67 demonstrates a set of interfaces that describe a vehicle, passengers, location, and destination. Properties and methods are declared using the familiar type annotations that have been used throughout this chapter. Constructors are declared using the new keyword.

Listing 1-67. Interfaces

```typescript
interface Point {
    // Properties
    x: number;
    y: number;
}

interface Passenger {
    // Properties
    name: string;
}

interface Vehicle {
    // Constructor
    new(): Vehicle;

    // Properties
    currentLocation: Point;
```

```
    // Methods
    travelTo(point: Point): void;
    addPassenger(passenger: Passenger): void;
    removePassenger(passenger: Passenger): void;
}
```

Interfaces do not result in any compiled JavaScript code; this is due to type erasure, which is described in Chapter 3. Interfaces are used at design time to provide autocompletion and at compile time to provide type checking.

Just like enumerations, interfaces remain open and all declarations with a common root are merged into a single structure. This means you must ensure that the combined interface is valid; you can't declare the same property in multiple blocks of the same interface (you'll receive a "duplicate identifier" error) and you can't define the same method (although you can add overloads to an existing one).

Declaring an interface in several blocks is not a particularly valuable feature when you are writing your own program, but when it comes to extending built-in definitions or external code, this feature is priceless. For example, Figure 1-7 shows the available items on a NodeList: the item method and the length property. The built-in interface definition for NodeList is shown in Listing 1-68; the length property, item method, and the indexer are all included.

```
1  const nodeList = document.getElementsByTagName('div');
2
3  nodeList.
        ⊗ entries   (method) NodeListOf<HTMLDivElement>.entrie…   ⓘ
          Returns an array of key, value pairs for every entry in the list
        ⊗ forEach
        ⊗ item
        ⊗ keys
        ● length
        ⊗ values
```

Figure 1-7. The native NodeList

Listing 1-68. Built-in NodeListOf<T> interface

```
interface NodeList {
    readonly length: number;
    item(index: number): Node;
    [index: number]: Node;
}
```

If interfaces were closed, you would be limited to the contract defined in the standard library that ships with TypeScript, but in Listing 1-69, an additional interface block extends the built-in NodeList interface to add an onclick property that is not available natively. The implementation isn't included in this example — it may be a new web standard that has yet to find its way into TypeScript's standard library or a JavaScript library that adds the additional functionality. As far as the compiler is concerned, the interface that is defined in the standard library and the interface that is defined in your TypeScript file are one interface. You can find out more about extending existing objects in Chapter 5, and about specifically extending native browser functionality in Chapter 6.

Listing 1-69. Extending the NodeList interface

```typescript
interface NodeList {
    onclick: (event: MouseEvent) => any;
}

const nodeList = document.getElementsByTagName('div');

nodeList.onclick = function (event: MouseEvent) {
    alert('Clicked'
};
```

You can also describe hybrid types with an interface, such as a function/object hybrid type. Listing 1-70 shows a very brief hybrid type that might have been an imaginary early version of jQuery, which is probably the most famous hybrid type implementation in the world.

Listing 1-70. Hybrid types

```typescript
// Hybrid type
interface SimpleDocument {
    (selector: string): HTMLElement;
    notify(message: string): void;
}

// Implementation
const prepareDocument = function (): SimpleDocument {
    let doc = <SimpleDocument>function (selector: string) {
        return document.getElementById(selector);
    };

    doc.notify = function (message: string) {
        alert(message);
    }

    return doc;
}

const $ = prepareDocument();

// Call $ as a function
const elem = $('myId');

// Use $ as an object
$.notify(elem.id);
```

It is worth reiterating that interfaces are not only for describing a contract you intend to implement in a class, they can be used to describe any structure you can conceive in your program whether they are functions, variables, objects, or combinations thereof. When a method accepts an options object as a parameter, which is common in JavaScript frameworks such as jQuery, an interface can be used to provide autocompletion for the complex object argument.

There is one other slightly obscure feature related to interfaces in TypeScript that is worth keeping in mind. An interface can inherit from a class in the same way a subclass can inherit from a superclass. When you do this, the interface inherits all the members of the class, but without any implementation. Anything added to the class will also be added to the interface. You'll find that this feature is particularly useful when used in conjunction with generics, which are explained later in this chapter.

Classes

Most of the preceding information on the TypeScript language has concerned various methods of annotating your code with type information. As you'll read in Chapter 3, although it is important to understand all the various type annotations, TypeScript has powerful type inference that can do a lot of the work for you. The structural elements, on the other hand, will become familiar tools molded to the shape of your hands. Classes are the most fundamental structural element when it comes to organizing you program.

There are quite a few aspects to learn when working with classes, but if you have any previous experience with class-based object orientation, many of the features will be recognizable, even if the details or syntax are new.

Constructors

All classes in TypeScript have a constructor, whether you specify one or not. If you leave out the constructor, the compiler will automatically add one. For a class that doesn't inherit from another class, the automatic constructor will be parameterless and will initialize any class properties. Where the class extends another class, the automatic constructor will match the superclass signature and will pass arguments to the superclass before initializing any of its own properties.

Listing 1-71 shows two classes that have a manually written constructor. It is a slightly longer example than many of the other code listings in this chapter, but it is worth reading through it before each aspect is explained.

Listing 1-71. Constructors

```
class Song {
    constructor(private artist: string, private title: string) {

    }

    play() {
        console.log('Playing ' + this.title + ' by ' + this.artist);
    }
}

class Jukebox {
    constructor(private songs: Song[]) {
    }

    play() {
        const song = this.getRandomSong();
        song.play();
    }
```

```
    private getRandomSong() {
        const songCount = this.songs.length;
        const songIndex = Math.floor(Math.random() * songCount);

        return this.songs[songIndex];
    }
}

const songs = [
    new Song('Bushbaby', 'Megaphone'),
    new Song('Delays', 'One More Lie In'),
    new Song('Goober Gun', 'Stereo'),
    new Song('Sohnee', 'Shatter'),
    new Song('Get Amped', 'Celebrity')
];

const jukebox = new Jukebox(songs);

jukebox.play();
```

One of the first things that may strike you about the example is that the constructor parameters are not mapped to member variables. If you prefix a constructor parameter with an access modifier, such as private, it will automatically be mapped for you. You can refer to these constructor parameters as if they were declared as properties on the class; for example, this.title, can be used anywhere within the Song class to obtain the song title on that instance. Listing 1-72 shows equivalent code where the parameters are manually mapped, but this is to illustrate the point that this creates a lot of redundant code, and you should avoid this approach.

Listing 1-72. Manually mapped constructor parameters

```
class Song {

    private artist: string;
    private title: string;

    constructor(artist: string, title: string) {
        // Don't do this!
        this.artist = artist;
        this.title = title;
    }

    play() {
        console.log('Playing ' + this.title + ' by ' + this.artist);
    }
}
```

Access Modifiers

Access modifiers change the visibility of class members. There are three access modifiers available in TypeScript:

- private
- protected
- public

The private modifier restricts the visibility to the same-class only. When you use the private modifier on a member, it won't appear in autocompletion (which is a strong hint that you can't use it) and attempts to access the member from outside the class will result in a compiler error. You cannot even access the member from a subclass.

The protected modifier allows the member to be used within the same-class, and within subclasses. Access from anywhere else is not allowed.

The public modifier, which is the default for class members, allows access from all locations. It is not necessary to specify the public keyword on a property or method unless you want to be explicit – but you will need to add it to constructor parameters to have them mapped to properties automatically.

When considering the visibility of class members, it is worth starting with the least visible access modifier, which is private. When a member is private, you can make changes to it knowing it is only used within the class you are changing. As you increase the visibility of members, you also increase the complexity of changes, and your blood pressure when you attempt to refactor your code. Access modifiers are a key component of encapsulation. When you are about to change a private member to become public, consider whether the code actually ought to be moved into the class instead.

Access modifiers are removed during compilation, so access is not controlled at runtime, but enforced logically during the compilation.

Properties and Methods

Instance properties are typically declared before the constructor in a TypeScript class. A property definition consists of three parts: an optional access modifier, the identifier, and a type annotation. For example: `public name: string;`. You can also initialize the property with a value: `public name = 'Jane';` When your program is compiled, the property initializers are moved into the top of the constructor, so they run before any code you place in the constructor. Instance properties can be accessed from within the class using the `this` keyword. If the property is public it can be accessed using the instance name.

You can also add static properties to your class, which are defined in the same way as instance properties, but with the `static` keyword between the access modifier (if one is specified) and the identifier. Static properties are accessed using the class name as shown in Listing 1-73, where the static `maxSongCount` property is accessed using `Playlist.maxSongCount` — even within a method on the class; this is because the property is not defined on each instance.

You can make both static and instance properties read-only to prevent the values being overwritten. The `maxSongCount` static property has been marked as `readonly` to prevent the value from being changed from 30.

Listing 1-73. Properties and methods

```
class Playlist {

    private songs: Song[] = [];

    static readonly maxSongCount = 30;
```

49

```
    constructor(public name: string) {
    }

    addSong(song: Song) {
        if (this.songs.length >= Playlist.maxSongCount) {
            throw new Error('Playlist is full');
        }

        this.songs.push(song);
    }
}

// Creating a new instance
const playlist = new Playlist('My Playlist');

// Accessing a public instance property
const name = playlist.name;

// Calling a public instance method
playlist.addSong(new Song('Therapy?', 'Crooked Timber'));

// Accessing a public static property
const maxSongs = Playlist.maxSongCount;

// Error: Cannot assign to a readonly property
Playlist.maxSongCount = 20;
```

Listing 1-73 also illustrates a typical method definition. Methods are defined a lot like functions, but they leave out the `function` keyword. You can annotate a method with all the parameters and return value type annotations that were discussed earlier in the section on functions. You can prefix the method name with an access modifier to control its visibility, which is public by default. Just as with instance properties, methods can be accessed from within the class using the `this` keyword; and if they are public they can be accessed outside of the class using the instance name.

You can create static methods by prefixing the method name with the `static` keyword. Static members can be called even when no instance of the class has been created and only a single instance of each static member exists in your program. All static members are accessed via the class name and not an instance name and static members have no access to nonstatic properties or methods.

TypeScript supports property getters and setters, if you are targeting ECMAScript 5 or above. The syntax for these is identical to method signatures as described in the following, except they are prefixed by either the get or set keyword. As shown in Listing 1-74, property getters and setters allow you to wrap property access with a method while preserving the appearance of a simple property to the calling code.

Listing 1-74. Property getters and setters

```
interface StockItem {
    description: string;
    asin: string;
}

class WarehouseLocation {
    private _stockItem: StockItem;
```

```typescript
    constructor(public aisle: number, public slot: string) {

    }

    get stockItem() {
        return this._stockItem;
    }

    set stockItem(item: StockItem) {
        this._stockItem = item;
    }
}

const figure = { asin: 'B001TEQ2PI', description: 'Figure' };

const warehouseSlot = new WarehouseLocation(15, 'A6');

warehouseSlot.stockItem = figure;
```

Class Heritage

There are two types of class heritage in TypeScript. A class can implement an interface using the implements keyword and a class can inherit from another class using the extends keyword.

When you implement an interface, the implements declaration is entirely optional due to the structural types in TypeScript. If you do specify the interface using the implements keyword, your class will be checked to ensure that it complies with the contract promised by the interface. Listing 1-75 shows how the Song class implements the Audio interface. The play method must be implemented in the Song class, and its signature must be compatible with the Audio interface declaration. A class can implement multiple interfaces, with each interface being separated by a comma, for example: implements Audio, Video.

Listing 1-75. Class heritage

```typescript
interface Audio {
    play(): any;
}

class Song implements Audio {
    constructor(private artist: string, private title: string) {
    }

    play(): void {
        console.log('Playing ' + this.title + ' by ' + this.artist);
    }

    static Comparer(a: Song, b: Song) {
        if (a.title === b.title) {
            return 0;
        }

        return a.title > b.title ? 1 : -1;
    }
}
```

```typescript
class Playlist {
    constructor(public songs: Audio[]) {
    }

    play() {
        var song = this.songs.pop();
        song.play();
    }

    sort() {
        this.songs.sort(Song.Comparer);
    }
}

class RepeatingPlaylist extends Playlist {

    private songIndex = 0;

    constructor(songs: Song[]) {
        super(songs);
    }

    play() {
        this.songs[this.songIndex].play;

        this.songIndex++;

        if (this.songIndex >= this.songs.length) {
            this.songIndex = 0;
        }
    }
}
```

■ **Note**   A method on a class can have fewer parameters than the interface specifies. This allows a class to ignore arguments that it doesn't require to execute the method. Any parameters that are specified must match the parameters in the interface.

You inherit from a class using the extends keyword, as shown in Listing 1-75. An extends clause makes your class a derived class, and it will gain all the properties and methods of the base class from which it inherits. You can override a public member of the base class by adding a member of the same name and kind as the base class member. The RepeatingPlaylist inherits from the Playlist class and uses the songs property from the base class using this.songs, but overrides the play method with a specialized implementation that plays the next song in a repeating loop.

The constructor on the RepeatingPlaylist class shown in Listing 1-75 could be omitted because the automatic constructor that would be generated would match it exactly.

If the subclass accepts additional arguments there are a couple of rules you need to follow. The super call to the base class must be the first statement in the subclass constructor and you cannot specify a more restrictive access modifier for a parameter on the subclass than it has on the base class.

There are some rules that must be followed for inheritance:

- A class can only inherit from a single superclass.
- A class cannot inherit from itself, either directly or via a chain of inheritance.

It is possible to create a class that inherits from another class and implements multiple interfaces. In this case, the class must be a subtype of the base class as well as each interface.

Abstract Classes

An abstract class can be used as a base class, but can't be instantiated directly. Abstract classes can contain implemented methods as well as abstract methods, which have no implementation and must be implemented by any subclass.

Listing 1-76 contains an abstract logger class with an abstract notify method, and an implemented protected getMessage method. Each subclass must implement the notify method, but can share the getMessage implementation from the base class.

Listing 1-76. Abstract classes

```
// Abstract class
abstract class Logger {
    abstract notify(message: string): void;

    protected getMessage(message: string): string {
        return `Information: ${new Date().toUTCString()} ${message}`;
    }
}

class ConsoleLogger extends Logger {
    notify(message) {
        console.log(this.getMessage(message));
    }
}

class InvasiveLogger extends Logger {
    notify(message) {
        alert(this.getMessage(message));
    }
}

let logger: Logger;

// Error. Cannot create an instance of an abstract class
logger = new Logger();

// Create an instance of a sub-class
logger = new InvasiveLogger();

logger.notify('Hello World');
```

Abstract classes are like interfaces, in that they contain a contract that may have no implementation. They can add to this with implementation code, and can specify access modifiers against the members: two things that interfaces cannot do.

Scope

If you call a class method from an event, or use it as a callback, the original context of the method can be lost, which results in problems using instance methods and instance properties. When the context is changed, the value of the this keyword is replaced.

Listing 1-77 shows a typical example of lost context. If the registerClick method is called directly against the clickCounter instance, it works as expected. When the registerClick method is assigned to the onclick event, the context is lost and this.count is undefined in the new context.

Listing 1-77. Lost context

```
class ClickCounter {
    private count = 0;

    registerClick() {
        this.count++;
        alert(this.count);
    }
}

const clickCounter = new ClickCounter();

document.getElementById('target').onclick = clickCounter.registerClick;
```

There are several techniques that can be used to preserve the context to enable this to work, and you may choose to use different approaches in different scenarios.

Property and Arrow Function

You can replace the method with a property and initialize the property using an arrow function as shown in Listing 1-78. This is a reasonable technique if you know that the class will be consumed with events or callbacks, but it is less of an option if your class has no knowledge of when and where it may be called.

Listing 1-78. Preserving context with a property and an arrow function

```
class ClickCounter {
    private count = 0;

    registerClick = () => {
        this.count++;
        alert(this.count);
    }
}
```

Function Wrapping at Point of Call

If you want to leave your class untouched, you can wrap the call to the instance method in a function to create a closure that keeps the context alongside the function. This is demonstrated in Listing 1-79, which allows the use of this within the registerClick method without converting the method to a property. This is preferable to mangling the class.

Listing 1-79. Preserving context with a closure

```
document.getElementById('target').onclick = function () {
        clickCounter.registerClick();
};
```

ECMAScript 5 Bind Function

Another technique that leaves the original class untouched is to use JavaScript's bind function, which is available in ECMAScript 5 and higher. The bind function sets the context for the method. It can be used more generally to permanently replace the context, but in Listing 1-80 it is used to fix the context for the registerClick method to be the clickCounter instance.

Listing 1-80. Preserving context with bind

```
const clickHandler = clickCounter.registerClick.bind(clickCounter);

document.getElementById('target').onclick = clickHandler;
```

Event Capturing

If you need to capture the event argument, the simplest way is to use an arrow function as shown in Listing 1-81. The registerClick method has been updated to take an identifier, which is obtained using the event target (or source element in older versions of Internet Explorer). This preserves the context and captures the event information in one terse statement.

Listing 1-81. Preserving context and capturing the event

```
class ClickCounter {
    private count = 0;

    registerClick(id: string) {
        this.count++;
        alert(this.count);
    }
}

const clickCounter = new ClickCounter();

document.getElementById('target').onclick = (e) => {
    const target = <Element>e.target || e.srcElement;
    clickCounter.registerClick(target.id);
};
```

Choosing a Solution

There are several techniques you can use to ensure that your context is preserved when using a class instance method for callbacks and events. There are no fixed rules about which of these is the correct one to use; it depends on the specific use and your own design preferences.

If you are targeting slightly older browsers, the bind function may not be an option, but if older browsers aren't an issue you may find it more graceful than a closure and it certainly makes your intent much clearer. The property and arrow-function technique is a neat trick, but perhaps allows too much knowledge of where the method is called to leak into your class.

One thing to consider when designing your program will be the number of instances of each class being created at runtime. If you are creating hundreds or thousands of instances it is more efficient for the methods to be normal instance methods, not arrow functions assigned to properties. This is because normal instance methods are defined once and used by all instances. If you use a property and arrow function, it will be duplicated on every instance. This duplication can become a big overhead when a large number of instances are created.

If you want to keep a clear divide between responsibilities, follow this guideline; when you need to preserve the scope of a callback, prefer to preserve it when setting up the callback, not by adjusting the class itself.

Type Information

Obtaining types at runtime is a topic to be treated with some care. If your program tests types to control the flow of the program, you should be hearing alarm bells in your head. Checking types and branching off in different directions based on the type is a strong indicator that you have broken encapsulation. With this in mind, the following section describes how you can check types and obtain type names at runtime.

To test the type of a class instance, you use the instanceof operator. The operator is placed between the instance and the type you want to test, as shown in Listing 1-82. The test returns true if you have an instance of the specified class, or if the specified class appears anywhere in the inheritance chain. In all other cases, it returns false.

Listing 1-82. Using the instanceof operator

```
class Display {
    name: string = '';
}

class Television extends Display {

}

class HiFi {

}

const display = new Display();
const television = new Television();
const hiFi = new HiFi();

let isDisplay;
```

```
// true
isDisplay = display instanceof Display;

// true (inherits from Display)
isDisplay = television instanceof Display;

// false
isDisplay = hiFi instanceof Display;
```

You can also test the presence of specific properties using the in keyword. Expanding on the previous example from Listing 1-82, we can test for the presence of a name property as shown in Listing 1-83. The in operator will return true if the class has the property or if it inherits from a class that has the property.

Listing 1-83. The in property

```
let hasName;

// true
hasName = 'name' in display;

// true
hasName = 'name' in television;

// false
hasName - 'name' in hiFi;
```

It is important to note that due to the code generation in the TypeScript compiler, an uninitialized property will not be detected because unless the property has a value, it does not appear in the compiled JavaScript code. In Listing 1-84 the hasName property will be false because, although a name property is declared, the name property is never initialized. If the name property had been assigned a value, hasName would be true.

Listing 1-84. Uninitialized property

```
class Display {
    name: string;
}

const display = new Display();

// false
const hasName = 'name' in display;
```

■ **Note**   Don't forget the quotes around the property name when using the in keyword as you will need to pass a string. Without the quotes, you would be testing the value of a variable, which may not even be defined.

If you want to obtain the type name at runtime, you may be tempted to use the typeof operator. Unfortunately, this will return the type name 'object' for all classes. This means you need to inspect the constructor of the instance to find the type name. This can be done as shown in Listing 1-85.

Listing 1-85. Obtaining runtime types

```
const tv = new Television();
const radio = new HiFi();

// Television
const tvType = tv.constructor.name;

// HiFi
const radioType = radio.constructor.name;
```

If you are using a minifier to squash your compiled JavaScript files, it is common for such tools to change the names of your classes, for example, the Television class may be minified to simply 'x'. If you intend to inspect the constructor names, you will need to disable the compression of function names in your minification tool.

Generics

Generic programming allows algorithms to be written in way that allows the types to be specified later. This allows the types to be processed identically without sacrificing type safety or requiring separate instances of the algorithm to handle each type. It is possible to constrain the possible types used by the algorithm by specifying a type constraint.

In TypeScript it is possible to create generic functions, including generic methods, generic interfaces, and generic classes.

Generic Functions

To make a function generic, you add a type parameter enclosed in angle brackets (< >) immediately after the function name. The type parameter can then be used to annotate function parameters, the return type, or types used within the function (or any combination thereof). This is illustrated in Listing 1-86.

When you call a generic function, you can specify the type argument by placing it in angle brackets after the function name. If the type can be inferred (e.g., by inspecting the types of the arguments passed to the function), the type argument becomes optional.

Listing 1-86. Generic functions

```
function reverse<T>(list: T[]) : T[] {
    const reversedList: T[] = [];

    for (let i = (list.length - 1); i >= 0; i--) {
        reversedList.push(list[i]);
    }

    return reversedList;
}

const letters = ['a', 'b', 'c', 'd'];
```

```
// d, c, b, a
const reversedLetters = reverse<string>(letters);

const numbers = [1, 2, 3, 4];

// 4, 3, 2, 1
const reversedNumbers = reverse<number>(numbers);
```

■ **Tip**   In both examples in Listing 1-86, the type arguments can be omitted because the compiler is able to infer the type based on the arguments passed to the function.

Generic Interfaces

To make a generic interface, the type parameters are placed directly after the interface name. Listing 1-87 shows a generic Repository interface that has two type parameters representing the type of a domain object and the type of an ID for that domain object. These type parameters can be used as annotations anywhere within the interface declaration.

When the CustomerRepository class implements the generic interface, it supplies the concrete Customer and CustomerId types as type arguments. The body of the CustomerRepository class is checked to ensure that it implements the interface based on these types.

Listing 1-87. Generic interfaces

```
class CustomerId {
    constructor(private customerIdValue: number) {
    }

    get value() {
        return this.customerIdValue;
    }
}

class Customer {
    constructor(public id: CustomerId, public name: string) {

    }
}

interface Repository<T, TId> {
    getById(id: TId): T;
    persist(model: T): TId;
}

class CustomerRepository implements Repository<Customer, CustomerId> {
    constructor(private customers: Customer[]) {

    }
```

```
    getById(id: CustomerId) {
        return this.customers[id.value];
    }

    persist(customer: Customer) {
        this.customers[customer.id.value] = customer;
        return customer.id;
    }
}
```

Generic Classes

If generic interfaces can save some duplication in your code, generic classes can save even more by supplying a single implementation to service many different type scenarios. The type parameters follow the class name and are surrounded by angle brackets. The type parameter can be used to annotate method parameters, properties, return types, and local variables within the class.

Listing 1-88 uses a generic class to provide a single implementation for all named ID types in a domain model. This allows all ids to be named without requiring individual implementations for each named type. This is a common pattern described by P. J. Plauger (*Programming on Purpose*, Prentice Hall, 1993) that prevents accidental substitution of values. This technique can be used in TypeScript, although there are some details to bear in mind when you implement the technique; these are discussed in Chapter 3.

Listing 1-88. Generic classes

```
class DomainId<T> {
    constructor(private id: T) {

    }

    get value(): T {
        return this.id;
    }
}

class OrderId extends DomainId<number> {
    constructor(orderIdValue: number) {
        super(orderIdValue);
    }
}

class AccountId extends DomainId<string> {
    constructor(accountIdValue: string) {
        super(accountIdValue);
    }
}

// Examples of compatibility

function onlyAcceptsOrderId(orderId: OrderId) {
    // ...
}
```

```
function acceptsAnyDomainId(id: DomainId<any>) {
    // ...
}

const accountId = new AccountId('GUID-1');
const orderId = new OrderId(5);

// Error: Argument of type 'AccountId' is not assignable to parameter of type 'OrderId'
onlyAcceptsOrderId(accountId);

// OK
onlyAcceptsOrderId(orderId);

// OK
acceptsAnyDomainId(accountId);
```

Type Constraints

A type constraint can be used to limit the types that a generic function, interface, or class can operate on. Listing 1-89 shows how an interface can be used to specify a contract that all types must satisfy to be used as a type argument. Type constraints are specified using the extends keyword, whether the constraint is an interface, a class, or a type annotation that describes the constraint.

If a type argument is specified that does not satisfy the constraint, the compiler will issue an error. The constraint also allows the TypeScript language service to supply autocompletion suggestions for the generically typed members.

Listing 1-89. Type constraints

```
interface HasName {
    name: string;
}

class Personalization {
    static greet<T extends HasName>(obj: T) {
        return 'Hello ' + obj.name;
    }
}
```

You can only specify a single class in a type constraint. Although you cannot specify multiple classes in a type constraint, you can create an interface that extends multiple classes and uses the interface as the constraint, which achieves the same result. Any types used with the constraint would then need to satisfy all the class signatures that have been combined into the single interface.

TypeScript Futures

There are plans to add further features to the TypeScript language. In the short term, most language changes will be made to keep TypeScript in step with the developments in the ECMAScript specification. The language will not be limited by ECMAScript developments though and the road map currently contains a range of features being considered for implementation to support a richer type system and improved tooling.

Summary

This chapter has introduced all the language features you need to write large-scale applications using TypeScript. You can revisit this chapter if you need to refer to any of these features. You should now have a firm grasp of type annotations, be able to use operators to perform shorthand type conversions, create routines inside of classes, and take advantage of generics to avoid near-duplicate implementations.

The next chapter provides further information on organizing your program, and Chapter 3 features a deep dive into the type system, which is especially important if your background is in nominally typed languages.

Key Points

- All JavaScript is valid TypeScript.

- Primitive types are closely linked to JavaScript primitive types.

- Types are inferred in TypeScript, but you can supply annotations to make types explicit or deal with cases the compiler can't handle.

- Interfaces can be used to describe complicated structures, to make type annotations shorter.

- All TypeScript arrays are generic.

- You can use enumerations as bit flags.

- There are special cases where type coercion applies, but in most cases type checking will generate errors for invalid use of types.

- You can add optional, default, and rest parameters to functions and methods.

- Arrow functions provide a short syntax for declaring functions, but can also be used to preserve the lexical scope.

- Enumerations, interfaces, and modules are open, so multiple declarations that have the same name in the same common root will result in a single definition.

- Classes bring structure to your TypeScript program and make it possible to use common design patterns.

- You can obtain type information at runtime, but this should be used responsibly.

■ ■ ■

CHAPTER 2

Code Organization

It is not the language that makes programs appear simple. It is the programmer that makes the language appear simple!

—Robert C Martin

This chapter deals with code organization. The subject deals with namespaces, modules, module loading, and packaging. The paramount concern for this chapter is to help you slice up your program into chunks that are easy to find, maintain, and consume.

There have been a few terminology changes since TypeScript was first made public, so to clarify the terms, here are descriptions of the main elements:

- A *namespace* (previously known as an internal module) creates a context for identifiers, reducing naming collisions in your program and providing a mechanism to organize your code into logical schemes. A namespace adds only one item to the global scope; and this item provides a hierarchical mechanism for accessing everything that is made public within the namespace.

- A module (previously known as an *external module*) is a completely isolated context that adds no items to the global scope. A module may import other modules, and export members that can be used outside of the module. Modules are supported by a module loader, with various options available to load modules in browsers, and with the CommonJS loader found on web servers running Node.

- A package is a mechanism for delivering a number of code files for consumption within another program. Most package managers have a format that involves a structured archive folder with the code and metadata. The package can be made available on either a public repository (as many open source projects are), or on a private repository such as a company-wide package repository.

A namespace can be divided among many files, with each contributing additional members to the namespace. A module is exactly equivalent to a single file. One of my goals in this chapter is to convince you to prefer modules over namespaces, as they provide several benefits immediately, and when your program grows.

Namespaces are a simple mechanism that work well with bundling. When you output your code to a single file, for example, by compiling your TypeScript code with the `--outFile` compiler flag. As you introduce more namespaces, the number of items in the global scope increases. When your program grows to a certain size, it becomes difficult to track the dependencies between your components and the output file can become unwieldy. While you can load your one massive file asynchronously, the entire program must be loaded before it can run. Namespaces can be a dangerous trap as they can feel frictionless when you first start writing your TypeScript program; but long term they will become a decision you regret.

© Steve Fenton 2018
S. Fenton, *Pro TypeScript*, https://doi.org/10.1007/978-1-4842-3249-1_2

Despite this warning, I will still explain how to use namespaces in this chapter, but this is not an endorsement of the feature. Any book on TypeScript would be incomplete with an explanation of namespaces, and even if I manage to convince you to avoid them, you will almost certainly come across them in some other codebase and you'll want to know how they work.

Namespaces

Namespaces can be used to group related features together. Each namespace is a singleton instance with all its contents enclosed within the scope of the namespace. By grouping variables, functions, objects, classes, and interfaces into namespaces, you can keep them out of the global scope and avoid naming collisions, although the root of each namespace is added to the global scope.

Namespaces are open ended and all declarations with the same name within a common root contribute toward a single namespace. This allows namespaces to be described in multiple files and will allow you to keep each file to a maintainable size.

Listing 2-1 shows two namespaces, both with a class named Example. Each namespace creates a separate context to allow the classes to have the same name. Each class is accessed as a member of the namespace, making the intended class unambiguous.

Listing 2-1. Namespaces

```
namespace First {
    export class Example {
        log() {
            console.log('Logging from First.Example.log()');
        }
    }
}

namespace Second {
    export class Example {
        log() {
            console.log('Logging from Second.Example.log()');
        }
    }
}

const first = new First.Example();

// Logging from First.Example.log()
first.log();

const second = new Second.Example();

// Logging from Second.Example.log()
second.log();
```

Namespaces can be organized into hierarchies: either by nesting them within each other, or by using a dotted-syntax when supplying the namespace identifier. These two alternatives are shown in Listing 2-2, with the first and second levels in the hierarchy being nested, and the third level being added using the dotted notation. In practical terms, all these declarations have added to the same hierarchy, as the calling code shows.

Listing 2-2. Nested and dotted hierarchies

```typescript
namespace FirstLevel {
    export namespace SecondLevel {
        export class Example {

        }
    }
}

namespace FirstLevel.SecondLevel.ThirdLevel {
    export class Example {

    }
}

const nested = new FirstLevel.SecondLevel.Example();

const dotted = new FirstLevel.SecondLevel.ThirdLevel.Example();
```

If you are using namespaces, mixing the styles of hierarchical namespace organization, and appending to namespaces across multiple files all adds to the psychological complexity of the program when it comes to fixing bugs or adding new behavior. The main driver for the hierarchy you create should be the ease of locating functionality with the aid of autocompletion. A good hierarchy will make your code easier to find and reduce the need to cross reference documentation.

You may have spotted that the nested module in Listing 2-2 has an export keyword. This keyword marks a namespace member as public. Without the export keyword, the namespace member can only be accessed from within the namespace (including subsequent additions to the same namespace). This differs from classes where members are public by default. Listing 2-3 is a realistic example of the application of these different levels of visibility, with the exported public members appearing first, followed by variables and classes that are only for use within the namespace.

Listing 2-3. Public and private members

```typescript
namespace Shipping {

    // Available as Shipping.Ship
    export interface Ship {
        name: string;
        port: string;
        displacement: number;
    }

    // Available as Shipping.Ferry
    export class Ferry implements Ship {
        constructor(
            public name: string,
            public port: string,
            public displacement: number) {
        }
    }
```

```
    // Only available inside of the Shipping module
    const defaultDisplacement = 4000;

    class PrivateShip implements Ship {
        constructor(
            public name: string,
            public port: string,
            public displacement: number = defaultDisplacement) {
        }
    }

}

const ferry = new Shipping.Ferry('Assurance', 'London', 3220);
```

The inverse of the export keyword is import. You can use an import statement to alias an item from another namespace as shown in Listing 2-4. The import statement references the Shipping.Ship class in the import statement and gives it the alias "Ship." The alias can then be used throughout the Docking namespace as a short name, so wherever Ship appears within the namespace, it refers to `Shipping.Ship`. This is particularly useful if you have long names or deep nesting in your program as it allows you to reduce the length of annotations. This reduces the noise in your code that repeating the namespace would cause. You can use any name in an import alias, although using a similar name to the imported member will make your code easier to comprehend.

Listing 2-4. Import alias

```
namespace Docking {
    import Ship = Shipping.Ship;

    export class Dock {
        private dockedShips: Ship[] = [];

        arrival(ship: Ship) {
            this.dockedShips.push(ship);
        }
    }
}

const dock = new Docking.Dock();
```

The import alias can also be used outside of modules to provide short names.

There are a few differences between code editors and integrated development environments when it comes to referencing namespaces from other files. Visual Studio automatically includes all TypeScript files within the project in the compilation, which means you don't need to specifically reference other files when you refer to them. Other code editors require a hint to help them discover the source of the code you are depending on. The format for these hints is a reference comment, as shown in Listing 2-5. Whether you need to use these hints or not, you will be responsible for making the code available at runtime.

Listing 2-5. Reference comments

```
///<reference path="Shipping.ts" />
```

If you are compiling your project into a single file using the TypeScript compiler, the reference comments serve an additional purpose of helping the compiler to order your output correctly, based on the dependencies. Because code generally needs to be defined before it is referenced, this ordering can be vital to your program working at runtime. You can read more about using the TypeScript compiler to generate a combined single output file in Appendix 2.

There is one final feature of namespaces to cover, which is declaration merging. On a simple level, any declaration that spans multiple blocks is a case of declaration merging, such as two interface blocks with the same name, which are merged into a single interface. Namespaces go beyond this simple merging by allowing merging with classes, functions, and enums. These hybrids may seem strange but represent an incredibly common JavaScript pattern.

Listing 2-6 demonstrates declaration merging between a namespace and a class. Both the class and namespace have the same name, which causes the merge. This allows code to instantiate a new instance of the class, or of members from the namespace.

Listing 2-6. Namespace/class merging

```
// Class/Namespace Merging
class Car {

}

namespace Car {
    export class Engine {

    }

    export class GloveBox {

    }
}

const car = new Car();
const engine = new Car.Engine();
const gloveBox = new Car.GloveBox();
```

Now you understand namespaces, refrain for a moment from implementing them because there is a better way to organize your code. Where namespaces limit the number of items in the global scope, modules go a step further and add nothing to the global scope. Modules also provide a solution to naming conflicts, as each file provides a new context for identifiers. Modules also have a killer-feature: you can load them asynchronously on demand. So, let's now take a look at modules.

Modules

Modules are the superior way to organize your code. They are the standard mechanism for server-side TypeScript and they are being adopted for use in the browser as part of the ECMAScript specification. Throughout this next section, I will hopefully convince you to choose modules instead of namespaces. Modules outperform namespaces in all respects. A namespace reduces the number of items added to the global scope, but modules are entirely self-contained and place nothing in the global scope. A namespace organizes your code at design time, but modules organize it at design time and at runtime. A namespace will scale your program to thousands of lines of code, but modules will take you past a million lines. Modules are the key to scaling really big programs. Although you can combine and minify all your JavaScript files to squash the size of a program, ultimately this will not scale forever.

To further organize your program, you can use a folder structure to manage your modules. You will only ever state this full path inside of an `import` statement, so the length shouldn't be a problem. All the other code that references an external module will refer to it by the alias given in the `import` statement.

- `./Transport/Maritime/Shipping`

- `./Transport/Maritime/Docking`

- `./Transport/Railways/Ticketing`

On top of all these benefits, modules are super easy to use. As soon as you add an import or export statement to a TypeScript file, it becomes a module. Listing 2-7 shows a sample shipping module. Everything inside of the module is part of the module's scope, and is not visible outside of the module unless they are exported. The Ship interface and Ferry class are made publicly available using the export keyword. Exported members can be variables, functions, classes, interfaces, or anything else you can give a name to.

Listing 2-7. Modules

```typescript
export interface Ship {
    name: string;
    port: string;
    displacement: number;
}

export class Ferry implements Ship {
    constructor(
        public name: string,
        public port: string,
        public displacement: number) {
    }
}

const defaultDisplacement = 4000;

class PrivateShip implements Ship {
    constructor(
        public name: string,
        public port: string,
        public displacement: number = defaultDisplacement) {
    }
}
```

To use a module, you can import it using one of a number of import styles. The import statement in Listing 2-8 imports the entire module and assigns it the alias "Shipping." The module members can be accessed via the Shipping variable.

Listing 2-8. Importing modules

```
// Import entire module
import * as Shipping from './Listing-2-007';

export class Dock {
    private dockedShips: Shipping.Ship[] = [];

    arrival(ship: Shipping.Ship) {
        this.dockedShips.push(ship);
    }
}
```

You can also selectively import module members, as shown in Listing 2-9. By naming a list of members within braces, and separated by a comma if there are more than one, you can use the short name of the member. This removes the need to specify the module alias each time you access a member.

Listing 2-9. Importing named module members

```
// Import a single export from a module
import { Ship } from './Listing-2-007';

export class Dock {
    private dockedShips: Ship[] = [];

    arrival(ship: Ship) {
        this.dockedShips.push(ship);
    }
}
```

If importing an individual member would result in a naming conflict, you can specify an alias for the member with the as keyword, as shown in Listing 2-10. Throughout the rest of the code after the import statement, you can refer to the member by the alias.

Listing 2-10. Imported members with an alias

```
// Import using an alias
import { Ship as Boat } from './Listing-2-007';

export class Dock {
    private dockedShips: Boat[] = [];

    arrival(ship: Boat) {
        this.dockedShips.push(ship);
    }
}
```

When you use module imports in TypeScript you can target different module loaders using the `--module` compiler flag. There are options to target CommonJS (Node), AMD (RequireJS), ESNext (native browser modules), or a few other module styles. There is more detail on the TypeScript compiler in Appendix 2.

Module Re-Exporting

Re-exporting allows you to re-expose another module, or a part of another module, without using it locally. Listing 2-11 shows how to export parts of another module, how to introduce an alias for the exported member, and how to export an entire module.

Listing 2-11. Re-exporting

```
// Re-export with an alias
export { Ship as Boat } from './Listing-2-007';

// Re-export an entire module
export * from './Listing-2-008';
```

You can use module re-exporting to combine several modules into a single wrapper module.

Default Exports

You can mark one member per module as a default export. The default export can be any member, such as a class, function, or value. Listing 2-12 shows a default export; it could also have been expressed on a separate line using `export default Yacht`.

Listing 2-12. Default export

```
export default class Yacht {
    constructor(
        public name: string,
        public port: string,
        public displacement: number) {
    }
}
```

When you import a default, you can use the shorthand statement shown in Listing 2-13. The compiler will warn you against this style of import if the module has no default export. You can effectively use any name in the import statement; it doesn't have to match the original name.

Listing 2-13. Importing a default

```
// Import a default export
import Yacht from './Listing-2-012';

// Error: Module has no default export
import Ship from './Listing-2-007';

const yacht = new Yacht('The Sea Princess', 'Tadley', 150);
```

If you don't have a good reason to use a default export, it is best to avoid them. Having to decide which kind of import statement you need to write for a module is an unnecessary cognitive scratch. The implicit renaming of the default during the import process can add additional complexity, especially as the imported name is not changed during a rename refactoring.

Exports Object

Some module kinds support an exports object, which wraps all the members being exported. This pattern is the predecessor of the default export, and it is common in both CommonJS and AMD module systems. You can use this pattern using the syntax shown in Listing 2-14, with an export = statement.

Listing 2-14. Export object

```
class Ferry {
    constructor(
        public name: string,
        public port: string,
        public displacement: number) {
    }
}

export = Ferry;
```

When consuming this style of module, you should use the import/require style of import that is shown in Listing 2-15.

Listing 2-15. Importing an export object

```
import Ferry = require('./Listing-2-014');

const ferry = new Ferry('Dartmouth Ferry', 'Dartmouth', 580)
```

TypeScript will generate different output for these statements, depending on the module kind you specify when compiling. You can read more about the TypeScript compiler in Appendix 2.

Module Loading

Although there are several kinds of module loaders, they all take care of getting hold of a module you depend on, and running your code once it has loaded. Because TypeScript is aware of all the major module styles, you can write the standard import and export statements and leave the compiler to handle the differences. This also means you can compile the same TypeScript code to target different module systems.

The most popular module kinds are described below:

- Native ECMAScript Modules. These are syntactically identical to the TypeScript format and are supported experimentally in the latest versions of all major browsers. While awaiting broad working support, either RequireJS or SystemJS can be used to load modules in browsers.

- AMD Modules. As well as managing module loading, the Asynchronous Module Definition style allows multiple modules to be loaded at the same time, even when they depend on each other. RequireJS is the most common implementation of AMD.

- CommonJS Modules. This is the prevalent module loading style for NodeJS and is supported by default.

- UMD Modules. The Universal Module Definition is a standard that works with both AMD and CommonJS modules. This allows the same output to be used with RequireJS and NodeJS without re-compilation.

- System Modules. This module style can be used in browsers and on NodeJS and has standardized handling for circular dependencies.

If you are choosing a module system for the first time, the two most flexible options are UMD or System as these can be used both in a browser and on the server.

Dynamic Module Loading

In many cases, you will only want to load a module in certain circumstances. You can avoid unnecessary network calls and file system access using dynamic module loading. To load modules on demand, you'll need to write a normal import statement, but add an additional conditional statement to actually load the module if your condition is met.

Listing 2-16 has the import statement to obtain the module, but this does not cause any code to be emitted. The call to require within the if-statement results in the module being loaded, and is only executed if the condition is true. To get all the normal type checking and autocompletion, a typeof annotation sets the type of the ferry variable. It is this additional variable that contains the type, and not the Ferry alias in the import statement.

Listing 2-16. Dynamic module loading

```
// Declaration for the require function (Node)
declare function require(moduleName: string): any;

// Import - doesn't actually emit code
import { Ferry } from './Listing-2-007';

const condition = true;

if (condition) {
    // Only imports if the condition is true
    const ferry: typeof Ferry = require("./Listing-2-007");

    const myFerry = new ferry('', '', 0);
}
```

Dynamic module loading forces your code to be more module aware than normal imports, so the code to perform dynamic loading changes depending on your module kind. Listing 2-18 shows the equivalent dynamic loading code to Listing 2-17, but this time for System modules. Because you can use SystemJS in browsers and on servers, this may be your best option if you plan to run your code cross-platform.

Listing 2-17. Dynamic module loading System modules

```
// Declaration for the require function (System JS)
declare const System: { import(module: string): Promise<any>; };

// Import - doesn't actually emit code
```

```
import { Ferry } from './Listing-2-007';

const condition = true;

if (condition) {
    // Only imports if the condition is true
    System.import('./Listing-2-007').then((ferry: typeof Ferry) => {
        const myFerry = new ferry('', '', 0);
    });
}
```

There is further detail on module loading in web browsers using AMD in Chapter 6 and module loading on the server with CommonJS in Chapter 7.

Mixing Namespace and Modules

I have included this section due to the number of questions I have received about this subject over the course of the past five years. Because so many programmers have a background in C# or Java, the question is perfectly understandable. In languages such as those, you physically organize code in files, but navigate it logically by namespace; the file structure has no particular meaning except as a tool to help the programmer find the code within the project. There are guidelines in some languages about keeping the file structure and namespaces similar, but file hierarchy and namespace hierarchy do not contribute to a single organizational element.

If you are using TypeScript modules, the file system becomes the namespace, and you navigate the namespace using autocompletion against the file system, as shown in Figure 2-1. Most development tools with TypeScript support will supply hints at each navigation level to help you locate the module you need, although the effectiveness of these hints is directly correlated to how well you organize and name your file hierarchy.

Figure 2-1. *TypeScript Module Navigation*

There is absolutely zero benefit to using namespaces alongside modules. All the benefits you get from namespaces are exceeded when you use modules. The primary purpose of a namespace is to provide scope, naming context, and discoverability, but this is already handled with modules:

- **Scope**. Modules add nothing to the global scope, so adding namespaces doesn't improve scope management.

- **Naming collisions**. Modules already provide a context per module for names, so namespaces don't improve this either.

- **Discoverability**. Modules already provide discoverability, and adding namespaces to this impairs the discoverability of members.

Although it can be tempting to transfer a practice that works well in another language, it should not be done blindly. One of the early goals of TypeScript was to make object-oriented programming in JavaScript more accessible to programmers with experience of class-based languages; but TypeScript is now a mature language with its own idioms, so when you are considering transposing ideas from another language it is worth weighing up the benefits. Mixing namespaces with modules has no upside, and several drawbacks, so avoid doing it.

Packaging

Whether you are dividing up your own private codebase for reuse, or making it available for others to use, packaging your code is now a fundamental TypeScript skill. In this section, I will show you all the elements you need to create an NPM package containing your code. NPM, or Node Package Manager, is the largest software registry on the planet, and is the de facto package management style for JavaScript, and therefore TypeScript. The examples are taken from the real-life TypeSpec project, which is a behaviour-driven development tool for TypeScript that parses plain-text business language (in the Gherkin syntax) and executes test steps to validate the program.

The full project can be found on GitHub: `https://github.com/Steve-Fenton/TypeSpec`

■ **Note**   Package management replaces the traditional workflow of searching online for a library, downloading the source code, unzipping the contents, and manually adding the source files to your own project. Not only can packages be obtained and added to your project in a single step, you can also make your dependencies explicit so other projects can consume your code without first having to obtain many libraries that your code requires to work. You can also manage the versions you depend on, for example, by upgrading a dependency to the latest stable release.

To follow all the steps in this section, you will need to install NodeJS, which includes NPM. NodeJS is a platform for server-side JavaScript, but you can use it locally to perform many tasks that will improve your productivity. You can download NodeJS from `https://nodejs.org/`

To create an NPM package, you need three things:

- README.md – a file that describes your project, written in markdown format.

- package.json – a file that describes your package using a JSON structure.

- Source code – the files that need to be in the package for it to be used within other programs.

When you are writing a package that will contain TypeScript code, it is best not to include the TypeScript source files. Instead, you should package the compiled JavaScript code, along with automatically generated type definitions. This allows your package to be consumed from JavaScript programs, and also means your TypeScript source code will not need to be re-compiled by any consumers.

The easiest way to generate a package is to copy your compiled output into a separate directory structure so it can easily be packaged without unnecessary files being present (the alternative would be to spend more time specifying which files should and shouldn't be included). A typical directory structure is shown in Figure 2-2, with the README.md and package.json files within the dist folder, and the .js and .d.ts files being copied into the src folder.

```
--dist
  |--README.md
  |--package.json
  |--src
      |--TypeSpec.d.ts
      |--TypeSpec.js
      |--...
```

Figure 2-2. *Directory structure for packaging*

Listing 2-18 shows a short version of a README.md file, with a simple title and description, along with instructions on how to install the package. Normally, the file should contain some basic usage instructions and links to more detailed documentation. The goal of this file should be to reduce the friction by providing answers to the kind of questions someone using your package for the first time may have.

Listing 2-18. README.md

```
# TypeSpec

A TypeScript BDD framework.

    npm install typespec-bdd

The aim is to properly separate the business specifications from the code,
but rather than code-generate (like Java or C# BDD tools), the tests will be
loaded and executed on the fly without converting the text into an
intermediate language or framework. This should allow tests to be written using any
unit testing framework - or even without one.
```

The package.json file is more structured and a number of the items are mandatory. Listing 2-19 shows a full package description, which includes information on the package, the author, and the location of documentation and issue logs. The license should be specified in the Software Package Data Exchange (SPDX) format.

Listing 2-19. package.json

```
{
  "author": "Steve Fenton",
  "name": "typespec-bdd",
  "description": "BDD framework for TypeScript.",
  "keywords": [
    "typespec",
    "typescript",
    "bdd",
    "behaviour",
    "driven"
  ],
  "version": "0.0.1",
  "homepage": "https://github.com/Steve-Fenton/TypeSpec",
  "bugs": "https://github.com/Steve-Fenton/TypeSpec/issues",
  "license": "(Apache-2.0)",
  "files": [
    "src/"
  ],
  "repository": {
    "url": "https://github.com/Steve-Fenton/TypeSpec"
  },
  "main": "src/TypeSpec.js",
  "types":  "src/TypeSpec.d.ts",
  "dependencies": { },
  "devDependencies": { },
```

```
  "optionalDependencies": { },
  "engines": {
    "node": "*"
  }
}
```

The package contents are described in the "files" element, which can contain folders and individual files, and by describing the entry point of the application in the "main" element. When working with TypeScript, you can provide the type definition for the entry point using the "types" element.

To prepare your files for packaging, you simply copy them into the distribution folder. This could be done using a post-build event in Visual Studio, as shown in Listing 2-20, or with a task executed by a task runner like Gulp.

Listing 2-20. Copy package contents

```
XCOPY $(ProjectDir)Scripts\TypeSpec\*.d.ts $(ProjectDir)dist\src\ /y
XCOPY $(ProjectDir)Scripts\TypeSpec\*.js $(ProjectDir)dist\src\ /y
XCOPY $(SolutionDir)README.md $(ProjectDir)dist\ /y
XCOPY $(ProjectDir)package.json $(ProjectDir)dist\ /y
```

Once the files are ready to be packaged, you simply run the package command in Listing 2-21. This will generate an archive file containing your package. You can use an archive reader to inspect the contents of the file and ensure everything is present as expected.

Listing 2-21. Packaging command

```
npm package
```

You can use the package either privately or publicly. This means you can use the same mechanism to package your open source projects for the whole world to use, or to add the package to your private repository. The command to publish an NPM package is shown in Listing 2-22. When you first run this command, you will be prompted to add credentials via the command line, as you can only publish packages for which you have the appropriate permissions.

Listing 2-22. Publishing command

```
npm publish
```

Although there appear to be several steps in packaging your code, once you have things set up, publishing a new version is as simple as updating the version number and re-running the publish command.

Decorators

When it comes to organizing code, most organization techniques are aligned either horizontally or vertically. A common horizontal organization technique is *n-tier* architecture, where the program is split into layers that handle the user interface, business logic, and data access. A rapidly growing vertical organization technique is micro-services, where each vertical slice represents a bounded context, such as "payments," "customers," or "users."

Decorators are relevant to both horizontal and vertical architectures, but can be particularly valuable in the context of vertical architectures. Decorators can be used to take care of cross-cutting concerns such as logging, authorization, or validation. When used correctly, this aspect-oriented style of programming can minimize the code required to satisfy these shared responsibilities.

TypeScript decorators can be used for aspect-oriented programming (AOP) and meta-programming, but we'll start with AOP as it provides a solid example of a real-world use of decorators.

■ **Note** TypeScript decorators are still experimental and may be subject to change before they become a stable feature. Depending on your TypeScript version, you may need to pass the experimentalDecorators compiler flag to allow this feature.

The syntax for decorators is straightforward. Listing 2-23 shows a decorator function, and a use of the decorator against the square method, with the decorator applied using the @ symbol.

Listing 2-23. Decorators

```
// Decorator Function
function log(target: any, key: string, descriptor: any) {
    // square
    console.log(key);
}

class Calculator {
    // Using the decorator
    @log
    square(n: number) {
        return n * n;
    }
}
```

Decorators can be applied to any of the following:

- Classes
- Accessors
- Properties
- Methods
- Parameters

Each kind of decorator requires a different function signature, as the decorator is provided with different parameters depending on the decorator use. This section will provide several practical examples that can be used as a starting point for your own decorators.

A more complete example of a property decorator is shown in Listing 2-24. As well as passing the name of the method in the key parameter, a property descriptor is passed in the descriptor parameter. The property descriptor is an object that contains the original method and some metadata. The method itself is found within the value property of the descriptor. When a method decorator returns a value, the value will be used as the descriptor. This means you can choose to observe, modify, or replace the original method.

In the case of the logging method decorator, the original method in the descriptor is wrapped with a logging function, which logs the fact the method was called as well as the arguments passed and the value returned. Each time the method is called, the information is logged.

Listing 2-24. Logging Method Decorator

```
function log(target: any, key: string, descriptor: any) {
    const original = descriptor.value;

    descriptor.value = function (...args: any[]) {
        // Call the original method
        const result = original.apply(this, args);

        // Log the call, and the result
        console.log(`${key} with args ${JSON.stringify(args)} returned
        ${JSON.stringify(result)}`);

        // Return the result
        return result;
    }

    return descriptor;
}

class Calculator {
    // Using the decorator
    @log
    square(num: number) {
        return num * num;
    }
}

const calculator = new Calculator();

// square with args [2] returned 4
calculator.square(2);

// square with args [3] returned 9
calculator.square(3);
```

This basic logging example means that the code within the calculator class need know nothing of the logging within the program. The logging logic can be kept entirely separate from the rest of the code in the program, and the logging code would be solely responsible for when and where information is logged.

Configurable Decorators

You can make a decorator configurable by converting your decorator function into a decorator factory. A decorator factory is a function that returns a decorator function. The factory can have any number of parameters that can be used in the creation of the decorator.

In Listing 2-25, the logging decorator has been converted into a decorator factory. The factory accepts a title that is prepended to the logging message.

Listing 2-25. Configurable decorators

```
function log(title: string) {
    return (target: any, key: string, descriptor: any) => {
        const original = descriptor.value;

        descriptor.value = function (...args: any[]) {
            // Call the original method
            const result = original.apply(this, args);

            // Log the call, and the result
            console.log(`${title}.${key}
                with args ${JSON.stringify(args)}
                returned ${JSON.stringify(result)}`);

            // Return the result
            return result;
        }

        return descriptor;
    };
}

class Calculator {
    // Using the configurable decorator
    @log('Calculator')
    square(num: number) {
        return num * num;
    }
}

const calculator = new Calculator();

// Calculator.square with args [2] returned 4
calculator.square(2);

// Calculator.square with args [3] returned 9
calculator.square(3);
```

When using a configurable decorator, the arguments are passed like a function call.

Class Decorators

To adapt the logging decorator for use with a class, the constructor must be wrapped with a logging constructor. This is slightly more complex than the method decorator, but the example in Listing 2-26 can be quickly adapted from logging to some other purpose.

The class decorator is only passed a single argument, representing the constructor of the class being decorated.

Listing 2-26. Class decorators

```
function log(target: any) {
    const original = target;

    // Wrap the constructor with a logging constructor
    const constr: any = (...args) => {
        console.log(`Creating new ${original.name}`);
        const c: any = () => {
            return original.apply(null, args);
        }
        c.prototype = original.prototype;

        return new c();
    }

    constr.prototype = original.prototype;

    return constr;
}

@log
class Calculator {
    square(n: number) {
        return n * n;
    }
}

// Creating new Calculator
var calc1 = new Calculator();

// Creating new Calculator
var calc2 = new Calculator();
```

As with method decorators, you can choose to modify, wrap, or replace the constructor passed in the class decorator. When replacing the constructor, you must maintain the original prototype as this is not done automatically.

Property Decorators

Property decorators can be split into a number of parts. In Listing 2-27 both the getter and the setter are replaced with logging implementations. To do this, the original property is deleted before the replacements are added with the original name.

Listing 2-27. Property decorators

```
function log(target: any, key: string) {
    let value = target[key];

    // Replacement getter
    const getter = function () {
```

```
            console.log(`Getter for ${key} returned ${value}`);
            return value;
        };

        // Replacement setter
        const setter = function (newVal) {
            console.log(`Set ${key} to ${newVal}`);
            value = newVal;
        };

        // Replace the property
        if (delete this[key]) {
            Object.defineProperty(target, key, {
                get: getter,
                set: setter,
                enumerable: true,
                configurable: true
            });
        }
    }
}

class Calculator {
    @log
    public num: number;

    square() {
        return this.num * this.num;
    }
}

const calc = new Calculator();

// Set num to 4
calc.num = 4;

// Getter for num returned 4
// Getter for num returned 4
calc.square();
```

Each time the getter or setter of the property is called, the access is logged. If you are only interested in decorating a getter or setter, you can apply accessor decorators individually to a getter or setter.

Summary

If you are confused about the sheer number of options when working with TypeScript, you can reduce the overload by sticking with the following recommend standard setup. Unless you have a good reason to do otherwise, use modules rather than namespaces; and never mix the two. Use a consistent import style to keep your dependency management simple, and avoid default exports.

By using the file system as a form of namespacing, your modules will be easier to find and consume; so pay attention to the naming of both files and folders.

When packaging your application, automate the generation of a distribution folder to contain the compiled JavaScript and TypeScript type definitions for your program. This allows you to easily publish from the distribution folder without having to filter the package contents.

Decorators allow you to implement aspect-oriented programming and provide a mechanism for meta-programming.

Key Points

- Internal modules are now called "namespaces."

- External modules are now called simply "modules."

- Don't mix modules and namespaces.

- There are several module loaders and they all have slightly different syntax; if you haven't chosen one yet, consider using SystemJS as it works everywhere. UMD is a good alternative as it works with AMD and CommonJS module systems.

- You can package your code to make it easier to reuse in other programs.

CHAPTER 3

The Type System

The fundamental problem addressed by a type theory is to ensure that programs have meaning. The fundamental problem caused by a type theory is that meaningful programs may not have meanings ascribed to them. The quest for richer type systems results from this tension.

—Mark Manasse

In this chapter, you will learn about the TypeScript type system, including some of the important ways in which it differs from other type systems that you may have encountered before. As TypeScript has drawn inspiration from a range of languages, it is worth understanding these subtle details because relying on your existing knowledge of other type systems may lead to some nasty surprises. These details are explored by comparing structural and nominal type systems and by looking at the details of optional static types, type erasure, and the powerful type inference provided by the TypeScript language service.

While many TypeScript features align with features, and proposed features, of the ECMAScript specification, the type system is unique to TypeScript. There are currently no plans to add type annotations, or any of the complex type-related features of TypeScript into the ECMAScript standard.

At the end of the chapter is a section about ambient declarations, which can be used to fill in type information for code that hasn't been written in TypeScript. This allows you to consume external code with type checking and autocompletion, whether it is old JavaScript code you already have, additions to the runtime platform, or third-party libraries and frameworks that you use within your program.

Type Systems

Type systems originate from type theory, which is credited to Bertrand Russell who developed the theory in the early 20th century and included it in his three-volume *Principia Mathematica* (Whitehead and Russell, Cambridge University Press, 1910). Type theory is a system in which each term is given a type and operations are restricted based on the types. TypeScript's annotations are strikingly similar to the style of the building blocks of type theory, as shown in Figure 3-1.

Type Theory	TypeScript
`x: nat`	`const x: number;`
`doubleUp: nat -> nat`	`doubleUp: (num: number) => number;`

Figure 3-1. *Type theory and TypeScript similarities*

© Steve Fenton 2018
S. Fenton, *Pro TypeScript*, https://doi.org/10.1007/978-1-4842-3249-1_3

In type theory, a symbol is annotated with a type just like with a TypeScript type annotation. The only difference in this respect is that type theory leaves out the const keyword and uses the nat type (a natural number) rather than the number type in TypeScript. Function annotations are also recognizable, with type theory leaving out the parentheses, which arguably improve the readability of the TypeScript example.

In general, a type system assigns a type to each variable, expression, object, function, class, or module in the system. These types are used alongside a set of rules designed to expose errors in the program. These checks can be performed at compile time (static checking) or at runtime (dynamic checking). Typical rules would include ensuring that the value used in an assignment is the same type as the variable it is being assigned to, or ensuring that a function call supplies arguments of the correct type based on the function signature.

All the types used within a type system act as contracts that state the accepted interactions between all the various components in the system. The kinds of errors that are detected based on these types are dependent on the rules in the type system and the level of complexity in the checking.

Optional Static Types

JavaScript is dynamically typed; variables do not have a fixed type, so no type restrictions can be applied to operations. You can assign a value of one type to a variable and later assign a value of a completely different type to the same variable. You can perform an operation with two incompatible values and get unpredictable results. If you call a function, there is nothing to enforce that you pass arguments of the correct type and you can even supply too many or too few arguments. These are demonstrated in Listing 3-1.

The JavaScript type system is incredibly flexible because of this, but sometimes this flexibility can cause problems.

Listing 3-1. JavaScript dynamic types

```
// Assignment of different types
let dynamic = 'A string';

dynamic = 52;

// Operations with different types
const days = '7';
const hours = 24;

// 168 (luckily, the hours string is coerced)
const week = days * hours;

// 77 (concatenate 7 and 7)
const fortnight = days + days;

// Calling functions
function getVolume(width, height, depth) {
        return width * height * depth;
}

// NaN (10 * undefined * undefined)
const volumeA = getVolume(10);

// 32 (the 8 is ignored)
const volumeB = getVolume(2, 4, 4, 8);
```

TypeScript provides a system for inferring and specifying types, but allows types to be optional. The optionality is important because it means you can choose when to enforce types and when to allow dynamic types. Unless you opt out of type checking, using the any type, the compiler will attempt to determine the types in your program and will check inferred types as well as the explicit types you specify using type annotations. Type annotations are described in Chapter 1.

All the checks are performed at compile time, which is what makes TypeScript statically typed. The compiler is responsible for constructing a schedule of all the types, checking expressions against these types and removing all the type information when it converts the code into valid JavaScript.

If you were to paste the JavaScript code from Listing 3-1 into a TypeScript file, you would receive errors for all the type errors found in the example. You can see the errors being flagged in the TypeScript listing in Figure 3-2 below.

```
1  // Assignment of different types
2  let dynamic = 'A string';
3
4  dynamic = 52;
5
6  // Operations with different types
7  const days = '7';
8  const hours = 24;
9
10 // 168 (luckily, the hours string is coerced)
11 const week = days * hours;
12
13 // 77 (concatenate 7 and 7)
14 const fortnight = days + days;
15
16 // Calling functions
17 function getVolume(width, height, depth) {
18     return width * height * depth;
19 }
20
21 // NaN (10 * undefined * undefined)
22 const volumeA = getVolume(10);
23
24 // 32 (the 8 is ignored)
25 const volumeB = getVolume(2, 4, 4, 8);
26
```

Figure 3-2. *TypeScript compiler errors*

■ **Note** One of the key points in TypeScript's type system is the optionality of the types. This effectively means you are not restricted to static types and can opt to use dynamic behavior whenever needed.

Structural Typing

TypeScript has a structural type system; this contrasts with most C-like languages, which are typically nominative. A nominative, or *nominal*, type system relies on explicitly named annotations to determine types. In a nominal system, a class would only be seen to implement an interface if it was decorated with the name of the interface (i.e., it must explicitly state that it implements the interface). In a structural type system, the explicit decoration is not required and a value is acceptable as long as its structure matches the specification of the required type.

A nominal type system is intended to prevent accidental type equivalence — just because something has the same properties does not mean it is valid — but as TypeScript is structurally typed accidental type equivalence is possible, and desirable.

In a nominal type system you could use named types to ensure that correct arguments were being passed, for example, you could create a CustomerId type to wrap the identifier's value and use it to prevent assignment of a plain number, or ProductId, CustomerTypeId, or any other type. A type with identical properties, but a different name, would not be accepted. In a structural type system, if the CustomerId wrapped a public property named value that contained the ID number, any other type that had a value property with an equivalent type would be acceptable.

If you wanted to use custom types for this kind of type safety in TypeScript, you would have to ensure the types were not accidentally equivalent by making them structurally unique. It is possible to do this using private members on a class to make it structurally unmatchable, but while the discussion on some support for nominal types continues, the most readable technique to create nominal types is that shown in Listing 3-2.

In the example class in Listing 3-2, the first method avoids accidental equivalence and will only accept a CustomerId, but the second method allows it to some extent by accepting any number. To call this second method, you must pass the value property of the identifier.

The DomainId type can be used to wrap any numeric identity in its current form. The CustomerId and ProductId are created using a type, and a factory method to create new instances. Attempting to pass the productId instance to the method accepting a CustomerId results in an error.

Listing 3-2. Using and avoiding equivalence

```
// DomainId type definition
type DomainId<T extends string> = {
  type: T,
  value: number,
}

// CustomerId
type CustomerId = DomainId<'CustomerId'>;
const createCustomerId = (value: number): CustomerId => ({ type: 'CustomerId', value });

// Product Id
type ProductId = DomainId<'ProductId'>;
const createProductId = (value: number): ProductId => ({ type: 'ProductId', value });

// Example class
class Example {
    static avoidAccidentalEquivalence(id: CustomerId) {
        // Implementation
    }
```

```
    static useEquivalence(id: number) {
        // Implementation
    }
}

var customerId = createCustomerId(1);
var productId = createProductId(5);

// Allowed
Example.avoidAccidentalEquivalence(customerId);

// Errors 'Supplied parameters do not match signature of call target'
Example.avoidAccidentalEquivalence(productId);

// Allowed
Example.useEquivalence(customerId.value);

// Allowed
Example.useEquivalence(productId.value);
```

While structural typing may seem to cause difficulties in a limited number of specialized situations, it has many advantages. For example, it is far easier to introduce compatible types without having to change existing code, and it is possible to create types that can be passed to external code without inheriting from an external class. It also outperforms nominal types in its ability to introduce a new supertype without changing the newly demoted subtypes, or the code that interacts with them.

One of the most significant benefits of structural typing is it saves myriad explicit type name decorations. It is possible to implement an interface without adding a specific type annotation, and anonymous objects can be created to match interfaces and classes without the need to add type annotations. You can use these objects if the properties and methods are of the same type, or compatible types, as the required type. A compatible type can be a subtype, a narrower type, or a structurally similar type.

One thing to avoid in a structurally typed language, such as TypeScript, is empty structures. An empty interface or an empty class is essentially a valid supertype of practically everything in your program, which means any object could be substituted for the empty structure at compile time because there is no contract to satisfy during type checking.

Structural typing complements the type inference in TypeScript. With these features, you can leave much of the work to the compiler and language service, rather than having to explicitly add type information and class heritage throughout your program.

■ **Note**   You can't rely on named types to create restrictions in a TypeScript program, only unique structures. For interfaces, this means creating uniqueness using a uniquely named property or method. For classes, any private member will make the structure unique.

Type Erasure

When you compile your TypeScript program into plain JavaScript, the generated code is different in two ways: *code transformation* and *type erasure*. The code transformation converts language features that are not available in the target JavaScript version into representations that are valid. For example, if you are targeting ECMAScript 5, where classes are not available, all your classes will be converted into immediately invoked function expressions that create appropriate representations using the prototypal inheritance available in ECMAScript 5. Type erasure is the process that removes all the type annotations from your code, as they are not understood by JavaScript.

Type erasure removes type annotations, custom types, and interfaces. These are only required at design time and at compile time for the purpose of static checking. At runtime types are not checked so the type information is not needed. You shouldn't encounter a problem at runtime because the logical use of types has been checked, except where you have opted out by using the any type.

Listing 3-3. TypeScript ordered array class

```
class OrderedArray<T> {
    private items: T[] = [];

    constructor(private comparer?: (a: T, b: T) => number) {
    }

    add(item: T): void {
        this.items.push(item);
        this.items.sort(this.comparer);
    }

    getItem(index: number): T {
        if (this.items.length > index) {
            return this.items[index];
        }
        return null;
    }
}

var orderedArray: OrderedArray<number> = new OrderedArray<number>();

orderedArray.add(5);
orderedArray.add(1);
orderedArray.add(3);

var firstItem: number = orderedArray.getItem(0);

alert(firstItem); // 1
```

Listing 3-3 shows an example TypeScript listing for an OrderedArray class. The class is generic, so the type of the elements in the array can be substituted. For complex types, an optional custom comparer can be supplied to evaluate the items in the array for the purposes of ordering, but for simple types it can be omitted. Following the class is a simple demonstration of the class in action. This code is compiled into the JavaScript shown in Listing 3-4. In the compiled output all of the type information is gone and the class has been transformed into a common JavaScript pattern called a *self-executing anonymous function*.

Listing 3-4. Compiled JavaScript code

```javascript
var OrderedArray = (function () {
    function OrderedArray(comparer) {
        this.comparer = comparer;
        this.items = [];
    }
    OrderedArray.prototype.add = function (item) {
        this.items.push(item);
        this.items.sort(this.comparer);
    };
    OrderedArray.prototype.getItem = function (index) {
        if (this.items.length > index) {
            return this.items[index];
        }
        return null;
    };
    return OrderedArray;
}());
var orderedArray = new OrderedArray();
orderedArray.add(5);
orderedArray.add(1);
orderedArray.add(3);
var firstItem = orderedArray.getItem(0);
alert(firstItem); // 1
```

Despite the type erasure and transformations performed during compilation, the JavaScript output is remarkably like the original TypeScript program. Almost all transformations from TypeScript to JavaScript are similarly considerate of your original code. Depending on the version of ECMAScript you are targeting, there may be more or fewer transformations, for example, the most recent features that TypeScript down-compiles to ECMAScript 3 and 5 wouldn't need to be transformed if you were to target ESNext during compilation.

Type Inference

Type inference is the polar opposite of type erasure. Type inference is the process by which types are determined at compile time in the absence of explicit type annotations.

Most basic examples of type inference, including the early examples in this book, show a simple assignment and explain how the type of the variable on the left of the assignment can be automatically set to the type of the literal value on the right-hand side. This kind of type inference is really "level one" for TypeScript, which is capable of far more complex determinations of the types in use.

TypeScript performs deep inspections to create a schedule of types in your program and compares assignments, expressions, and operations using this schedule of types. During this process, there are some clever tricks that are employed when a direct type is not available, which allow the type to be found indirectly. One such trick is *contextual typing*, where TypeScript uses the context of an expression to determine the types.

Listing 3-5 shows how types can be inferred in progressively more indirect ways. The return value of the add function is determined by working backward from the return statement. The type of the return statement is found by evaluating the type of the expression a + b, which in turn is done by inspecting the types of the individual parameters.

In the very last expression in Listing 3-5, the result parameter type in the anonymous function can be inferred using the context in which the function is declared. Because it is declared to be used by the execution of callsFunction, the compiler can see that it is going to be passed as a string; therefore the result parameter will always be a string type. A third example comes from the declaration of CallsFunction; because the variable has been typed using the CallsFunction interface, the compiler infers the type of the cb parameter based on the interface.

Listing 3-5. Bottom-up and top-down inference

```
function add(a: number, b: number) {
    /* The return value is used to determine
       the return type of the function */
    return a + b;
}

interface CallsFunction {
    (cb: (result: string) => any): void;
}

// The cb parameter is inferred to be a function accepting a string
var callsFunction: CallsFunction = function (cb) {
    cb('Done');

    // Error: Argument of type '1' is not assignable to parameter of type 'string'
    cb(1);
};

// The result parameter is inferred to be a string
callsFunction(function (result) {
    return result;
});
```

Best Common Type

When type information is being inferred, there are a limited number of situations where the best common type must be determined. Listing 3-6 shows how the values in the array literal are considered in order to generate the best common type between all of the array's values .

Listing 3-6. Best common types

```
// number[]
let x = [0, 1, null];

// (string | number)[]
let y = [0, 1, null, 'a'];
```

The process of determining the best common type is not just used for array literal expressions; they also are used to determine any case where multiple values have different types, such as the return type of a function or method that contains multiple return statements.

Contextual Types

Contextual types are a good example of how advanced type inference can be. Contextual typing occurs when the compiler bases its types on the location of an expression. In Listing 3-7, the type of the event parameter is determined by the known signature of the window.onclick definition. The inference is not just limited to the parameters; the entire signature, including the return value, can be inferred because of the existing knowledge of the window.onclick signature.

Listing 3-7. Contextual types

```
window.onclick = function(event) {
        var button = event.button;
};
```

If you inspect the type information for Listing 3-7, you'll find that the event parameter is a MouseEvent, the scope of this is Window, and the return type is any.

Widened Types

The term *"widened type"* refers to situations in TypeScript where the type of a function call, expression, or assignment is null or undefined. In these cases, the type inferred by the compiler will be the widened any type. In Listing 3-8, the widened variable will have a type of any.

Listing 3-8. Widened types

```
function example() {
    return null;
}

var widened = example ();
```

When to Annotate

Because type inference has been a key feature of TypeScript since day one, the discussion on when to make types explicit with type annotations can take place without controversy. This has been a tricky topic for statically typed languages that have later decided to add some level of support for type inference.

The final decision about the level of type annotations you add to your program should be made jointly between all team members, but you may wish to use the following suggestions as a starting point for your discussion.

- Start by adding no type annotations (full inference.)
- Add type annotations where the inferred type would be any.
- Add type annotations for public method return types.
- Add type annotations for public method parameters.

The key to a healthy relationship with types is to use as few type annotations as possible. If the type *can* be inferred, allow it to be inferred. Put your faith in the compiler as far as you can and you'll soon discover that you can trust it to do a good job. You can get the compiler to warn you about cases where it can't find a type using a special flag (--noImplicitAny) that prevents the any type from being inferred. You can read more about code quality flags in Appendix 2.

The final note on type annotations is to require as little as possible. If you only need an object to have a name member, don't annotate it with a more restrictive type, such as Customer. Be specific with your return types, but accept the most general arguments that you can.

Duplicate Identifiers

Overall, you should do your best to avoid name clashes in your program. TypeScript supplies the tools to make name clashes unnecessary by allowing you to move your program out of the global scope and into modules. However, there are some interesting features around identifiers in TypeScript, including many situations where you are permitted to use the same name within the same scope.

In most cases, the use of an existing class or variable name within the same scope will result in a "Duplicate identifier" error. No particular structure gets preferential treatment; the latter of the two identifiers will be the source of the error. If you re-use a namespace multiple times in your program, this will not result in a duplicate identifier error because all of the individual blocks are logically merged into a single namespace.

Another valid use of a duplicate identifier is with interfaces. Once again, the compiler knows that there will be no duplicate identifier at runtime because interfaces are erased during compilation; its identifier will never appear in the JavaScript output. The use of a duplicate identifier for an interface and a variable is a common pattern in the TypeScript library, where the standard types are defined using an interface and then allocated to a variable declaration with a type annotation. Listing 3-9 shows the TypeScript library definition for DeviceMotionEvent. The interface for DeviceMotionEvent is immediately followed by a variable declaration with the same DeviceMotionEvent identifier.

Listing 3-9. TypeScript DeviceMotionEvent

```
interface DeviceMotionEvent extends Event {
    readonly acceleration: DeviceAcceleration | null;
    readonly accelerationIncludingGravity: DeviceAcceleration | null;
    readonly interval: number | null;
    readonly rotationRate: DeviceRotationRate | null;
    initDeviceMotionEvent(type: string, bubbles: boolean, cancelable: boolean, acceleration:
DeviceAccelerationDict | null, accelerationIncludingGravity: DeviceAccelerationDict | null,
rotationRate: DeviceRotationRateDict | null, interval: number | null): void;
}

declare var DeviceMotionEvent: {
    prototype: DeviceMotionEvent;
    new(typeArg: string, eventInitDict?: DeviceMotionEventInit): DeviceMotionEvent;
};
```

Ambient Declarations are explained in more detail later in this chapter, but this technique works just as well without the declare keyword before the variable declaration. The use of interfaces in the standard library is a deliberate choice. Interfaces are open, so it is possible to extend the definitions in additional interface blocks. If a new web standard was published that added a motionDescription property to the DeviceMotionEvent object, you wouldn't have to wait for it to be added to the TypeScript standard library; you could simply add the code from Listing 3-10 to your program to extend the interface definition.

All the interface definition blocks from the same common root are combined into a single type, so the DeviceMotionEvent still has all the original properties from the standard library and also has the motionDescription property from the additional interface block.

Listing 3-10. Extending the DeviceMotionEvent

```
interface DeviceMotionEvent {
    motionDescription: string;
}

// The existing DeviceMotionEvent has all of its existing properties
// plus our additional motionDescription property
function handleMotionEvent(e: DeviceMotionEvent) {
    var acceleration = e.acceleration;
    var description = e.motionDescription;
}
```

Type Checking

Once a schedule of types has been gathered from your program, the TypeScript compiler is able to use this schedule to perform type checking. At its simplest, the compiler is checking that when a function is called that accepts a parameter of type number; all calling code passes an argument with a type that is compatible with the number type.

Listing 3-11 shows a series of valid calls to a function with a parameter named input, with a type of number. Arguments are accepted if they have a type of number, enum, null, undefined, or any. Remember, the any type allows dynamic behavior in TypeScript, so it represents a promise from you to the compiler saying that the values will be acceptable at runtime.

Listing 3-11. Checking a parameter

```
function acceptNumber(input: number) {
    return input;
}

// number
acceptNumber(1);

// enum
acceptNumber(Size.XL);

// null
acceptNumber(null);
```

As types become more complex, type checking requires deeper inspection of the objects. When an object is checked, each member of the object is tested. Public properties must have identical names and types; public methods must have identical signatures. When checking the members of an object, if a property refers to a nested object, the inspection continues to work down into that object to check compatibility.

Listing 3-12 shows three differently named classes and a literal object that show all are compatible as far as the compiler is concerned.

Listing 3-12. Compatible types

```
class C1 {
    name: string;

    show(hint?: string) {
        return 1;
    }
}

class C2 {
    constructor(public name: string) {

    }

    show(hint: string = 'default') {
        return Math.floor(Math.random() * 10);
    }
}

class C3 {
    name: string;

    show() {
        return <any> 'Dynamic';
    }
}

var T4 = {
    name: '',
    show() {
        return 1;
    }
};

var c1 = new C1();
var c2 = new C2('A name');
var c3 = new C3();

// c1, c2, c3 and T4 are equivalent
var arr: C1[] = [c1, c2, c3, T4];

for (var i = 0; i < arr.length; i++) {
    arr[i].show();
}
```

The notable parts of this example include the name property and the show method. The name *property* must exist on the object, it must be public, and it must be a string type. It doesn't matter whether the property is a constructor property. The show method must return a type compatible with number. The parameters must also be compatible — in this case the optional hint parameter can be matched using a default parameter or by omitting the parameter entirely. If a class had a mandatory hint parameter, it would not be compatible with the types in Listing 3-12. As shown in the fourth type, literal objects can be compatible with classes as far as the compiler is concerned, as long as they pass the type comparison.

CHAPTER 3 ■ THE TYPE SYSTEM

Type checking is not limited to positive matching, where the supplied type must have the structure of the required type. An increasing number of negative checks are being added to the compiler that enables it to detect a different class of error. For example, the excess property warning will highlight properties that are not anticipated on an object, which is a great way to catch situations where you have mis-typed a property name. This kind of checking may introduce additional errors as you upgrade the version of TypeScript you use in your projects, but if you persevere and review the messages the compiler is sending you, you will eventually find subtle bugs that the compiler has managed to catch for you.

Ambient Declarations

Ambient declarations can be used to add type information to existing JavaScript code. Commonly, this is used to add type information for your own existing code, or for a third-party library that you want to consume in your TypeScript program.

Ambient declarations can be gradually constructed by starting with a simple imprecise declaration and turning up the dial on the details over time. Listing 3-13 shows an example of the least precise ambient declaration you can write for the jQuery framework. The declaration simply notifies the compiler that an external variable will exist at runtime without supplying further details of the structure of the external variable. This will suppress errors for the $ variable, but will not supply deep type checking or useful autocompletion.

Listing 3-13. Imprecise ambient declaration

```
declare var $: any;

$('#id').html('Hello World');
```

All ambient declarations begin with the declare keyword. This tells the compiler that the following code block contains only type information and no implementation. Blocks of code created using the declare keyword will be erased during compilation and result in no JavaScript output. At runtime, you are responsible for ensuring the code exists and that it matches your declaration.

To get the full benefit of compile-time checking, you can create a more detailed ambient declaration that covers more of the features of the external JavaScript that you use. If you are building an ambient declaration, you can choose to cover the features you use the most, or the higher-risk features that you judge to be the most likely source of type errors. This allows you to invest in defining the type information that gives you the most return on your time investment.

In Listing 3-14 the jQuery definition has been extended to cover the two elements used in the first example: the selection of an element using a string query containing the element's id and the setting of the inner HTML using the html method. In this example, a class is declared called jQuery, this class has the html method that accepts a string. The $ function accepts a string query and returns an instance of the jQuery class.

Listing 3-14. Ambient class and function

```
declare class jQuery {
    html(html: string): void;
}

declare function $(query: string): jQuery;

$('#id').html('Hello World');
```

95

When this updated ambient declaration is used, autocompletion supplies type hints as shown in Figure 3-3. Any attempt to use a variable, function, method, or property that isn't declared will result in a compiler error and all arguments and assignments will also be checked.

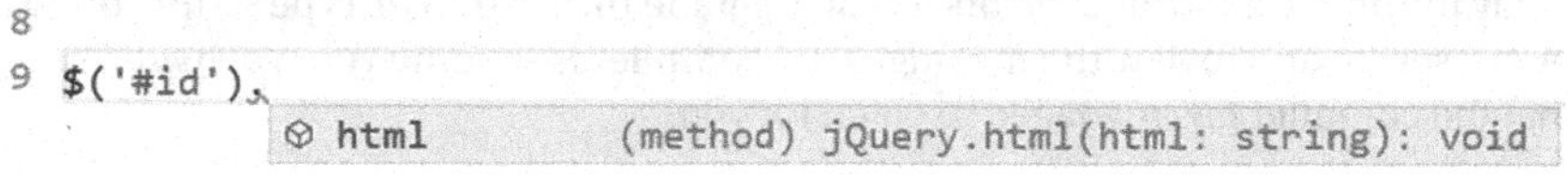

```
8
9 $('#id').
         ⊘ html           (method) jQuery.html(html: string): void
```

Figure 3-3. *Ambient declaration autocompletion*

It is possible to create ambient declarations for variables, functions, classes, enumerations, and both internal and external modules. Interfaces appear to be missing from this list, but interfaces are already analogous to ambient declarations as they describe a type without resulting in any compiled code. This means you can write ambient declarations using interfaces, but you would not use the declare keyword for interfaces.

■ **Note**   In reality, it actually makes more sense to declare jQuery as an interface rather than a class because you cannot instantiate instances of jQuery using var jq = new jQuery(); All you would need to do is change the declare class keywords to the interface keyword because neither an ambient class nor an interface needs any implementation.

Declaration Files

Although it is possible to place ambient declarations in any of your TypeScript files, there is a special naming convention for files that contain only ambient declarations. The convention is to use a .d.ts file extension. Each module, variable, function, class, and enum in the file must be preceded by the declare keyword, and this is enforced by the TypeScript compiler.

To use a declaration file from within your program, you can refer to the file just like any other TypeScript file. You can use reference comments, or make the file the target of an import statement. When using import statements to target a file, the declaration file should be placed in the same folder and have the same name as the JavaScript file as shown in Figure 3-4.

jquery.d.ts   jquery.js

Figure 3-4. *Declaration files*

Definitely Typed

If you plan to write an ambient declaration for any of the common JavaScript libraries or frameworks, you should first check to see if someone has already done the hard work by visiting the online library for ambient declarations, Definitely Typed:

`http://definitelytyped.org/`

The Definitely Typed project, started by Boris Yankov, contains countless definitions for popular JavaScript projects including Angular, Backbone, Bootstrap, Breeze, D3, Ember, jQuery, Knockout, Node, Underscore, and many others. There are even declarations for unit testing frameworks such as Jasmine, Mocha, and qUnit. Some of these external sources are incredibly complex, so using an existing declaration can save a great deal of time. The repository is now supported by Microsoft. You can search for the correct definition name and installation instructions at:

`https://aka.ms/types`

The easiest way to bring an existing type definition into your project is with NPM, as shown in Listing 3-15.

Listing 3-15. installing type definitions

```
npm install --save @types/jquery
```

Summary

Working within the TypeScript type system requires at least a passing knowledge of the difference between nominal and structural typing. Structural typing can make some designs a little tricky, but it doesn't prevent you from using any patterns that you may wish to transfer from a nominally typed system. Type inference allows you to leave out type annotations in favor of allowing the types to be inferred throughout your program.

When you compile your program, the types are checked against the explicit and implicit types, allowing a large class of errors to be detected early. You can opt out of type checking for specific parts of your program using the any type.

You can add type information for JavaScript code by creating or obtaining ambient declarations for the JavaScript code. Usually these ambient declarations would be stored in a declaration file that sits alongside the JavaScript file.

Key Points

- Static type checking is optional.

- TypeScript is structurally typed.

- All type information is removed during compilation.

- You can let the compiler work out the types for you using type inference.

- Ambient declarations add type information to existing JavaScript code.

■ ■ ■

CHAPTER 4

Object Orientation in TypeScript

*There are two ways of constructing a software design: One way is to make it so simple that
there are obviously no deficiencies and the other way is to make it so complicated that
there are no obvious deficiencies. The first method is far more difficult. It demands the
same skill, devotion, insight, and even inspiration as the discovery of the simple physical
laws which underlie the complex phenomena of nature.*

—Tony Hoare

Object-oriented programming allows concepts from the real world to be represented by code that contains
both the data and related behavior. The concepts are normally modeled as classes, with properties for the
data and methods for the behavior, and the specific instances of these classes are called objects.

There have been many discussions about object orientation over the years and I'm sure that the
debate remains lively enough to continue for many years to come. Because programming is a heuristic
process, you will rarely find one absolute answer. This is why you will hear the phrase "it depends" so
often in software development. No programming paradigm fits every situation so anyone telling you that
functional programming, object-oriented programming, or some other programming style is the answer to
all problems simply hasn't been exposed to a large enough variety of complex problems. Because of this,
programming languages are becoming increasingly multiparadigm.

Object-oriented programming is a formalization of many good practices that emerged early on in
computer programming. It supplies the concepts to make these good practices easier to apply. By modeling
real-world objects from the problem domain using objects in the code, the program can speak the same
language as the domain it serves. Objects also allow encapsulation, or information hiding, which prevents
different parts of a program from modifying data that another part of the program relies on.

The simplest explanation in favor of programming concepts such as object orientation comes not from
the world of software, but from psychology. G. A. Miller published his famous paper, "The Magical Number
Seven, Plus or Minus Two" (*Psychological Review*, 1956) describing the limitations on the number of pieces
of information we can hold in short-term memory at any one time. Our information processing ability is
limited by this number of between five and nine items of information that we can hold on to concurrently.
This is the key reason for any technique of code organization and in object orientation it should drive you
toward layers of abstraction that allow you to skim high-level ideas first and dive further into the levels of
detail when you need to. If you organize it well, a programmer maintaining the code will need to hold onto
less concurrent information when attempting to understand your program.

© Steve Fenton 2018
S. Fenton, *Pro TypeScript*, https://doi.org/10.1007/978-1-4842-3249-1_4

Robert C. Martin (Uncle Bob) presented this idea in a slightly different way during a group-refactoring session when he said well-written, "polite" code was like reading a newspaper. You could scan the higher-level code in the program as if they were headlines. A programmer maintaining the code would scan through the headlines to find relevant areas in the code and then drill down to find the implementation details. The value in this idea comes from small readable functions that contain code at a similar level of abstraction. The newspaper metaphor supplies a clear vision of what clean code looks like, but the principle of reducing the amount of cognitive overhead is still present.

Object Orientation in TypeScript

TypeScript supplies all the key tools that you need to use object-orientation in your program.

- Classes

- Instances of classes

- Methods

- Inheritance

- Open recursion

- Encapsulation

- Delegation

- Polymorphism

Classes, instances of classes, methods, and inheritance were discussed in detail in Chapter 1. These are the building blocks of an object-oriented program and are made possible in a simple way by the language itself. All you need for each of these concepts is one or two language keywords.

The other terms in this list are worthy of further explanation, particularly in respect of how they work within the TypeScript type system. The following sections expand on the concepts of open recursion, encapsulation, delegation, and polymorphism along with code examples that demonstrate each concept.

■ **Note**   Although this chapter discusses object orientation in detail, don't forget that JavaScript, and therefore TypeScript, is a multiparadigm language. In particular, there are some excellent function programming features available that you shouldn't overlook, even if you are writing object-oriented code.

Open Recursion

Open recursion is a combination of recursion and late binding. When a method calls itself within a class, that call can be forwarded to a replacement defined in a subclass. Listing 4-1 is an example of a class that reads the contents of a directory. The FileReader class reads the contents based on the supplied path. Any files are added to the file tree, but where directories are found, there is a recursive call to this.getFiles. These calls would continue until the entire path, including all subfolders, are added to the file tree. The fs.reaaddirSync and fs.statSync methods belong to NodeJS, which is covered in more detail in Chapter 7.

■ **Note**   I used the Sync versions of the NodeJS file system calls, `readdirSync` and `statSync`, because they make the examples much simpler. In a real program, you should consider using the standard equivalents, `readdir` and `stat`, which are asynchronous and accept a callback function.

The `LimitedFileReader` is a subclass of the `FileReader` class. When you create an instance of the `LimitedFileReader` class, you must specify a number that limits the depth of the file tree represented by the class. This example shows how the call to `this.getFiles` uses open recursion. If you create a `FileReader` instance, the call to `this.getFiles` is a simple recursive call. If you create an instance of the `LimitedFileReader`, the same call to `this.getFiles` within the `FileReader.getFiles` method will actually be dispatched to the `LimitedFileReader.getFiles` method.

Listing 4-1. Open recursion

```typescript
import * as fs from 'fs';

interface FileItem {
    path: string;
    contents: string[];
}

class SyncFileReader {
    getFiles(path: string, depth: number = 0) {
        const fileTree = [];

        const files = fs.readdirSync(path);

        for (let file of files) {
            const stats = fs.statSync(file);

            let fileItem: FileItem;

            if (stats.isDirectory()) {
                // Add directory and contents
                fileItem = {
                    path: file,
                    contents: this.getFiles(file, (depth + 1))
                };
            } else {
                // Add file
                fileItem = {
                    path: file,
                    contents: []
                };
            }

            fileTree.push(fileItem);
        }
```

```
        return fileTree;
    }
}

class LimitedFileReader extends SyncFileReader {
    constructor(public maxDepth: number) {
        super();
    }

    getFiles(path: string, depth = 0) {
        if (depth > this.maxDepth) {
            return [];
        }

        return super.getFiles(path, depth);
    }
}

// instatiating an instance of LimitedFileReader
const fileReader = new LimitedFileReader(1);

// results in only the top level, and one additional level being read
const files = fileReader.getFiles('path');
```

This example of open recursion can be summarized as the following:

- When you create a new SyncFileReader: fileReader.getFiles is a call to SyncFileReader.getFiles

  - **this**.getFiles within **SyncFileReader** is a call to **SyncFileReader**.getFiles

- When you create a new LimitedFileReader

  - fileReader.getFiles is a call to LimitedFileReader.getFiles

  - super.getFiles is a call to SyncFileReader.getFiles

  - **this**.getFiles within **SyncFileReader** is a call to **LimitedFileReader**. getFiles

The beauty of open recursion is that the original class remains unchanged and needs no knowledge of the specialization offered by the subclass. The subclass gets to reuse the code from the superclass, which avoids duplication.

Encapsulation

Encapsulation is fully supported in TypeScript. A class instance can contain properties as well as methods that operate on those properties; this is the encapsulation of data and behavior. The properties can also be hidden using the private access modifier, which hides the data from code outside of the class instance.

A common use of encapsulation is data hiding: preventing access to data from outside of the class except via explicit operations. The example in Listing 4-2 shows a Totalizer class that has a `private total` property, which cannot be modified by code outside of the Totalizer class. The property can change when external code calls the methods defined on the class. This removes the risk of the following

- External code adding a donation without adding the tax rebate;

- External code failing to validate the amount is a positive number;

- The tax rebate calculation appearing in many places in calling code;

- The tax rate appearing in many places in external code.

Listing 4-2. Encapsulation

```
class Totalizer {
    private total = 0;
    private taxRateFactor = 0.2;

    addDonation(amount: number) {
        if (amount <= 0) {
            throw new Error('Donation exception');
        }

        const taxRebate = amount * this.taxRateFactor;
        const totalDonation = amount + taxRebate;

        this.total += totalDonation;
    }

    getAmountRaised() {
        return this.total;
    }
}

const totalizer = new Totalizer();

totalizer.addDonation(100.00);

const fundsRaised = totalizer.getAmountRaised();

// 120
console.log(fundsRaised);
```

Encapsulation is the tool that can help you to prevent the largest amount of duplicated code in a program, but it doesn't do it magically. You should hide your properties using the `private` keyword to prevent external code changing the value or controlling the program's flow using the value. One of the most common kinds of duplication is logical branching, for example. the `if` and `switch` statements, which control the program based on a property that should have been hidden using the `private` keyword. When you change the property, you then need to hunt down all these logical branches, which creates a worrying ripple of change throughout your code.

The greatest benefit to encapsulation is that it hugely simplifies the task of understanding code. A private member on a class allows you to understand the exact use of the member without looking at any code outside of that class. You can guarantee that every use of the member is right in front of you, and if there are no uses of the member you can delete it, safe in the knowledge that no other code depends on it.

As soon as you increase the visibility of a member, you can no longer understand how it is used without looking at a much wider collection of code. If you are authoring a package that is consumed within other programs, you cannot possibly understand all the uses of the member, so things are infinitely more complicated than it is for private members.

Delegation

One of the most important concepts in terms of re-use in your program is *delegation*. Delegation describes the situation where one part of your program hands over a task to another part. In true delegation, the wrapper passes a reference to itself into the delegate, which allows the delegate to call back into the original wrapper, for example, the wrapper class would call the delegate class, passing the keyword this into the delegate, allowing the delegate to call public methods on the wrapper class. This allows the wrapper class and delegate class to behave as a subclass and superclass.

Where the wrapper doesn't pass a reference to itself, the operation is technically known as *forwarding* rather than delegation. In both delegation and forwarding you may call a method on one class, but that class hands off the processing to another class, as shown in Listing 4-3. Delegation and forwarding are often good alternatives to inheritance if the relationship between two classes fails the "is a" test.

■ **Note**   The "is a" test in object-orientation involves describing the relationship between objects to validate that the subclass is indeed a specialized version of the superclass. For example, "a Cat *is a* Mammal" and "a Savings Account *is a* Bank Account." It is usually clear when the relationship is not valid, for example, "a Motor Car *is a* Chassis" doesn't work, but "a Car *has a* Chassis" does. A "has a" relationship requires delegation (or forwarding), not inheritance.

Listing 4-3. Delegation

```
interface ControlPanel {
    startAlarm(message: string): any;
}

interface Sensor {
    check(): any;
}

class MasterControlPanel {
    private sensors: Sensor[] = [];

    constructor() {
        // Instantiating the delegate HeatSensor
        this.sensors.push(new HeatSensor(this));
    }
```

```typescript
    start() {
        for (let sensor of this.sensors) {
            sensor.check();
        }

        window.setTimeout(() => this.start(), 1000);
    }

    startAlarm(message: string) {
        console.log('Alarm! ' + message);
    }
}

class HeatSensor {
    private upperLimit = 38;
    private sensor = {
        read: function() { return Math.floor(Math.random() * 100); }
    };

    constructor(private controlPanel: ControlPanel) {
    }

    check() {
        if (this.sensor.read() > this.upperLimit) {
            // Calling back to the wrapper
            this.controlPanel.startAlarm('Overheating!');
        }
    }
}

const controlPanel = new MasterControlPanel();

controlPanel.start();
```

Listing 4-3 is a simple example of delegation. The ControlPanel class passes itself into the HeatSensor constructor, which enables the HeatSensor class to call the startAlarm method on the ControlPanel when required. The ControlPanel can coordinate any number of sensors, and each sensor can call back into the ControlPanel to set off the alarm if a problem is detected.

It is possible to expand on this to demonstrate various decision points where either inheritance or delegation may be selected. Figure 4-1 describes the relationships between various car components. The *chassis* is the plain skeleton that a motor car is built on, the bare framework for a car. When the engine, driveshaft, and transmission are attached to the chassis, the combination is called a *rolling chassis*.

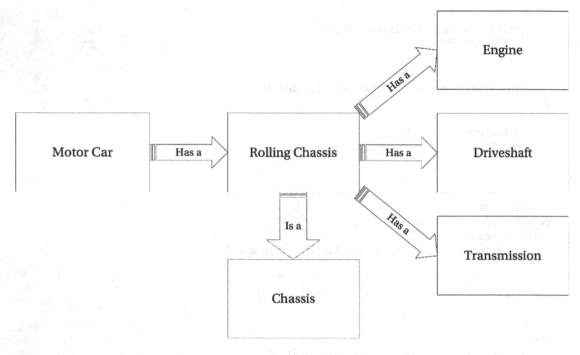

Figure 4-1. *Encapsulation and inheritance*

For each relationship in the diagram, try reading both the *is a* and the *has a* alternatives to see if you agree with the relationships shown. We suspend grammar for the duration of these checks in object-oriented programming, so you'll never need to use "is an," or "has an."

Polymorphism

In programming, polymorphism refers to the ability to specify a contract and have many different types implement that contract. The code using a class that implements some contract should not need to know the details of the specific implementation. In TypeScript, polymorphism can be achieved using several different forms:

- An interface implemented by many classes;

- An interface implemented by many objects;

- An interface implemented by many functions;

- A superclass with many specialized subclasses;

- Any structure with many similar structures.

The final bullet point, "any structure with many similar structures," refers to TypeScript's structural type system, which will accept structures compatible with a required type. This means you can achieve polymorphism with two functions with the same signature and return type (or two classes with compatible structures, or two objects with similar structures) even if they do not explicitly implement a named type, as shown in Listing 4-4.

Listing 4-4. Polymorphism

```
interface Vehicle {
    moveTo(x: number, y: number);
}

// Explicit interface implementation
class Car implements Vehicle {
    moveTo(x: number, y: number) {
        console.log('Driving to ' + x + ' ' + y);
    }
}

class SportsCar extends Car {

}

// Doesn't explicitly implement the Vehicle interface
class Airplane {
    moveTo(x: number, y: number) {
        console.log('Flying to ' + x + ' ' + y);
    }
}

class Satellite {
    moveTo(x: number) {
        console.log('Targeting ' + x);
    }
}

function navigate(vehicle: Vehicle) {
    vehicle.moveTo(59.9436499, 10.7167959);
}

const car = new SportsCar();
navigate(car);

const airplane = new Airplane();
navigate(airplane);

const satellite = new Satellite();
navigate(satellite);
```

Listing 4-4 illustrates polymorphism in TypeScript. The navigate function accepts any type compatible with the Vehicle interface. Specifically, this means any class or object that has a method named moveTo that accepts *up to* two arguments of type number.

■ **Note** It is important to remember that a method is structurally compatible with another if it accepts fewer arguments. In many languages, you would be forced to specify the redundant parameter even though it isn't used in the method body, but in TypeScript you can omit it. The calling code may still pass the argument if the contract specifies it, which preserves polymorphism.

The navigate function in Listing 4-4 sends the specified Vehicle to the Norwegian Computing Centre in Oslo — where polymorphism was created by Ole-Johan Dahl and Kristen Nygaard.

All the types defined in the example are compatible with the Vehicle definition; Car explicitly implements the interface, SportsCar inherits from Car so it also implements the Vehicle interface. Airplane does not explicitly implement the Vehicle interface, but it has a compatible moveTo method and will be accepted by the navigate function The Satellite class represents a vehicle with a fixed "y" coordinate, which means only the "x" coordinate can be controlled. This type is still compatible as types with fewer arguments are allowed in TypeScript. The acceptance of compatible types based on their structure is a feature of TypeScript's structural type system, which is described in Chapter 3.

SOLID Principles

Object orientation, as with any programming paradigm, doesn't prevent confusing or unmaintainable programs. This is the reason for the five heuristic design guidelines commonly referred to as the SOLID principles.

The SOLID principles were catalogued by Robert C. Martin, and described in a series of online articles, and in several books (http://www.objectmentor.com/resources/articles/Principles_and_Patterns.pdf), 2000; *Agile Principles, Patterns, and Practices in C#* (Prentice Hall, 2006). The "SOLID" acronym was spotted by Michael Feathers some time later. Luckily, the order of the principles isn't important, so they can be ordered to suit this more memorable form. The principles were intended to be the basic tenets that underpin object-oriented programming and design. In general, the principles provide guidance for creating readable and maintainable code.

It is important to remember that software design is a heuristic process. It is not possible to create rules that can be followed like a checklist. The SOLID principles are guidelines to help you think about your program's design in terms of object orientation and can help you to make an informed design decision that works in your specific context. The principles also supply a shared language that can be used to discuss designs with other programmers.

The five SOLID principles are these:

- *Single responsibility principle*—a class should have one, and only one, reason to change.

- *Open–closed principle*—it should be possible to extend the behavior of a class without modifying it.

- *Liskov substitution principle*—subclasses should be substitutable for their superclasses.

- *Interface segregation principle*—many small, client-specific interfaces are better than one general-purpose interface.

- *Dependency inversion principle*—depends on abstractions, not concretions.

The five SOLID principles are discussed individually in the sections that follow.

The Single Responsibility Principle (SRP)

The SRP requires that a class should have only one reason to change. When designing your classes, you should aim to put related features together, ensuring that they are likely to change for the same reason, and keep features apart if they will change for different reasons. A program that follows this principle has classes that perform just a few related tasks. Such a program is likely to be highly cohesive.

The term *cohesion* refers to a measure of the relatedness of features within a class or module. If features are unrelated, the class has low cohesion and is likely to change for many different reasons. High cohesion results from the proper application of the SRP.

When you are adding code to your program, you need to make a conscious decision about where it belongs. Most violations of this principle do not come from obvious cases where a method is clearly mismatched to its enclosing class. It is far more common for a class to gradually overstep its original purpose over a period of time, and under the care of many different programmers.

You don't need to limit your thinking to classes when considering the SRP, as the principle has fractality. You can apply the principle to methods, ensuring that they do just one thing and therefore have just one reason to change. You can also apply the principle to modules, ensuring that at a general level the module has a single area of responsibility.

Listing 4-5 shows a typical violation of the SRP. At first glance, all the methods seem to belong to the Movie class, because they all perform operations using the properties of a movie. However, the appearance of persistence logic blurs the line between the use of the Movie class as an object, and its use as a data structure.

Listing 4-5. Single responsibility principle (SRP) violation

```
class Movie {
    private db: DataBase;

    constructor(private title: string, private year: number) {
        this.db = DataBase.connect('user:pw@mydb', ['movies']);
    }

    getTitle() {
        return this.title + ' (' + this.year + ')';
    }

    save() {
        this.db.movies.save({ title: this.title, year: this.year });
    }
}

// Movie
const movie = new Movie('The Internship', 2013);

movie.save();
```

To fix this class before it grows into a bigger problem, the two concerns can be divided between the Movie class that takes care of movie-related behavior and a MovieRepository that is responsible for storing the data as shown in Listing 4-6. If features are added to the Movie class, the MovieRepository requires no changes. If you were to change your data storage device, the Movie class wouldn't need to change.

Listing 4-6. Separate reasons for change

```typescript
class Movie {
    constructor(private title: string, private year: number) {
    }

    getTitle() {
        return this.title + ' (' + this.year + ')';
    }
}

class MovieRepository {
    private db: DataBase;

    constructor() {
        this.db = DataBase.connect('user:pw@mydb', ['movies']);
    }

    save(movie: Movie) {
        this.db.movies.save(JSON.stringify(movie));
    }
}

// Movie
const movie = new Movie('The Internship', 2013);

// MovieRepository
const movieRepository = new MovieRepository();

movieRepository.save(movie);
```

Keeping an eye on the class-level responsibilities is usually straightforward if you keep in mind the single responsibility principle, but it can be even more important at the method level, ensuring that each method performs just one task and is named in a way that reveals the intended behavior of the method. Uncle Bob coined the phrase "extract 'til you drop," which refers to the practice of refactoring your methods until each one has so few lines it can only do a single thing. This practice of refactoring methods extensively is easily worth the effort of reworking the design.

The Open–Closed Principle (OCP)

The OCP is often summed up by the sentence: *software entities should be open for extension but closed for modification.* In pragmatic terms, no matter how much you design your program up front, it is almost certain that it won't be entirely protected from modification. However, the risk of changing an existing class is that you will introduce an inadvertent change in behavior that ripples across the code that depends on the class. This can be mitigated somewhat (but not entirely) by automated tests, which is described in Chapter 10.

To follow the OCP, you need to consider the parts of your program that are likely to change. For example, you would attempt to identify any class that contains a behavior that you may want to replace or extend in the future. The slight hitch with this is that it is usually not possible to predict the future, and there is a danger that if you introduce code intended to pay off later, it almost always will not. Trying to guess what may happen can be troublesome either because it turns out the code is never needed or because the real future turns out to be incompatible with the prediction. So, you will need to be pragmatic about this principle, which sometimes means introducing the code to solve a problem only when you first encounter the problem in real life.

With these warnings in mind, a common way to follow the OCP is to make it possible to substitute one class with another to get different behaviors. This is a reasonably simple thing to do in most object-oriented languages and TypeScript is no exception. Listing 4-7 shows a reward card point calculation class named RewardPointsCalculator. The standard number of reward points is "four points per whole dollar spent in the store." When the decision is made to offer double points to some VIP customers, instead of adding a conditional branch within the original RewardPointsCalculator class, a subclass named DoublePointsCalculator is created to deal with the new behavior. The subclass in this case calls the original getPoints method on the superclass, but it could just as easily ignore the original class entirely and calculate the points any way it wishes.

If the decision was made to only give reward points on certain qualifying purchases, a class could handle the filtering of the transactions based on their type before calling the original RewardPointsCalculator — again, extending the behavior of the application rather than modifying the existing RewardPointsCalculator class.

Listing 4-7. Open–closed principle (OCP)

```
class RewardPointsCalculator {
    getPoints(transactionValue: number) {
        // 4 points per whole dollar spent
        return Math.floor(transactionValue) * 4;
    }
}

class DoublePointsCalculator extends RewardPointsCalculator {
    getPoints(transactionValue: number) {
        const standardPoints = super.getPoints(transactionValue);
        return standardPoints * 2;
    }
}

const pointsCalculator = new DoublePointsCalculator();

// 800
alert(pointsCalculator.getPoints(100.99));
```

By following the OCP, a program is more likely to contain maintainable and reusable code. By avoiding rework within an existing class, you also avoid the shock waves that can echo throughout the program following a change. Code that is known to work is left untouched and new code is added to handle the new requirements.

The Liskov Substitution Principle (LSP)

In *Data Abstraction and Hierarchy* Barbara Liskov (http://www.sr.ifes.edu.br/~mcosta/disciplinas/20091/tpa/recursos/p17-liskov.pdf, 1988) wrote,

> *What is wanted here is something like the following substitution property: If for each object o1 of type S there is an object o2 of type T such that for all programs P defined in terms of T, the behavior of P is unchanged when o1 is substituted for o2 then S is a subtype of T.*

—Barbara Liskov

The essence of this is that if you substitute a subclass for a superclass, the code that uses the class shouldn't need to know that the substitution has taken place. If you find yourself testing the type of an object in your program, there is a high probability that you are violating the LSP. The specific requirements of this principle are described later, using the example of a super Animal class, and a subclass of Cat that inherits from Animal.

- *Contravariance of method arguments in the subtype*: If the superclass has a method accepting a Cat, the subclass method should accept an argument of type Cat or Animal, which is the superclass for Cat.

- *Covariance of return types in the subtype*: If the superclass has a method that returns an Animal, the subclass method should return an Animal, or a subclass of Animal, such as Cat.

- *The subtype should throw either the same exceptions as the supertype, or exceptions that are subtypes of the supertype exceptions*: In TypeScript, you are not limited to using exception classes; you can simply specify a string to throw an exception. It is possible to create classes for errors in TypeScript, as shown in Listing 4-8. The key here is that if calling code has an exception handling block, it should not be surprised by the exception thrown by a subclass. There is more information on exception handling in Chapter 8.

Listing 4-8. Error classes

```
class ApplicationError implements Error {
    constructor(public name: string, public message: string) {

    }
}

throw new ApplicationError('Example Error', 'An error has occurred');
```

The LSP supports the OCP by ensuring that new code can be used in place of old code when a new behavior is added to a program. If a subclass couldn't be directly substituted for a superclass, adding a new subclass would result in changes being made throughout the code and may even result in the program flow being controlled by conditions that branch based on the object types.

The Interface Segregation Principle (ISP)

It is quite common to find that an interface is in essence just a description of an entire class. This is usually the case when the interface was written after the class. Listing 4-9 shows a simple example of an interface for a printer that can copy, print, and staple documents. Because the interface is just a way of describing all the behaviors of a printer, it grows as new features are added, for example, folding, inserting into envelopes, faxing, scanning, and e-mailing may eventually end up on the Printer interface.

Listing 4-9. Printer interface

```
interface Printer {
    copyDocument();
    printDocument(document: Document);
    stapleDocument(document: Document, tray: number);
}
```

The ISP states that we should not create these big interfaces, but instead write a series of smaller, more specific, interfaces that are implemented by the class. Each interface would describe an independent grouping of behavior, allowing code to depend on a small interface that provides just the required behavior. Different classes could provide the implementation of these small interfaces, without having to implement additional unrelated functionality.

The Printer interface from Listing 4-9 makes it impossible to implement a printer that can print and copy, but not staple — or even worse, the staple method must be implemented to throw an error that states the operation cannot be completed. The likelihood of a printer satisfying the Printer interface decreases over time as the interface grows larger, and it becomes hard to add a new method to the interface because it affects multiple implementations. Listing 4-10 shows an alternative approach that groups methods into more specific interfaces that describe a number of contracts that could be implemented individually by a simple printer or simple copier, as well as by a super printer that can do everything.

Listing 4-10. Segregated interfaces

```typescript
interface Printer {
    printDocument(document: Document);
}

interface Stapler {
    stapleDocument(document: Document, tray: number);
}

interface Copier {
    copyDocument();
}

class SimplePrinter implements Printer {
    printDocument(document: Document) {
        //...
    }
}

class SuperPrinter implements Printer, Stapler, Copier {
    printDocument(document: Document) {
        //...
    }

    copyDocument() {
        //...
    }

    stapleDocument(document: Document, tray: number) {
        //...
    }
}
```

When you follow the ISP, client code is not forced to depend on methods it doesn't intend to use. Large interfaces tend to encourage calling code that is organized in similar large chunks, whereas a series of small interfaces allows the client to implement small maintainable adapters to communicate with the interface.

The Dependency Inversion Principle (DIP)

In a conventional object-oriented program, the high-level components depend on low-level components in a hierarchical structure. The coupling between components results in a rigid system that is hard to change, and one that fails when changes are introduced. It also becomes hard to reuse a module because it cannot be moved into a new program without also bringing along a whole series of dependencies.

Listing 4-11 shows a simple example of conventional dependencies. The high-level LightSwitch class depends on the lower-level Light class.

Listing 4-11. High-level dependency on low-level class

```
class Light {
    switchOn() {
        //...
    }

    switchOff() {
        //...
    }
}

class LightSwitch {
    private isOn = false;

    constructor(private light: Light) {
    }

    onPress() {
        if (this.isOn) {
            this.light.switchOff();
            this.isOn = false;
        } else {
            this.light.switchOn();
            this.isOn = true;
        }
    }
}
```

The DIP simply states that high-level modules shouldn't depend on low-level components, but instead depend on abstractions. In turn, the abstractions should not depend on details, but on yet more abstractions. In simple terms, you can satisfy the DIP by depending on an interface, rather than a class.

Listing 4-12 demonstrates the first step of DIP in practice, simply adding a LightSource interface to break the dependency between the LightSwitch and Light classes. We can continue this design by abstracting the LightSwitch into a Switch interface; the Switch interface would depend on the LightSource interface, not on the low-level Light class.

Listing 4-12. Implementing the dependency inversion principle (DIP)

```
interface LightSource {
    switchOn();
    switchOff();
}
```

```typescript
class Light implements LightSource {
    switchOn() {
        //...
    }

    switchOff() {
        //...
    }
}

class LightSwitch {
    private isOn = false;

    constructor(private light: LightSource) {
    }

    onPress() {
        if (this.isOn) {
            this.light.switchOff();
            this.isOn = false;
        } else {
            this.light.switchOn();
            this.isOn = true;
        }
    }
}
```

The DIP extends the concepts of the OCP and the LSP. By depending on abstractions, code is less tightly bound to the specific implementation details of a class. This principle has a big impact, yet it is relatively simple to follow, as all you need to do is supply an abstract class or an interface (or interfaces, bearing in mind the interface segregation principle) to depend on rather than a concrete class.

Design Patterns

In software, design patterns provide a catalog of known problems along with a design solution for each problem described. These patterns are not overly prescriptive; instead they provide a set of tools that you can arrange in a different way each time you use them. The definitive source for the most common design patterns is the original "Gang of Four" book, *Design Patterns: Elements of Reusable Object-Oriented Software* (Gamma, Helm, Johnson, & Vlissides, Addison Wesley, 1995).

It is possible to transfer these design patterns to JavaScript, as shown by Diaz and Harmes (*Pro JavaScript Design Patterns*, Apress, 2007), and if it can be done in plain JavaScript it can be done in TypeScript. The translation from traditional design pattern examples to TypeScript is more natural in many cases, due to the class-based object orientation offered in TypeScript.

TypeScript is a natural fit for design patterns because it supplies all the language constructs required to use all the creational, structural, and behavioral patterns in the original catalog as well as many more documented since then. A small sample of design patterns is described in the following section, along with TypeScript code examples.

The following example demonstrates the strategy pattern and the abstract factory pattern. These are just 2 of the 24 patterns described in the original Gang of Four book. The patterns are described in general below and then used to improve the design of a small program.

■ **Note**   Although you may have an up-front idea about the design patterns that may improve the design of your program, it is far more common and often more desirable to let the patterns emerge as your program grows. If you predict the patterns that may be required, you could be guessing wrong. If you let the code reveal problems as you extend it, you are less likely to create large numbers of unnecessary classes, and you are less likely to get lost down the rabbit hole following the wrong design.

The Strategy Pattern

The strategy pattern allows you to encapsulate different algorithms in a way that makes each one substitutable for another. In Figure 4-2 the Context class would depend on Strategy, which provides the interface for concrete implementations. Any class that implements the interface could be passed to the Context class at runtime.

An example of the strategy pattern is shown in the practical example later in this section.

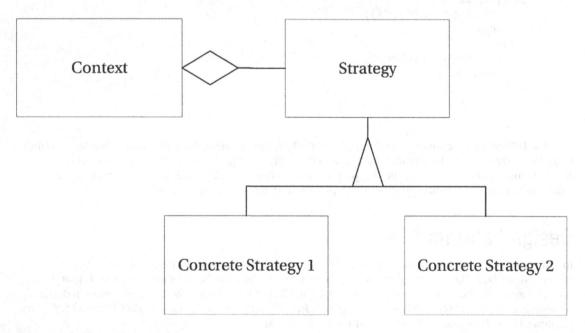

Figure 4-2. *The strategy pattern*

The Abstract Factory Pattern

The abstract factory pattern is a creational design pattern. It allows you to specify an interface for the creation of related objects without specifying their concrete classes. The aim of this pattern is for a class to depend on the behavior of the abstract factory, which will be implemented by different concrete classes that are either changed at compile time or runtime.

An example of the abstract factory pattern is shown in the practical example in Figure 4-3 and in the following text.

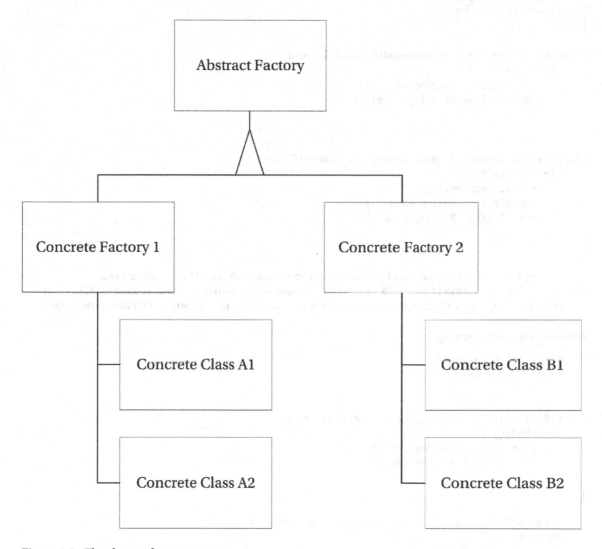

Figure 4-3. *The abstract factory pattern*

Practical Example

To illustrate the use of Strategy and Abstract Factory design patterns, we will use a car wash example. The car wash can run different grades of wash depending on how much the driver spends. Listing 4-13 illustrates the wheel cleaning strategy, which consists of an interface for wheel cleaning classes, and two strategies that provide either a basic or executive clean.

Listing 4-13. Wheel cleaning

```
interface WheelCleaning {
    cleanWheels(): void;
}

class BasicWheelCleaning implements WheelCleaning {
    cleanWheels() {
        console.log('Soaping Wheel');
        console.log('Brushing wheel');
    }
}

class ExecutiveWheelCleaning extends BasicWheelCleaning {
    cleanWheels() {
        super.cleanWheels();
        console.log('Waxing Wheel');
        console.log('Rinsing Wheel');
    }
}
```

Listing 4-14 shows the strategies for cleaning the bodywork of the car. This is similar to the WheelCleaning example in Listing 4-13, but it does not necessarily need to be. Neither the WheelCleaning nor BodyCleaning code will change when we convert the example to use the abstract factory pattern later.

Listing 4-14. Body cleaning

```
interface BodyCleaning {
    cleanBody(): void;
}

class BasicBodyCleaning implements BodyCleaning {
    cleanBody() {
        console.log('Soaping car');
        console.log('Rinsing Car');
    }
}

class ExecutiveBodyCleaning extends BasicBodyCleaning {
    cleanBody() {
        super.cleanBody();
        console.log('Waxing car');
        console.log('Blow drying car');
    }
}
```

Listing 4-15 shows the CarWashProgram class before it is updated to use the abstract factory pattern. This is a typical example of a class that knows too much. It is tightly coupled to the concrete cleaning classes and is responsible for creating the relevant classes based on the selected program.

Listing 4-15. CarWashProgram class before the abstract factory pattern

```typescript
class CarWashProgram {
    constructor(private washLevel: number) {

    }

    runWash() {
        let wheelWash: WheelCleaning;
        let bodyWash: BodyCleaning;

        switch (this.washLevel) {
            case 1:
                wheelWash = new BasicWheelCleaning();
                wheelWash.cleanWheels();

                bodyWash = new BasicBodyCleaning();
                bodyWash.cleanBody();

                break;
            case 2:
                wheelWash = new BasicWheelCleaning();
                wheelWash.cleanWheels();

                bodyWash = new ExecutiveBodyCleaning();
                bodyWash.cleanBody();

                break;
            case 3:
                wheelWash = new ExecutiveWheelCleaning();
                wheelWash.cleanWheels();

                bodyWash = new ExecutiveBodyCleaning();
                bodyWash.cleanBody();

                break;
        }
    }
}
```

The abstract factory itself is an interface that describes the operations each concrete factory can perform. In Listing 4-16 the `ValetFactory` interface provides method signatures for obtaining the class providing the wheel-cleaning feature and the class providing the body-cleaning feature. A class that requires wheel cleaning and body cleaning can depend on this interface and remain de-coupled from the classes that specify the actual cleaning.

Listing 4-16. Abstract factory

```typescript
interface ValetFactory {
    getWheelCleaning() : WheelCleaning;
    getBodyCleaning() : BodyCleaning;
}
```

In Listing 4-17, three concrete factories are declared that provide either a bronze-, silver-, or gold-level wash. Each factory provides appropriate cleaning classes that match the level of wash required.

Listing 4-17. Concrete factories

```typescript
class BronzeWashFactory implements ValetFactory {
    getWheelCleaning() {
        return new BasicWheelCleaning();
    }

    getBodyCleaning() {
        return new BasicBodyCleaning();
    }
}

class SilverWashFactory implements ValetFactory {
    getWheelCleaning() {
        return new BasicWheelCleaning();
    }

    getBodyCleaning() {
        return new ExecutiveBodyCleaning();
    }
}

class GoldWashFactory implements ValetFactory {
    getWheelCleaning() {
        return new ExecutiveWheelCleaning();
    }

    getBodyCleaning() {
        return new ExecutiveBodyCleaning();
    }
}
```

Listing 4-18 shows the updated class with the abstract factory pattern in action. The CarWashProgram class no longer has any knowledge of the concrete classes that will perform the car-cleaning actions. The CarWashProgram is now constructed with the appropriate factory that will provide the classes to perform the clean. This could either be done via a compile-time mechanism or a dynamic runtime one.

Listing 4-18. Abstract factory pattern in use

```typescript
class CarWashProgram {
    constructor(private cleaningFactory: ValetFactory) {

    }

    runWash() {
        const wheelWash = this.cleaningFactory.getWheelCleaning();
        wheelWash.cleanWheels();

        const bodyWash = this.cleaningFactory.getBodyCleaning();
        bodyWash.cleanBody();
    }
}
```

Mixins

Mixins provide an alternate way of composing your application that isn't explicitly covered in books on design patterns.

Mixins take their name from a customizable ice-cream dessert that was first available at Steve's Ice Cream in Somerville, Massachusetts. The idea behind the mix-in dessert was that you choose an ice cream and add another product to flavor it, for example, a candy bar. The mix-in, or smoosh-in, ice-cream concept has gone global since its appearance on Steve Herrell's menu back in 1973.

In programming, mixins are based on a very similar concept. Augmented classes are created by adding together a combination of mixin classes that each provide a small reusable behavior. These mixin classes are partly an interface and partly an implementation.

TypeScript Mixins

There are two styles on mixins available within TypeScript: the original simple mixins, and the newer real mixins. Simple mixins are implemented with the aid of one additional function that performs the wiring. The function to apply the mixins is shown in Listing 4-19. This function walks the instance members of each of the mixin classes passed in the baseCtors array and adds each of them to the derivedCtor class. You will use this function each time you want to apply mixins to a class, and you'll see this function used in the examples throughout this section.

Listing 4-19. Mixin enabler function

```
function applyMixins(derivedCtor: any, baseCtors: any[]) {
    baseCtors.forEach(baseCtor => {
        Object.getOwnPropertyNames(baseCtor.prototype).forEach(name => {
            derivedCtor.prototype[name] = baseCtor.prototype[name];
        });
    });
}
```

Once you have added this function somewhere within your program, you are ready to start using mixins. In Listing 4-20 a series of small reusable mixin classes are defined. There is no specific syntax for these classes. In this example, we define a series of possible behaviors, Sings, Dances, and Acts. These classes act as the menu of behaviors that can be mixed together to create different flavors composed of different combinations.

Listing 4-20. Reusable classes

```
class Sings {
    sing() {
        console.log('Singing');
    }
}

class Dances {
    dance() {
        console.log('Dancing');
    }
}
```

```
class Acts {
    act() {
        console.log('Acting');
    }
}
```

On their own, these classes are too small to be useful, but they adhere very closely to the single responsibility principle. You are not restricted to a single method, but the idea is that each class represents one behavior that you can sum up in the class name. To make these mixins useful, you need to compose them into usable augmented classes.

In TypeScript, you compose your mix class using the implements keyword, followed by a comma-separated list of mixins. The implements keyword pays homage to the fact that mixins are like interfaces that come with an implementation. You will also need to supply temporary properties that match all the mixins that you combine, as shown in Listing 4-21. These properties will be replaced when the applyMixins function is called directly after the class declaration.

There is nothing to ensure that you call the applyMixins function with the same collection of classes that you listed in the implements statement. You are responsible for keeping the two lists synchronized.

Listing 4-21. Composing classes

```
class Actor implements Acts {
    act: () => void;
}

applyMixins(Actor, [Acts]);

class AllRounder implements Acts, Dances, Sings {
    act: () => void;
    dance: () => void;
    sing: () => void;
}

applyMixins(AllRounder, [Acts, Dances, Sings]);
```

The Actor and AllRounder classes have no real implementation, only placeholders for the implementation that is supplied by the mixins. This means that there is only one place in the program that needs to be changed for any given behavior. Using an augmented class is no different from using any other class in your program, as shown in Listing 4-22.

Listing 4-22. Using the classes

```
const actor = new Actor();
actor.act();

const allRounder = new AllRounder();
allRounder.act();
allRounder.dance();
allRounder.sing();
```

■ **Note** You may have spotted that mixins look a little bit like multiple inheritance. Multiple inheritance is not permitted in TypeScript. The key to mixins is the use of the `implements` keyword, rather than the `extends` keyword, which makes them like interfaces rather than superclasses.

When to Use Mixins

Mixins already have some support in TypeScript — but what should you bear in mind when using them? First and foremost, the mechanism for adding the implementation to the augmented class is not checked, so you must be very careful about calling the `applyMixins` function with the correct list of class names. This is one area that you will want to fully test to avoid any nasty surprises.

The decision about whether to use mixins or classical inheritance usually comes down to the relationship between the classes. When deciding between inheritance and delegation, it is common to use the "is a" verses "has a" test. As described earlier in this chapter.

- A car **has a** chassis.

- A rolling chassis **is a** chassis.

Inheritance would only be used where the "is a" relationship works in a sentence, and delegation would be used where "has a" makes more sense. With mixins, the relationship is best described by a "can do" relationship, for example:

- *An actor can do acting.*

  Or

- *An actor acts.*

You can reinforce this relationship by naming your mixins with names such as `Acting` or `Acts`. This makes your class read like a sentence, for example, "Actor implements Acting."

Mixins are supposed to allow small units to be composed into larger ones, so the following scenarios are good candidates for using mixins:

- Composing classes with optional features, mixins are options.

- Reusing the same behavior on many classes.

- Creating many variations based on similar lists of features.

Restrictions

You cannot use mixins with private members because the compiler will generate an error if the members are not implemented in the augmented class. The compiler will also generate an error if both the mixin and the augmented class define a private member with the same name.

The other restriction on mixins is that although method implementations are mapped to the augmented class, property values are not mapped; this is demonstrated in Listing 4-23. When you implement a property from a mixin you need to initialize it in the augmented class. To avoid confusion, it is best to define a required property in the mixin, but provide no default value.

Listing 4-23. Properties not mapped

```
class Acts {
    public message = 'Acting';

    act() {
        console.log(this.message);
    }
}

class Actor implements Acts {
    public message: string;
    act: () => void;
}

applyMixins(Actor, [Acts]);
const actor = new Actor();

// Logs 'undefined', not 'Acting'
actor.act();
```

If the property does not need to be tied to the instance, you can use static properties as these would remain available from within the methods that are mapped from the mixin to the augmented class. Listing 4-24 is an update to Listing 4-23 that solves the problem using a static property. If you do need different values on each instance, the instance property should be initialized within the augmented class.

Listing 4-24. Static properties are available

```
class Acts {
    public static message = 'Acting';

    act() {
        alert(Acts.message);
    }
}

class Actor implements Acts {
    act: () => void;
}

applyMixins(Actor, [Acts]);

const actor = new Actor();

// Logs 'Acting'
actor.act();
```

Real Mixins

Real mixins provide a more solid mechanism for supporting composition using mixins. The equivalent mixin for creating an actor is shown in Listing 4-25. The Constructor type is a generic type for an object with a constructor that accepts zero or more arguments. The mixin is defined in the Acts function, which extends any suppled class with a message property and an act method.

To apply the mixin to a class, you simply call the Acts function, passing the target class. Whenever you call the resulting mix class, it will have its original members, along with the additional members of the mixin.

Listing 4-25. Real mixins.

```
type Constructor<T = {}> = new (...args: any[]) => T;

function Acts<TBase extends Constructor>(Base: TBase) {
    return class extends Base {
        message: string = 'Acting';
        act() {
            alert(this.message);
        }
    };
}

class Person {
    constructor(private name: string) {

    }
}

const Actor = Acts(Person);

const actor = new Actor('Alan');

// Acting
actor.act();
```

To show a comparative case of creating a mix class with multiple mixins, the complete real mixins equivalent of the singing, dancing, acting simple mixin is shown in Listing 4-26.

Listing 4-26. The full real mixins

```
type Constructor<T = {}> = new (...args: any[]) => T;

function Sings<TBase extends Constructor>(Base: TBase) {
    return class extends Base {
        sing() {
            alert('Singing');
        }
    };
}
```

```typescript
function Dances<TBase extends Constructor>(Base: TBase) {
    return class extends Base {
        dance() {
            alert('Dancing');
        }
    };
}

function Acts<TBase extends Constructor>(Base: TBase) {
    return class extends Base {
        act() {
            alert('Acting');
        }
    };
}

class Person {
    constructor(private name: string) {

    }
}

const Actor = Acts(Person);

const AllRounder = Acts(Sings(Dances(Person)));

const actor = new Actor('Alan');
actor.act();

const allRounder = new AllRounder('Gene');
allRounder.act();
allRounder.dance();
allRounder.sing();
```

The benefits of real mixins include the removal of the possibility of forgetting to call the apply mixins function, and the support for all members. The syntax takes some work, but once you have the constructor type, the rest is reasonably trivial.

Summary

All the building blocks of object orientation are present in TypeScript. The language tools make it possible to apply all the principles and practices of object orientation that you have learned using other languages into your program, using the SOLID principles to guide your composition, and applying design patterns as a reference for well-established solutions to common problems.

Object orientation, in itself doesn't solve the problems of writing and maintaining a program that solves complex problems. It is just as possible to write poor code using object orientation as it is to write bad code in any other programming paradigm; this is why the patterns and principles are so important. The elements of object orientation in this chapter complement the testing techniques in Chapter 10.

You can practice and improve your object-oriented design skills as well as your unit testing skills using coding katas. These are described in Appendix 4 and there are some example katas for you to try out.

Key Points

- TypeScript has all the tools needed to write object-oriented programs.
- The SOLID principles aim to keep your code malleable and prevent it from rotting.
- Design patterns are existing, well-known solutions to common problems.
- You don't have to implement a design pattern exactly as it is described.
- Mixins provide an alternative mechanism for composition.

CHAPTER 5

■ ■ ■

Understanding the Runtime

The difference between a bad programmer and a good programmer is understanding. That is, bad programmers don't understand what they are doing and good programmers do.

—Max Kanat-Alexander

Once your TypeScript program has been compiled to plain JavaScript, you can run it anywhere. JavaScript happily runs in a browser or on a server; you just have to bear in mind that the available features differ depending on where the code runs. This chapter explains some of the differences you will encounter between browser and server runtimes and also explains some important concepts that are common to all runtimes, such as the event loop, scope, and events.

Runtime Features

Even an aged browser will give you access to the Document Object Model (DOM), mouse and keyboard events, forms, and navigation. A modern browser will add offline storage, an indexed database, HTTP requests, geolocation, and suite of application programming interfaces (APIs) for device sensors such as light, accelerometer, and proximity. JavaScript isn't just the most common language in web browsers; it has been running on servers since the early 1990s. JavaScript's prominence as a server-side language has really gained traction with NodeJS, which is a server technology built on the V8 JavaScript engine. Running on the server gives you access to databases, the file system, cryptography, domain name resolution, streams, and countless other modules and utilities. Figure 5-1 illustrates how JavaScript as a language is made powerful by the APIs supplied by browsers or servers.

Unless you explicitly use an API that allows thread creation, such as web workers or a child process, the statements in your program will be queued to execute on a single thread. Running a program on a single thread removes many of the headaches that would be caused by multiple threads trying to manipulate the same state, but it does mean you need to remember that your code could be queued. A long-running event handler can block other events from firing in a timely manner, and the order in which the queue gets executed can vary in subtle ways. The queue is usually processed in first-in first-out order, but different runtime environments may revisit the queue at different times. For example, one environment may return to the queue only when a function has been completed, but another may revisit the queue whenever a function transfers control, for example, by calling another function. In the latter case, another statement may be executed before the second function is called. Despite the alarming nature of these potential differences, it is rare to find that they cause any problems in practice.

© Steve Fenton 2018
S. Fenton, *Pro TypeScript*, https://doi.org/10.1007/978-1-4842-3249-1_5

As well as processing the queue containing all the events, the runtime may have other tasks to perform that need to be processed on the same thread; for example, a browser may need to redraw the screen. If you have a function that takes too long to run, you could affect the redraw speed of the browser. To allow a browser to draw 60 frames per second, you would need to keep the execution of any function to less than 17 ms. Keeping functions fast is very easy in practice, except where you deal with an API with blocking calls, such as localStorage, or if you execute a long-running loop.

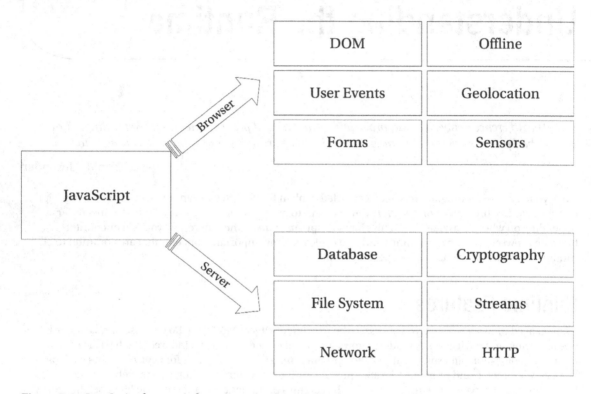

Figure 5-1. *JavaScript features in browser vs. server environments*

One of the most common side effects of the single-threaded approach at runtime is that intervals and timers may appear to take longer than the specified time to execute. This is because they must wait in the queue to be executed. Listing 5-1 shows a test function that times the execution of a delayed logging statement. Calling the test function sets up the 50-ms timer and measures how long it takes to fire. Running this code several times will show you that you get a result in the range of 50 to 52 ms, which is what you'd expect.

Listing 5-1. Queued timer

```
function test() {
    const testStart = performance.now();

    window.setTimeout(function () {
        console.log(performance.now() - testStart);
    }, 50);
}

test();
```

To simulate a long-running process, a loop that runs for 100 ms has been added to the test function in Listing 5-2. The loop starts after the timer is set up, but because nothing is de-queued until the original test function is completed, the timer executes much later than before. The times logged in this example are typically in the range of 118 to 130 ms.

Listing 5-2. Queued timer, delayed, waiting for the test method to finish

```
function test() {
    const testStart = performance.now();

    window.setTimeout(function () {
        console.log(performance.now() - testStart);
    }, 50);

    // Simulated long running process
    const start = +new Date();
    while (+new Date() - start < 100) {
        // Delay for 100ms
    }
}

test();
```

■ **Note** The performance.now high-resolution timer is supported in the latest versions of all major browsers. This method of measuring execution times is more accurate than using the Date object. Dates are based on the system clock, which is synchronized as often as every 15 minutes. If synchronization occurs while you are timing an operation, it will affect your result. The performance.now value comes from a high-resolution timer that can measure submillisecond intervals, starts at 0 when the page begins to load, and isn't adjusted during synchronization.

Scope

The term *scope* refers to the set of available identifiers that can be resolved in a given context. In most C-like languages, identifiers are block scoped, meaning they are available within the same set of curly braces that they are defined in. Variables declared within a set of curly braces are not available outside of those braces, but statements within the curly braces can access variables declared outside of the braces. Listing 5-3 shows this general C-like scoping in action.

This is not the case when you use the var keyword in JavaScript (and therefore TypeScript). If the code in Listing 5-3 was executed in a JavaScript runtime, the value logged in both statements would be the same; in particular, you would see "*Outer: 2*", rather than "*Outer: 1*". This is because scope of variables created with the var keyword is defined by functions, rather than blocks.

Listing 5-3. C-like scope

```
var scope = 1;

{
    var scope = 2;
```

```
    // Inner: 2
    console.log('Inner: ' + scope);
}

// Outer: 1
console.log('Outer: ' + scope);
```

Listing 5-4 shows the same example, but with a function to provide scope for the inner variable. The function creates a new context, making the inner scope variable independent of the outer scope variable. In this example, the logging statements work as they would in other C-like languages.

Listing 5-4. Functional scope

```
var scope = 1;

(function () {
    var scope = 2;

    // Inner: 2
    console.log('Inner: ' + scope);
}());

// Outer: 1
console.log('Outer: ' + scope);
```

There are two new variable declarations in the ECMAScript specification, let and const. Both let and const are block scoped and will save you from the many pitfalls of function-scoped variables. The const keyword has the additional advantage of preventing reassignment, which means the variable cannot be overwritten (although its value can change).

You can use both let and const in your TypeScript code. If you are targeting an older version of JavaScript, the compiler will use down-level compilation to rename your variables to prevent them being affected by the change in context. Listing 5-5 revisits the original example, using the const keyword in place of the var keyword, resulting in the correct logging of "Inner: 2" and "Outer: 1".

Listing 5-5. Block-level scope

```
const scope = 1;

{
    const scope = 2;

    // Inner: 2
    console.log('Inner: ' + scope);
}

// Outer: 1
console.log('Outer: ' + scope);
```

The down-level compilation of Listing 5-5 replaces the const keyword with the var keyword, but renames the second variable scope_1, as shown in Listing 5-6; this prevents the inner variable from overwriting the outer one. The compiler is smart enough to avoid naming collisions, so if you already had a variable that you had named scope_1, the compiler would pick a different name.

Listing 5-6. Down-level compilation of block-scoped variables

```
var scope = 1;
{
    var scope_1 = 2;
    // Inner: 2
    console.log('Inner: ' + scope_1);
}
// Outer: 1
console.log('Outer: ' + scope);
```

Because you can use block-scoped variables in TypeScript regardless of the target runtime, there should be no reason to use the var keyword in your TypeScript program.

■ **Note** As mentioned in Chapter 1, the recommended coding style is to use the `const` keyword for all variables, and only open a variable to reassignment with the `let` keyword if you decide to allow it.

Using block-scoped variables also prevents var hoisting, which treated all variables as being declared at the very top of their scope. This technically allowed variables to be used before the line of code that declared them, although their value would be undefined. Listing 5-7 shows an example of var hoisting.

Listing 5-7. Variable hoisting

```
function lemur() {
    // undefined, but technically allowable
    console.log(kind);

    var kind = 'Ruffed Lemur';
}

lemur();
```

The TypeScript compiler will issue a warning if you access a block-level variable before it is declared, preventing this kind of subtle error, and the even more confusing error in Listing 5-8, where you might expect the global variable to be used in the log statement. The coincidental reuse of a name from a wider scope when using the var keyword has caused some of the most famously tricky bugs I have ever investigated in my career.

Listing 5-8. Variable hoisting and global scope confusion

```
var kind = 'Ring Tailed Lemur';

function lemur() {
    // undefined, not 'Ring Tailed Lemur'
    console.log(kind);

    var kind = 'Ruffed Lemur';
}

lemur();
```

■ **Note**   In your program, the best way to avoid confusion is to avoid adding to the global scope wherever possible. The absence of global variables means the TypeScript compiler can warn you about usage of variables before they are declared and accidental omission of the var or let keywords.

Callbacks

Almost all modern JavaScript APIs, including the new browser APIs that supply access to readings from device sensors, avoid blocking by accepting a callback that will be executed once an operation has finished. A callback is simply a function that you pass as an argument, and which is called when an operation has completed.

To illustrate the benefits of callbacks, Figure 5-2 shows the program flow while waiting for a blocking sensor to respond to a request. Because the request is blocking the main thread for the duration of the request, no other statements can be executed. Blocking the event queue for more than a few milliseconds is undesirable and must be avoided for long operations. Operations involving calls to the file system, hardware devices, or calls across a network connection all have the potential to block your program for unacceptable lengths of time.

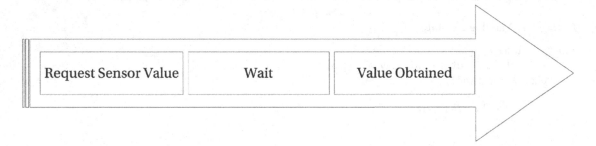

Figure 5-2. *Blocking call*

Callbacks are very useful for avoiding these blocking requests. Figure 5-3 shows how this pattern is used to avoid blocking the main thread during a long-running process. When the request is made, a function is passed along with the request. The main thread is then able to process the event queue as normal. When the long-running process ends, the callback function is then called, being passed any relevant arguments. This adds the callback to the event queue, where it is executed in turn.

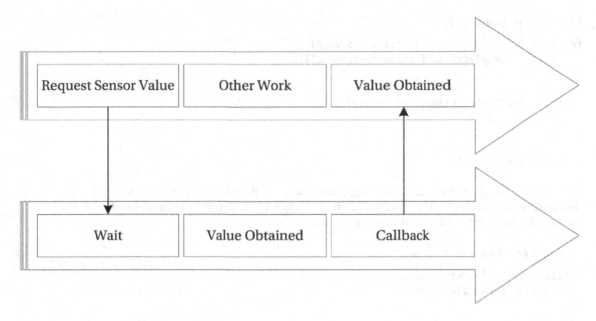

Figure 5-3. *Using a callback*

Although callbacks are commonly used to avoid blocking the program during a long-running process, you can freely pass a function as an argument anywhere in your program. Listing 5-9 demonstrates this. The go function accepts a function argument. The `callback` parameter has a type annotation that restricts the functions that can be passed to only those that accept a `string` argument. The `callbackFunction` satisfies this type annotation.

In the body of the go function, the callback is executed using the `call` method, which is available on all functions in JavaScript.

Listing 5-9. Passing a function as an argument

```
function go(callback: (arg: string) => void) {
    callback.call(this, 'Example Argument');
}

function callbackFunction(arg: string) {
    alert(arg);
}

go(callbackFunction);
```

There are three common ways to execute the callback from within the go function. In Listing 5-9, the call method was used. When you use `call`, you must supply a variable that will be used to set the context of the `this` keyword within the callback. You can follow the context argument with any number of additional arguments; these will be passed into the callback. You can also use the `apply` method, which is almost identical to `call`, except you pass the arguments as an array, as shown in Listing 5-10. If your result is already an array, this results in the values being exploded in to separate arguments.

Listing 5-10. Using apply

```
function go(callback: (arg: string) => void) {
    callback.apply(this, ['Example Argument']);
}

function callbackFunction(arg: string) {
    alert(arg);
}

go(callbackFunction);
```

The third method of executing a callback is to simply call the function with parentheses, as demonstrated in Listing 5-11. This technique doesn't allow the context to be set, so depending on the context, the scope may different to your expectation.

Listing 5-11. Simple function call

```
function go(callback: (arg: string) => void) {
    callback('Example Argument');
}

function callbackFunction(arg: string) {
    alert(arg);
}

go(callbackFunction);
```

There is an additional use for the apply method outside of the context of callbacks. Because it accepts an array containing arguments, you can use apply to extract arguments from an array. This is demonstrated in Listing 5-12. To find the maximum number in the numbers array, you would either write a loop to test each one or pass each value individually into the Math.max function using each index. Using the apply method means you can simply pass the numbers array and have the apply method convert the array into the argument list. Because you aren't using apply to modify the scope, you can pass null as the first argument.

Listing 5-12. Using apply to convert array to arguments

```
const numbers = [3, 11, 5, 7, 2];

// A fragile way of finding the maximum number
// const max = Math.max(numbers[0], numbers[1], numbers[2], numbers[3], numbers[4]);

// A solid way to find the maximum
const max = Math.max.apply(null, numbers);

// 11
console.log(max);
```

The pattern of using callbacks is one example of functions passed as arguments. The next section describes how powerful this language feature is and how it can be used in other ways.

Passing Functions as Arguments

Functions are first-class citizens in JavaScript, which means they can be passed as arguments, returned from another function as a return value, assigned to variables, and stored as properties on an object. Passing a function as an argument is the mechanism used to provide callbacks.

You can use the ability to pass functions as arguments to create a simple implementation of the observer pattern, storing a collection of subscribers and publishing an event to them all from a single class. This simple observer design is shown in Listing 5-13. Any number of subscribers can be added, and when the publisher receives a message, it distributes it to all the subscribers.

Listing 5-13. Simple observer

```
interface Subscriber {
    (message: string): void;
}

class Publisher {
    private subscribers: Subscriber[] = [];

    addSubscriber(subscriber: Subscriber) {
        this.subscribers.push(subscriber);
    }

    notify(message: string) {
        for (let subscriber of this.subscribers) {
            subscriber(message);
        }
    }
}

const publisher = new Publisher();

// Using an arrow function
publisher.addSubscriber((message) => console.log('A: ' + message));

// Using an inline function
publisher.addSubscriber(function (message) {
    console.log('B: ' + message);
});

// A: Test message
// B: Test message
publisher.notify('Test message');
```

■ **Note**   When you pass a function as an argument, you must omit the parentheses; for example, go(callbackFunction) rather than go(callbackFunction()); otherwise the function is executed and the return value is passed instead.

First-class functions are one of the most powerful features in any language. You can create higher-order functions that accept functions as arguments and return functions as results; this allows greater flexibility as well as granular code reusability in your program. You can also refer to Chapter 1 to find out more about function currying, and arrow functions.

Promises

Promises were introduced to reduce several problems caused by callbacks. When using a chain of callbacks, code can become deeply nested and difficult to follow. When error handling is considered, the callbacks often repeat error handling code, further increasing the cognitive overhead of understanding the program.

The native Promise object is only available in versions of ECMAScript after version 5. If you are targeting these more recent versions of the specification, you can use the purely native version of promises. Otherwise, you'll need to apply a polyfill to add the desired feature.

To fully explore promises, we'll need to work through a fairly substantial example. By the end of this exercise you'll understand how to consume promises, and how to create them. Even though the examples in this section are very simple (they just log some data to the console), you'll be able to see the problems caused by callback chains, and how promises fix the nesting and readability.

Simple Callbacks

The first example involves simple callbacks. This example allows a callback to be used to return control to calling code once an asynchronous operation completes. We will evolve this program to solve various problems shortly.

Listing 5-14 is the starting point for our fictitious API that asynchronously obtains some data. The getData method takes an id, and a callback that will be executed once the data is available. The code that relies on the data must be placed inside of this callback.

Listing 5-14. Fictitious API v1.0

```
interface FictitiousData {
    id: number;
    name: string;
}

class FictitiousAPI {
    static data: { [index: number]: FictitiousData } = {
        1: { id: 1, name: 'Aramis' },
        2: { id: 2, name: 'Athos' },
        3: { id: 3, name: 'Porthos' },
        4: { id: 4, name: 'D\'Artagnan' }
    };

    static getData(id: number, callback: (data: FictitiousData) => void) {
        // Simulating async data access with a timeout
        window.setTimeout(() => {
            const result = this.data[id];

            if (typeof result == 'undefined') {
                throw new Error('No matching record');
            }
```

```
        callback(result);
    }, 200);
}
}
```

A simple use of the API is shown in Listing 5-15. Once the asynchronous getData function is ready, it executes the callback function, which logs the data to the console.

Listing 5-15. Single call

```
// Single call: 'Aramis'
FictitiousAPI.getData(1, function (data) {
    console.log(data.name);
});
```

One of the problems associated with the callback pattern is that it isn't possible to handle any exceptions that occur within the asynchronous code. No matter where you insert a try/catch statement, you won't be able to handle the error in this version of the API.

Listing 5-16. Error Handling

```
// Error handling (doesn't work)
try {
    FictitiousAPI.getData(5, function (data) {
        console.log(data.name);
    })
} catch (ex) {
    console.log('This statement is not reached, the error is not caught!');
}
```

When you need to chain several calls using callbacks, the code quickly becomes nested and hard to read. Listing 5-17 is a nesting of similar calls to get data, but nested callbacks can also occur when you need to use several different asynchronous APIs.

Listing 5-17. Nested callbacks

```
FictitiousAPI.getData(1, (data) => {
    console.log(data.name);

    FictitiousAPI.getData(2, (data) => {

        if (data.name == 'Athos') {
            console.log(data.id + ' ' + data.name);
        } else {
            console.log(data.name);
        }

        FictitiousAPI.getData(3, (data) => {
            console.log(data.name);

            FictitiousAPI.getData(4, (data) => {
                console.log(data.name);
```

```
                    FictitiousAPI.getData(5, (data) => {
                        console.log(data.name);
                    })
                });
            });
        });
});
```

The output from this program is shown below:

```
==== OUTPUT ====
Aramis
2 Athos
Porthos
D'Artagnan
Error: No matching record
```

The first step in evolving this code is to make it possible to handle errors that occur within the API. After this, we can look at improving it with promises.

Callbacks and Error Handling

To solve the problem of error handling, we will introduce an additional parameter to the callback function. This is a common pattern in programs that use callbacks extensively. By placing the error parameter first, the success condition can have a variable number of parameters without affecting where the calling code should expect to find information about a problem.

Listing 5-18 shows the complete second version of the API, which now includes the error string as the first parameter. Instead of raising an error, the error message is passed as the first argument in the event of a problem. In success cases, no error string is passed.

Listing 5-18. Fictitious API v2.0

```
interface FictitiousData {
    id: number;
    name: string;
}

class FictitiousAPI {
    static data: { [index: number]: FictitiousData } = {
        1: { id: 1, name: 'Aramis' },
        2: { id: 2, name: 'Athos' },
        3: { id: 3, name: 'Porthos' },
        4: { id: 4, name: 'D\'Artagnan' }
    };

    static getData(id: number, callback: (error: string, data: FictitiousData) => void) {
        // Simulating async data access with a timeout
        window.setTimeout(() => {
            const result = this.data[id];
```

```
            if (typeof result == 'undefined') {
                callback('No matching record', null);
                return;
            }

            callback(null, result);
        }, 200);
    }
}
```

To put this new error handling pattern in practice, the simple call in Listing 5-19 now needs to test for an error before using the data argument.

Listing 5-19. Single call with error handling

```
// Single call: 'Aramis'
FictitiousAPI.getData(1, function (error, data) {
    if (error) {
        console.log('Caught ' + error);
        return;
    }

    console.log(data.name);
});
```

The same test appears in Listing 5-20 and successfully handles the error that was previously impossible to handle. We can now undertake different actions on success and on error.

Listing 5-20. Working error handling

```
// Error handling
FictitiousAPI.getData(5, function (error, data) {
    if (error) {
        console.log('Caught ' + error);
        return;
    }

    console.log(data.name);
});
```

The downside to this pattern is the proliferation of error handling code, which makes our nested callback situation even more verbose, as shown in Listing 5-21. Even though this code example is still satisfying a very basic function, it is now a complicated listing that is hard to comprehend.

Listing 5-21. Nested callbacks with error handling

```
FictitiousAPI.getData(1, (error, data) => {
    if (error) {
        console.log('Caught ' + error);
        return;
    }

    console.log(data.name);
```

141

```
FictitiousAPI.getData(2, (error, data) => {
    if (error) {
        console.log('Caught ' + error);
        return;
    }

    if (data.name == 'Athos') {
        console.log(data.id + ' ' + data.name);
    } else {
        console.log(data.name);
    }

    FictitiousAPI.getData(3, (error, data) => {
        if (error) {
            console.log('Caught ' + error);
            return;
        }

        console.log(data.name);

        FictitiousAPI.getData(4, (error, data) => {
            if (error) {
                console.log('Caught ' + error);
                return;
            }

            console.log(data.name);

            FictitiousAPI.getData(5, (error, data) => {
                if (error) {
                    console.log('Caught ' + error);
                    return;
                }

                console.log(data.name);
            })
        });
    });
});
```

The output from this program is substantially similar to before and is shown below, the only difference being the error is now handled:

```
==== OUTPUT ====
Aramis
2 Athos
Porthos
D'Artagnan
Caught No matching record
```

The next step in evolving this code is to drastically improve its readability using promises.

Promises

Introducing promises to the API is quite a simple task. In Listing 5-22, the signature of the getData method has been cleaned up by removing all parameters that were introduced for callbacks. This makes the signature better describe what is required to perform the operation: in this case, just the id.

The body of the method has been wrapped in a new promise object, which always has a signature with two function parameters. The first function will be used to fulfill the promise when the request is successful. The second function is used to reject the promise when there is an error. All promises have this signature, but in TypeScript you can further enhance these functions with more specific type information.

In Listing 5-22 the fulfill function has a typed parameter data, which will contain FicitiousData, and the reject function has a string reason. The type annotations here will ensure autocompletion members are correct in the code that uses this promise. You can also use a type argument when creating a promise to add this type information.

Listing 5-22. Fictitious API v3.0

```
interface FictitiousData {
    id: number;
    name: string;
}

class FictitiousAPI {
    static data: { [index: number]: FictitiousData } = {
        1: { id: 1, name: 'Aramis' },
        2: { id: 2, name: 'Athos' },
        3: { id: 3, name: 'Porthos' },
        4: { id: 4, name: 'D\'Artagnan' }
    };

    static getData(id: number) {
        return new Promise((fulfil: (data: FictitiousData) => void, reject: (reason: string)
=> void) => {
            // Simulating async data access with a timeout
            window.setTimeout(() => {
                const result = this.data[id];

                if (typeof result == 'undefined') {
                    reject('No matching record');
                }

                fulfil(result);
            }, 200);
        });
    }
}
```

When we call the getData method, we are now given back a promise, as shown in Listing 5-23. In place of a callback, the promise object has a then method, which accepts a function. In this simple case, the primary benefit of the promise is that it separates the concerns of the getData signature, and the then signature. There are more substantial benefits to come.

Listing 5-23. Single call with then

```
// Single call: 'Aramis'
FictitiousAPI.getData(1)
    .then(function (data) {
        console.log(data.name);
    });
```

To handle errors that occur when satisfying a promise, the catch method can be used, as shown in Listing 5-24. We now have three items that all handle individual concerns, rather than the previous callback design where the concerns were all intermingled.

Listing 5-24. Error handling with catch

```
// Error handling (works)
FictitiousAPI.getData(5)
    .then(function (data) {
        console.log(data.name);
    })
    .catch(function (error) {
        console.log('Caught ' + error);
    })
```

To better demonstrate these benefits, the full promise chain is shown in Listing 5-25. The code is minimally nested (two levels at the maximum, compared to five levels in the previous version that used callbacks with error handling). Each of the then functions is comparatively easy to comprehend and all of the exception handling is contained within the single catch.

Listing 5-25. Promise chain

```
FictitiousAPI.getData(1)
    .then((data) => {
        console.log(data.name);
        return FictitiousAPI.getData(2);
    })
    .then((data) => {
        if (data.name == 'Athos') {
            console.log(data.id + ' ' + data.name);
        } else {
            console.log(data.name);
        }

        return FictitiousAPI.getData(3);
    })
    .then((data) => {
        console.log(data.name);
        return FictitiousAPI.getData(4);
    })
    .then((data) => {
        console.log(data.name);
        return FictitiousAPI.getData(5);
    })
```

```
    .catch((error) => {
        console.log('Caught ' + error);
    });
```

The output of the updated program is identical to before, but the program is far easier to read.

```
==== OUTPUT ====
Aramis
2 Athos
Porthos
D'Artagnan
Caught No matching record
```

Although this example uses a single catch, to reproduce the behavior of the original callback example, you can insert additional catch blocks to handle errors earlier in the chain if you want to continue processing the chain afterwards. Promises are very flexible in this respect.

Even in the case of nesting and error handling, promises are more than a match for callbacks, but there are some other benefits to promises that simply aren't possible with callbacks.

Multiple Promises

An alternative to chaining multiple promises is to aggregate their results with a wrapper promise that is responsible for obtaining the values from the individual sub-promises. There is a mechanism built into promises that allows this to be done with a simple call to Promise.all.

Listing 5-26 shows the promise chain from Listing 5-25 collapsed into a call to Promise.all. Once all promises have been settled the then block is executed with the results. If there are any errors, the catch block is called immediately; this is a fail-fast mechanism. This is a good way to express that your code requires all the promises to be fulfilled in order to continue.

Listing 5-26. Promise.all

```
Promise.all([
    FictitiousAPI.getData(1),
    FictitiousAPI.getData(2),
    FictitiousAPI.getData(3),
    FictitiousAPI.getData(4)
]).then((values) => {
    for (let val of values) {
        console.log(val.name);
    }
}).catch((error) => {
    console.log('Caught ' + error);
});
```

No matter how long each individual promise takes to fulfill, the values passed in the then block will be ordered the same as the promises that were passed in. In the case of Listing 5-26, the results will always be ordered Aramis, Athos, Porthos, D'Artagnan, even if the asynchronous operations succeeded in a different order.

Fastest Promise

If you are calling several asynchronous operations and are only interested in getting the fastest result, you can use the `Promise.race` method.

Listing 5-27 shows the promise chain from Listing 5-25 used in a promise race. The first promise to settle causes the race to also settle with either the fulfilled value or the rejection reason of the fastest promise. Even though the first result is available immediately, in the background the other operations continue, which means they still consume resources even after your race has a winner.

Listing 5-27. Fastest promise

```
Promise.race([
    FictitiousAPI.getData(1),
    FictitiousAPI.getData(2),
    FictitiousAPI.getData(3),
    FictitiousAPI.getData(4)
]).then((data) => {
    console.log(data.name);
}).catch((error) => {
    console.log('Caught ' + error);
});
```

Promises offer a superior mechanism for handling asynchronous chains, reducing nesting, and both simplifying and standardizing error handling. There are also some useful standard compositions of promises that allow you to fire off many asynchronous operations and converge on a single then block when the promises are all fulfilled.

Promises are set to become the de facto mechanism for asynchronous APIs, with browsers set to implement promise-based improvements to features. For example, the XMLHttpRequest mechanism shown in Listing 5-28 is likely to be replaced with a fetch API that uses promises for the same operation.

Listing 5-28. XMLHttpRequest

```
const request = new XMLHttpRequest();

request.onload = function() {
    if (request.status !== 200) {
        // Status code not likely to be usable, i.e. a redirect
        console.log('Status Code:', request.status);
        return;
    }

    const data = JSON.parse(request.responseText);
    console.log(data);
};

request.onerror = (error) => {
    // Network failure or status code is error
    console.log('Error making request: ', error);
};

request.open('get', './api/musketeers.json', true);
request.send();
```

The fetch API equivalent is shown in Listing 5-29. Although this feature is experimental at the time of writing, its introduction is imminent. Please be aware that the final specification may differ from this example.

Listing 5-29. Fetch API

```
fetch('./api/musketeers.json')
    .then((response) => {
        if (response.status !== 200) {
            // Status code not likely to be usable, i.e. a redirect or an error
            console.log('Status Code:', response.status);
            return;
        }

        return response.json();
    }).then((data) => {
        console.log(data);
    })
    .catch((error) => {
        // i.e. network failure
        console.log('Error making request', error);
    });
```

As the promise pattern becomes more familiar, changes such as the Fetch API will make interactions more familiar and predictable. Unlike the XMLHttpRequest, which almost always causes programmers to double-check the documentation, you can follow the pattern through the Fetch API as it is just a promise chain. You can expect similar changes to any APIs that offer asynchronous operations.

Events

Events are a fundamental concept in the JavaScript runtime, so they are of great interest to any TypeScript programmer. Event listeners are commonly attached to user-initiated events such as touch, click, keypress, and other interactions on a web page, but events can also be used as a mechanism for decoupling code that needs to trigger processing and the code that undertakes the work.

Events are handled across two distinct phases — capturing and bubbling.

1. During capturing, the event is sent to the topmost elements in the document hierarchy first and then to more deeply nested elements.

2. During bubbling, it is sent to the target element first and then to its ancestors.

The phase is supplied as a property of the event argument and can be accessed using e.eventPhase where your event argument is named e.

At the risk of overstating the point about running in an event loop on a single thread, it is worth remembering that multiple event listeners attached to the same event will execute sequentially, not in parallel, and a long-running listener may delay the execution of the subsequent listeners attached to the same event. When an event is triggered, each event listener is queued in the same order it is attached; if the first listener takes 2 s to run, the second listener is blocked for at least 2 s and will only execute once it reaches the top of the event queue.

Listing 5-30. Event listeners

```
class ClickLogger {
    constructor() {
        document.addEventListener('click', this.eventListener);
    }

    eventListener(e: Event) {
        // 3 (Bubbling Phase)
        const phase = e.eventPhase;

        const tag = (<HTMLElement>e.target).tagName;

        console.log(`Click event in phase ${phase} detected on element ${tag} by
ClickLogger.`);
    }
}

const clickLogger = new ClickLogger();
```

Listing 5-30 shows a class that attaches one of its methods, eventListener, to the click event on the document. When used in conjunction with the HTML page in Listing 5-31; this ClickLogger class will output messages based on the element clicked, for example:

- Click event detected on element DIV by ClickLogger.

- Click event detected on element P by ClickLogger.

- Click event detected on element BLOCKQUOTE by ClickLogger.

- Click event detected on element FOOTER by ClickLogger.

Listing 5-31. Example document

```
<!DOCTYPE html>
<html lang="en">
<head>
    <meta charset="utf-8" />
    <title>Event Demo</title>
</head>
<body>
    <div>
        Clicking on different parts of this document logs appropriate messages.
        <blockquote>
            <p>
                Any fool can write code that a computer can understand.
                Good programmers write code that humans can understand.
            </p>
            <footer>
                -Martin Fowler
            </footer>
        </blockquote>
    </div>
</body>
</html>
```

> ■ **Note** The correct way to add an event listener is the `addEventListener` call. Versions of Internet Explorer prior to version 9 use an alternative `attachEvent` method. You can target both of these methods of attaching an event using the custom `addEventCrossBrowser` function shown in Listing 5-32. An improved version of this function appears in Chapter 5.

Listing 5-32. Cross-browser events

```
function addEventCrossBrowser(element, eventName, listener) {
    if (element.addEventListener) {
        element.addEventListener(eventName, listener, false);
    } else if (element.attachEvent) {
        element.attachEvent('on' + eventName, listener);
    }
}

class ClickLogger {
    constructor() {
        addEventCrossBrowser(document, 'click', this.eventListener);
    }

    eventListener(e: Event) {
        // 3 (Bubbling Phase)
        const phase = e.eventPhase;

        const tag = (<HTMLElement>e.target).tagName;

        console.log('Click event detected on element ' + tag + ' by ClickLogger.');
    }
}

const clickLogger = new ClickLogger();
```

You are not limited to the finite list of supported events in any given runtime; you can listen for, and dispatch, your own custom events too.

TypeScript's Custom-Event Mechanism

Listing 5-33 shows the custom-event mechanism. In some environments, it is as simple as using `addEventListener` and `dispatchEvent`. You can pass custom data as part of the event to use in the listener.

Listing 5-33. Custom events

```
// Polyfill for CustomEvent:
// https://developer.mozilla.org/en/docs/Web/API/CustomEvent
(function () {
    function CustomEvent(event, params) {
        params = params || { bubbles: false, cancelable: false, detail: undefined };
        const evt = <any>document.createEvent('CustomEvent');
```

```typescript
        evt.initCustomEvent(event, params.bubbles, params.cancelable, params.detail);
        return evt;
    };

    CustomEvent.prototype = (<any>window).Event.prototype;

    (<any>window).CustomEvent = CustomEvent;
})();

// Fix for lib.d.ts
interface StandardEvent {
    new(name: string, obj: {}): CustomEvent;
}
var StandardEvent = <StandardEvent><any>CustomEvent;

// Code for custom events is below:

enum EventType {
    MyCustomEvent
}

class Trigger {
    static customEvent(name: string, detail: {}) {
        const event = new StandardEvent(name, detail);

        document.dispatchEvent(event);
    }
}

class ListeningClass {
    constructor() {
        document.addEventListener(
            EventType[EventType.MyCustomEvent],
            this.eventListener,
            false);
    }

    eventListener(e: Event) {
        console.log(EventType[EventType.MyCustomEvent] + ' detected by ClickLogger.');
        console.log('Information passed: ' + (<any>e).detail.example);
    }
}

var customLogger = new ListeningClass();

Trigger.customEvent(
    EventType[EventType.MyCustomEvent],
    {
        "detail": {
            "example": "Example Value"
        }
    }
);
```

You can choose to use events, or code events, such as the simple observer from the earlier example in Listing 5-13, to distribute work throughout your program.

Event Phases

An event is dispatched to an event target along a propagation path that flows from the root of the document to the target element. Each progression along the path from the root to the target element is part of the capture phase of the event and the phase will be 1. Then the event reaches the event target, and the phase changes to the target phase, which is phase 2. Finally, the event flows in the reverse direction from the event target back to the root in the bubbling phase, which is phase 3.

These event phases are shown in Figure 5-4. The additional elements in the blockquote are not part of the hierarchy between the root and the event target, so they are not included in the propagation path.

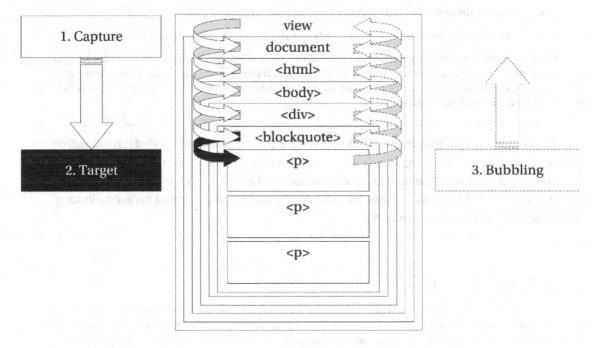

Figure 5-4. Event phases

Events provide a powerful mechanism for decoupling the code in your program. If you trigger events rather than directly call code to perform an action, it is a simple task to divide the action into small event listeners with a single responsibility. It is also a trivial matter to add additional listeners later.

Extending Objects

Almost everything in JavaScript is an object that consists of a set of properties. Each property is a key-value pair with a string key and value of any type, including primitive types, objects, and functions. If the value is a function, it is commonly called a method. Whenever you create a class in TypeScript, it is represented using JavaScript objects, but there are also many built-in objects that you can use.

The native objects all remain open, which means you can extend them as easily as you can your own objects. You need to take care when extending a native object for the following reasons:

- If everyone extended native objects, the chances are the extensions would overwrite each other or combine in incompatible ways.

- It is possible that the native object definition may later clash with yours, and your implementation will hide the native implementation.

So, although it is possible to extend native objects, in general it is only recommended as a technique to be used as a *polyfill*, which is a way of adding current features to older runtimes. Although you may decide to live by a less restrictive rule, it is worth writing extensions to native objects in the style of a polyfill so you can at least detect when one of the following happens:

- Native functionality is added with a name that clashes with your extension.

- Another programmer adds another extension with the same name.

- A third-party library or framework adds an extension with the same name.

The third item in particular suggests you shouldn't write native object extensions if you are shipping your program to be used as a library by other programmers. If library authors routinely extended native objects, there would be a high chance of a clash and the winner would simply be the last extension to load, as it would overwrite all previous ones.

■ **Note**   The term *polyfill* (named after a wall smoothing and crack filling cement called Polyfilla) was coined by Remy Sharp (*Remy Sharp's Blog*, `http://remysharp.com/2010/10/08/what-is-a-polyfill/`, 2010) as a term to describe a technique used to add missing native behavior in a way that defers to the native implementation when it becomes available. For example, you would attempt to detect the feature inside a browser and only add to it if it was missing.

Extending the Prototype

In Listing 5-34, the native NodeList, which contains a list of HTML elements, has been extended to add an each method that executes a callback function for each element in the list. The extension is added to the NodeList.prototype, which means it will be available on all NodeList instances. Calling document. querySelectorAll returns a NodeList of matching elements, and now the each method can be used to display the contents of each element using the getParagraphText function. The use of the each method means the for loop can be defined in just a single place.

Rather than passing each element into the callback function as an argument, the call method is used to bind the element to the function's context, which means the getParagraphText function can use the this keyword to refer to the element.

Listing 5-34. Extending objects in JavaScript

```
NodeList.prototype.each = function (callback) {
    for (let node of this) {
        callback.call(node);
    }};
```

```
const getParagraphText = function () {
    console.log(this.innerHTML);
};

const paragraphs = document.querySelectorAll('p');
paragraphs.each(getParagraphText);
```

When you add this code to a TypeScript program, errors will be generated to warn you that the each method doesn't exist on the NodeList interface. You can remove these errors and get intelligent autocompletion by adding to the interface in your program, as shown in Listing 5-35. The added benefit is that if the native object is updated in a way that clashes with your extension, the TypeScript compiler will warn you about the duplicate declaration.

Listing 5-35. Extending objects in TypeScript

```
interface NodeList {
    each(callback: () => any): void;
}

NodeList.prototype.each = function (callback) {
    for (let node of this) {
        callback.call(node);
    }
};

const getParagraphText = function () {
    console.log(this.innerHTML);
};

const paragraphs = document.querySelectorAll('p');
paragraphs.each(getParagraphText);
```

In this example, the this keyword within the each method has no type because it can't be inferred. This can be improved as shown in Listing 5-36. By moving the elements from the contextual this keyword into a parameter, the autocompletion and type checking in your program is improved. This also means the function can be reused more easily. Both the NodeList and the generic NodeListOf interfaces have been extended to give the tightest possible type checking.

Listing 5-36. Improved TypeScript object extensions

```
interface NodeList {
    each(callback: (element: HTMLElement) => any): void;
}

interface NodeListOf<TNode extends Node> {
    each(callback: (element: TNode) => any): void;
}

NodeList.prototype.each = function (callback: (elem: HTMLElement) => any) {
    for (let node of this) {
        callback.call(node, node);
    }
};
```

```
const getParagraphText = function (elem: HTMLParagraphElement) {
    console.log(elem.innerHTML);
};

const paragraphs = document.querySelectorAll('p');
paragraphs.each(getParagraphText);
```

To make this solution more like a polyfill, the code should check for the existence of the each method before adding it. This is how you would add an interim feature that is planned but not yet available on your target runtime. You can see this in action in Listing 5-37.

Listing 5-37. Turning an extension into a polyfill

```
if (!NodeList.prototype.each) {
    NodeList.prototype.each = function (callback: (elem: HTMLElement) => any) {
        for (let node of this) {
            callback.call(node, node);
        }
    };
}
```

Extending objects via the prototype is a technique that can be used on any object in TypeScript, even your own, unless it is sealed. Extending prototypes is a convoluted way to add behavior to objects that are under your control. You may be tempted to use the technique to extend a library that you consume, as it would allow you to upgrade the library later without losing your own additions.

Sealing Objects

If you are concerned about your code being extended, you can prevent extensions being made to your instances by using Object.seal. Listing 5-38 shows a typical extension that someone else may make to your code, and Listing 5-39 shows how to prevent it. Object.seal prevents new properties from being added and marks all existing properties as nonconfigurable. It is still possible to modify the values of the existing properties.

Listing 5-38. Extended instance

```
class Lemur {
    constructor(public name: string) {

    }
}

const lemur = new Lemur('Sloth Lemur');

// new property
lemur.isExtinct = true;

// true
console.log(lemur.isExtinct);
```

Listing 5-39. Sealing an instance

```
class Lemur {
    constructor(public name: string) {

    }
}

const lemur = new Lemur('Sloth Lemur');

Object.seal(lemur);

// new property
lemur.isExtinct = true;

// undefined
console.log(lemur.isExtinct);
```

You can check whether an object is sealed using the Object.isSealed method, passing in the object you want to check. There are a series of similar operations that may be useful — each could be used in Listing 5-38 in place of the Object.seal call to get the results described in the following example.

- Object.preventExtensions/Object.isExtensible is a more permissive version of Object.seal, allowing the properties to be deleted and to be added to the prototype.

- Object.freeze/Object.isFrozen is a more restrictive alternative to Object.seal that prevents properties from being added or removed and also prevents values being changed.

There is an excellent overview of creating, extending, and sealing JavaScript objects in *Expert JavaScript* by Mark Daggett (Apress, 2013).

Alternatives to Extending

It would be somewhat irresponsible to advise against extending native objects without presenting an alternative solution to the problem. This section shows an example of the classList property that is available on HTML elements in modern web browsers. The polyfill is shown, and then an alternative solution is supplied that uses a façade to marshal the call between either the native classList or the substitute version.

Listing 5-40 shows a call to retrieve the list of classes from an element that will fail in old browsers. The classList API actually supplies options to add, remove, and toggle classes — but for this example just the retrieval of the array of class names is shown.

Listing 5-40. Using the native classList

```
const elem = document.getElementById('example');

console.log(elem.classList);
```

One common solution to the potential absence of this feature is to use a polyfill. Listing 5-41 shows a simple polyfill that tests for the presence of the classList API and then adds it to the HTMLElement or Element prototype. The replacement function splits the string of class names to create an array, or it returns an empty array if there are no class names.

Listing 5-41. ClasList Polyfill

```
if (typeof document !== "undefined" && !("classList" in document.documentElement)) {
    const elementPrototype = (HTMLElement || Element).prototype;
    if (elementPrototype) {
        Object.defineProperty(elementPrototype, 'classList', {
            get: function () {
                const list = this.className ? this.className.split(/\s+/) : [];
                console.log('Polyfill: ' + list);
            }
        });
    }
}

const elem = document.getElementById('example');

console.log(elem.classList);
```

Although using a polyfill is the right solution in this particular case (due to its close match to the native behavior and safety check that ensures it doesn't overwrite the native implementation if it is present), it is worth looking at the alternative design too. In many cases, the solution in Listing 5-42 is a more stable option as it won't ever clash with native or library code. The downside to this approach is that the calling code must be changed to reference the façade.

Listing 5-42. ClassList Façade

```
class Elements {
    static getClassList(elem: HTMLElement) {
        if ('classList' in elem) {
            return elem.classList;
        }
        return elem.className ? elem.className.split(/\s+/) : [];
    }
}

const elem = document.getElementById('example');

console.log(Elements.getClassList(elem));
```

The façade option has one major benefit in addition to being better isolated than the polyfill. The intent of this code is clear. When it comes to maintaining your code, the less cluttered and more straightforward method in the Elements class trumps the polyfill every time. Clean and maintainable code is always preferable to a clever but complex solution.

Summary

The JavaScript runtime is well known for its quirks and surprises, but on the whole the TypeScript compiler will shield you from most of the common faux pas. Using block-level variable declarations and keeping the global scope clear will help the compiler to help you, so it is worth using the structural features of TypeScript such as classes as well as either modules or namespaces, to enclose functions and variables.

Most of your code will execute on a single thread, and both callbacks and promises help to avoid blocking this thread during long-running operations. Promises are more readable than callbacks and help to keep different concerns separated. Keeping functions short not only makes your program easier to maintain, it can also make your program more responsive as each time a function is called, it is added to the back of the event queue and the runtime has an opportunity to process the oldest entry on the queue before it ages too much.

You can listen to native events and create custom events, or you can use the observer pattern to dispatch and listen to custom events in your program.

You can extend objects, including native objects, but it is often more appropriate to use mediating code to marshal the call to avoid clashing with other libraries or future extensions to native code. You can prevent extensions on your own objects by sealing, freezing, or preventing extensions.

Key Points

- Avoid the functionally scoped var keyword as TypeScript makes block-level variables available even for older versions of JavaScript.

- Callbacks can help to avoid blocking the main thread.

- Events can prevent tight coupling, whether using native events or your own publisher.

- You can extend all JavaScript objects and almost everything in JavaScript is an object.

- You can seal or freeze objects to prevent further changes.

- You can polyfill missing behavior to make new features available on old platforms.

■ ■ ■

CHAPTER 6

Running TypeScript in a Browser

All modern web browsers—on desktops, game consoles, tablets and smart phones—include JavaScript interpreters, making JavaScript the most ubiquitous programming language in history.

—David Flanagan

Although there are many different environments you might target with your TypeScript program, one of the widest categories of runtime will surely be the web browser. This chapter introduces the general design of the web browser before introducing practical examples for interacting with web pages, making asynchronous requests to the web server, storing data on the user's local machine, and accessing hardware sensors. At the end of the chapter there is information about modularizing your program and loading modules on demand.

■ **Note**   Some of the features described in this chapter are experimental and have limited browser support. To find out which browsers support any specific feature, visit the "Can I use" project by Alexis Deveria (`http://caniuse.com/`, 2014).

The Anatomy of a Web Browser

Web browsers have quickly evolved from the simple document displays of the 1990s to fully fledged application environments and 3D gaming displays today. The reliance on plugins, applets, and downloads is diminishing fast as video, audio, and gaming all join documents, images, and applications inside of the HTML document inside of a web browser.

It is worth knowing a little about web browsers if your program is going to rely on them to work, but if the details of browsers and the history of some of the important features aren't causing a general feeling of excitement or if you already know everything there is to know about browsers, feel free to skip to the next section, which is more hands-on. If you'd like to know a bit more about how web browsers work, read on.

Web browsers are typically made up of the components shown in Figure 6-1. User interface

- Browser engine
- Rendering engine
- Widget engine
- JavaScript interpreter
- Networking
- Storage

© Steve Fenton 2018
S. Fenton, *Pro TypeScript*, https://doi.org/10.1007/978-1-4842-3249-1_6

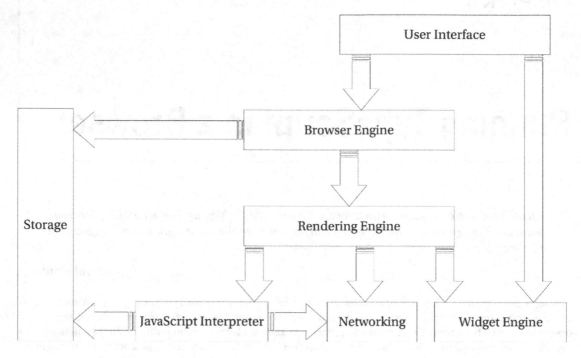

Figure 6-1. *Web browser components*

The user interface includes all the buttons and text boxes that appear on all web browser windows, for example, the address bar, back and forward buttons, and the refresh button. The browser engine and rendering engine handle the content display, which takes up the main area of the web browser's display. The widget engine supplies common user controls to the user interface and to the rendering engine, such as text inputs, drop-down lists, and buttons.

To display a web page, the browser engine relies on the rendering engine to display the HTML along with the appropriate styles defined in the cascading style sheets (CSS) or by the user if they are overriding page styles. The rendering engine relies on networking to fetch resources such as the web page, stylesheets, JavaScript files, and images. The widget engine is used whenever a user interaction component is needed, such as a text box. The JavaScript interpreter runs the downloaded JavaScript, which in turn may access storage, networking, and any other available application programming interfaces (APIs).

On the whole, the user interface, browser engine, rendering engine, and widget engine do a grand job and you don't need to know all of the minute details; the one exception to this is a process known as *reflows*, which can affect the perceived performance of your program.

Reflows and Frames Per Second

Each time the layout of the web page is changed by JavaScript or CSS, the layout is flagged as being invalid, but isn't immediately updated. The reflow, which recalculates the size and position of all elements in the document, would typically occur just before drawing the page. Additional reflows can be triggered if the JavaScript code requests the size or position of an element when the layout has the invalid flag. This additional reflow is needed to ensure the information supplied for the size or position is up to date.

Listing 6-1 shows a function that has a typical reflow problem, invalidating the layout on two occasions and causing two reflows. Each time a value is set on the document that can affect the layout, the layout is flagged as being invalid. Each time a value is retrieved from the document when the layout is invalid, the reflow is triggered. Although the example in the listing results in two reflows, if the mistake is repeated, it can result in many more. Reflows slow down your program and the page, which needs to wait for its turn to re-render.

Listing 6-1. Triggering multiple reflows

```
const image = document.getElementById('mainImage');
const container = document.getElementById('content');

function updateSizes() {
    // Flags the layout as invalid
    image.style.width = '50%';

    // Causes a reflow to get the value
    const imageHeight = image.offsetHeight;

    // Flags the layout as invalid
    container.classList.add('highlight');

    // Causes a reflow to get the value
    const containerHeight = container.offsetHeight;

    return {
        'imageHeight': imageHeight,
        'containerHeight': containerHeight
    };
}

const result = updateSizes();
```

Multiple reflows can be avoided by performing the layout-invalidating operations before attempting to retrieve any values from the document, as shown in Listing 6-2. By grouping the operations that invalidate the layout at the start of the function and before any operations that require a reflow, we reduce the total number of reflows required during the function.

Listing 6-2. Triggering a single reflow

```
const image = document.getElementById('mainImage');
const container = document.getElementById('content');

function updateSizes() {
    // Operations that invalidate the layout
    image.style.width = '50%';
    container.classList.add('highlight');

    // Operations that require a reflow
    const imageHeight = image.offsetHeight;
    const containerHeight = container.offsetHeight;
```

```
    return {
        'imageHeight': imageHeight,
        'containerHeight': containerHeight
    };
}

const result = updateSizes();
```

A basic test of these two examples can be obtained by looping each one to run every 200ms. Although there is hardly any difference between them, the first version with multiple reflows reduces the refresh rate to 53 frames-per-second, and the second maintains 57 frames-per-second (a static web page renders at 59 frames-per-second on the computer I used to test this code).

The only situation that forces you to use multiple reflows is one in which you need to obtain a measurement after making a change: for example, finding the width of an element after you have changed its contents and then using the width to reposition the element, which cannot be done without a reflow. You can still carefully plan your operations to reduce the overall number of reflows to the minimum number possible.

When measuring your browser-based program, the frames-per-second measurement is a good indicator of the perceived responsiveness of your web application. This measure is available in your browser tools.

The Interesting Components

The JavaScript interpreter along with the network and storage APIs are the most interesting components of a web browser when it comes to TypeScript. Each is described in more detail in the following sections.

The JavaScript Interpreter

The JavaScript interpreter, or JavaScript engine as it is also known, has a lot of work to do. Not only does it parse and execute the JavaScript program; it must manage objects and memory, work the event loop, and handle interactions with APIs such as storage, network, and sensors.

One of the things that make JavaScript programming in the browser so interesting (and at times frustrating) is that you will encounter many different JavaScript interpreters. In some rare cases, you may even encounter no interpreter and your program won't run. Having to support many interpreters can increase the amount of testing you need to perform as you will need to check that your program works in each web browser. However, there are upsides to the plethora of interpreters. One of the upsides is that browser vendors all want to be able to claim that their particular implementation of a JavaScript engine is the fastest; and as a result interpreters have become many times faster as they each fight for the top spot.

The main things to watch for when relying on these different interpreters to run your program are the following:

- They may only support an older version of the ECMAScript standard.

- They can implement additional features that are not part of the ECMAScript specification.

- They all run different code at different speeds especially on different operating systems.

- At some point in time you will encounter an end user who has JavaScript switched off entirely.

■ **Note** ECMAScript 5 is supported in the current version of all major browsers. ECMAScript 6 (or ECMAScript 2015) is supported by all front runners, but you lose Internet Explorer and many fringe browsers. ECMAScript 2016 has full support in Firefox only at the time of writing, with Chrome, Opera, and Edge all satisfying 75–95% of the standard. Very little support is available for the next set of candidate recommendations. Remember: TypeScript's down-level compilation will let you use many new features with compilation targeting ECMAScript 5 or 6.

A Brief History of Networking

The evolution of networking in the web browser can be tracked through several stages. The earliest mechanism for updating a part of the web page, without replacing the entire document, was to use a frameset. Framesets were a proposal for the HTML 3.0 specification. Websites would typically have a three-part frameset with individual frames for the header, navigation, and content. When a link was selected in the navigation frame, the content frame would be replaced with a new web page without reloading the header or the navigation. Framesets had the dual purpose of allowing parts of the display to update independently and also allowed reusable widgets such as headers and navigation to be included without server-side processing.

A major problem with framesets was that the web address for the page was not updated as the user navigated because the user was still viewing the frameset, no matter which pages were being displayed in the frames within the frameset. When users bookmarked a page, or shared a link to a page, it would not lead them back to the display they navigated to, but instead simply displayed the landing page for the website. Additionally, framesets caused various problems for screen readers and text browsers.

The replacement for framesets was inline frames (the iframe element). Inline frames were placed inside the body of another document and could be updated independently. It was still possible to use iframes in ways that caused similar problems to framesets, but they did offer a very useful new feature to emerge.

In the days before networking in JavaScript, enterprising and creative programmers would use iframes to give the appearance of live updates. For example, a hidden iframe pointing to a server-generated web page would be refreshed using a timer every 10 seconds. Once the page had loaded, JavaScript would be used to grab new data from the iframe and update parts of the visible page based on the hidden page in the iframe. The architecture of this mechanism is shown in Figure 6-2.

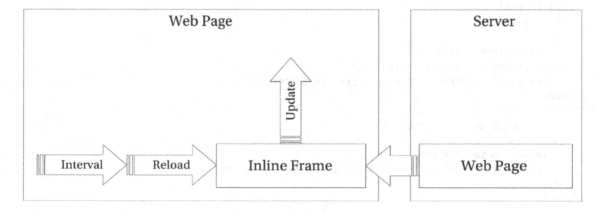

Figure 6-2. Updating a web page by refreshing a second page in an iframe

It was this creative use of inline frames to transfer data from the server to a web page that inspired the invention of XMLHTTP communication (Internet Explorer 5) and later the standardized XmlHttpRequest. These asynchronous requests were revolutionary because of the part they played in enabling web-based applications. There are various complications with using asynchronous requests, which are detailed later in this chapter, but their importance cannot be overstated.

The latest networking technology to hit the web browser is web sockets, which provides a persistent full-duplex communication between the browser and the server. This allows simultaneous communication in both directions. Web sockets are also discussed in more detail later in this chapter.

Storing Data on the Client

For a long time, the only storage available to a JavaScript program was a few miserly kilobytes in a cookie that could disappear without warning at any time. Many browsers offer a setting that clears all cookies each time the browser is closed. At best, cookies could be used to store a token to keep a user logged in for a time, and this was really its only major usefulness to a web application.

In modern browsers, there are several options for storage on the user's machine from simple key/value local storage to NoSQL indexed databases. Even the initial limit of a few megabytes can be increased with the user's permission. Concrete examples of storage options are explained later in this chapter.

The ability to store a reasonable amount of data on the user's machine allows caching of data locally. This can speed up your program and reduce the number of round trips to the server. It also allows your web application to run offline and synchronize with the server the next time a connection is available.

The Document Object Model

The Document Object Model, or DOM, is a web browser interface for interacting with HTML and XML documents. The interface allows you to find elements, obtain and update information about their contents, and attributes and listen to user events. If you are interacting with a web page from your program, you are using the DOM.

All the examples in this section use the HTML document in Listing 6-3.

Listing 6-3. HTML document for DOM examples

```html
<!DOCTYPE html>
<html lang="en">
<head>
    <meta charset="utf-8" />
    <title>Running in a Browser</title>
    <link rel="stylesheet" href="app.css" type="text/css" />
</head>
<body>
    <h1>Running in a Browser</h1>

    <div id="content"></div>
    <script data-main="app" src="/Scripts/require.js"></script>
</body>
</html>
```

The document is an HTML5 web page with a level-one heading and a division with an id of "content." The aim of the following examples is to obtain a reference to this element, make changes to it, and listen to events generated within it.

Finding Elements

One of the most common interactions with the DOM is finding an element within the document. There are several ways to get an element as shown in Listing 6-4. Using document.getElementById has long been the standard method of obtaining an element on the web page and in TypeScript this returns an object of the HTMLElement type. Although this is a common way to find elements, it specifically only obtains elements based on their id attribute.

The traditional alternative to document.getElementById has been document.getElementsByTagName. Whereas obtaining elements based on the id is too specific; finding them by tag name is typically too general. For this reason, the document.querySelector and document.querySelectorAll methods were introduced in the Selectors API specification, allowing CSS query selectors to be used to find elements. When there are multiple possible matches, document.querySelector returns the first matching element, whereas document.querySelectorAll returns all matching elements.

Listing 6-4. Finding DOM elements

```
// HTMLElement
const a = document.getElementById('content');

// Element
const b = document.querySelector('#content');

// HTMLDivElement (due to type assertion)
const c = <HTMLDivElement>document.querySelector('#content');
```

When you obtain elements using getElementById, it will return the general HTMLElement type. Using querySelector will get you the even more general Element type. The TypeScript compiler is not able to determine the exact kind of element that is returned. If you want to use members from a specific type of element, you can use a type assertion to tell the compiler which element type to expect. This doesn't guarantee that the type will be correct at runtime; it just gives you the right autocompletion information and type checking.

Type assertions are not required when you use document.getElementsByTagName because TypeScript uses specialized overload signatures to return the correct type based on the tag name you supply. This is shown in Listing 6-5, where the NodeList is returned with elements of the HTMLDivElement type automatically.

Listing 6-5. Getting elements by HTML tag

```
// NodeListOf<HTMLDivElement>
const elements = document.getElementsByTagName('div');

// HTMLDivElement
const a = elements[0];
```

The final type you will come across is the NodeListOf<Element> returned from the document. querySelectorAll method, as shown in Listing 6-6. Despite this, you can still use a type assertion to work with the specialized HTML element of your choice.

Listing 6-6. Getting elements using CSS selectors

```
// NodeListOf<Element>
var elements = document.querySelectorAll('#content');

// Element
var a = elements[0];

// HTMLDivElement
var b = <HTMLDivElement>elements[0];
```

■ **Note** You may have noticed that the various methods of finding elements in the DOM all return different types of objects and different collections. This is not an idiosyncrasy of TypeScript, but represents the underlying DOM specifications. In many cases, you will have more knowledge of the element than the compiler and a type assertion can be used to make the type more specific.

If you want to avoid the liberal sprinkling of type assertions, you can wrap your calls with generic functions to marshal your calls to the DOM API. Listing 6-7 shows wrapper functions that allow you to supply type hints in the form of generic type arguments.

Listing 6-7. Generic Wrapper Functions

```
function QueryOf<T extends Element>(query: string) {
    return <T>document.querySelector(query);
}

const elem = QueryOf<HTMLDivElement>('div#content');

function QueryAllOf<T extends Element>(query: string) {
    return <NodeListOf<T>>document.querySelectorAll(query);
}

const elems = QueryAllOf<HTMLDivElement>('div');
```

When using these wrapper functions, you will receive return values of the expected type. You could extend these functions to include element validation to ensure the elements found are of the expected type.

Changing Elements

Once you have located an element, or elements, that you want to change, there are several options available to you to update the contents of each element.

Listing 6-8 shows a simple replacement of the entire contents of the element by supplying a new string of HTML. The existing contents of the element will be discarded in favor of the string you supply. There are downsides to this approach; not only does this involve hard-coding HTML strings in your program, but also there can be security risks if you use this method to insert user-generated or third-party content. On the positive side, this is the simplest way to completely replace the entire contents of an element.

Listing 6-8. Updating the element's HTML

```
const element = <HTMLDivElement> document.querySelector('#content');

element.innerHTML = '<span>Hello World</span>';
```

In many cases, rather than replacing the entire contents of an element, you will want to add to the element without losing the existing contents. Listing 6-9 shows multiple additions to the content division, which results in all the new elements being appended. The listing also shows the use of the document. createElement method to generate elements, rather than using strings.

Listing 6-9. Using appendChild

```
const element = <HTMLDivElement>document.querySelector('#content');

// Create and add the first element
const newElement1 = document.createElement('div');
newElement1.textContent = 'Hello World';

element.appendChild(newElement1);

// Create and add the second element
const newElement2 = document.createElement('div');
newElement2.textContent = 'Greetings Earth';

element.appendChild(newElement2);
```

When you use element.appendChild, the newest element appears last. To add the newest element to the top of the element, you can use the element.insertBefore method as shown in Listing 6-10. The first argument passed to insertBefore is the new element, and the second argument is the element used to position the new element. In the example the current first child element is used to ensure the new element appears first, but you can use the same method to place a new element anywhere in the DOM.

Listing 6-10. Using insertBefore

```
const element = <HTMLDivElement>document.querySelector('#content');

const newElement2 = document.createElement('div');
newElement2.textContent = 'Greetings Earth';

element.insertBefore(newElement2, element.firstChild);
```

If you plan to create a nested set of elements to add to the page, it is more efficient to construct the whole hierarchy before adding it to the DOM. This will ensure you only invalidate the layout once, which in turn means the page is redrawn fewer times to reflect your changes.

Events

There are many different ways of attaching event listeners, with some browsers lagging behind the standards-compliant method of adding listeners. The addEventListener method is the standards-compliant way to add an event listener for a DOM event, although some older browsers still rely on the attachEvent method (which also requires that the event name is prefixed with 'on').

To solve the problems of cross-browser compatibility, Remy Sharp created an addEvent method that not only eases the browser differences, but also allows collections of elements to be passed as an argument, not just single elements. Listing 6-11 is an adapted version of Remy's original script with the addition of type information for the method.

Listing 6-11. Cross-Browser enhanced events

```
export const addEvent: (elem: Window | Document | Element | NodeListOf<Element>,
    eventName: string, callback: Function) => void = (function () {
    if (document.addEventListener) {
        // Handles modern browsers
        return function (elem, eventName, callback) {
            if (elem && elem.addEventListener) {
                // Handles a single element
                elem.addEventListener(eventName, callback, false);
            } else if (elem && elem.length) {
                // Handles a collection of elements (recursively)
                for (let i = 0; i < elem.length; i++) {
                    addEvent(elem[i], eventName, callback);
                }
            }
        };
    } else {
        // Handles some old browsers
        return function (elem, eventName, callback) {
            if (elem && elem.attachEvent) {
                // Handles a single element
                elem.attachEvent('on' + eventName, function () {
                    return callback.call(elem, window.event);
                });
            } else if (elem && elem.length) {
                // Handles a collection of elements (recursively)
                for (let i = 0; i < elem.length; i++) {
                    addEvent(elem[i], eventName, callback);
                }
            }
        };
    }
})();
```

The two major branches of the addEvent method handle the browser differences, with a check inside each branch that handles either a single element of a collection of elements. When all browsers support the addEventListener method, the second half of the method will become redundant.

This addEvent method will be used wherever events are needed in this chapter.

Frameworks and Libraries

There are many frameworks and libraries that can help with all these DOM interactions. A select few are described below, although there are many more to choose from. The incredible selection of libraries is summed up neatly by Martin Beeby.

If you pick a noun and add .js or .io, you'll probably get a library.

—Martin Beeby

Despite a sometimes-overwhelming range of libraries, the high-quality ones tend to float to the top, thanks to a discerning and vocal community. Most of the available libraries can be added to your program using your preferred package manager, such as NPM; or you can just download the scripts and add them manually. For a third-party library that is written in plain JavaScript, you can usually find a matching type definition too, thanks to the Definitely Typed project.

http://definitelytyped.org/

If you are using Visual Studio, Package Installer by Mads Kristensen is an extension that will speed up your package management. Figure 6-3 shows the "Quick Install Package" dialog for RequireJS, and Figure 6-4 shows how to obtain the type definition using the @types scope on NPM.

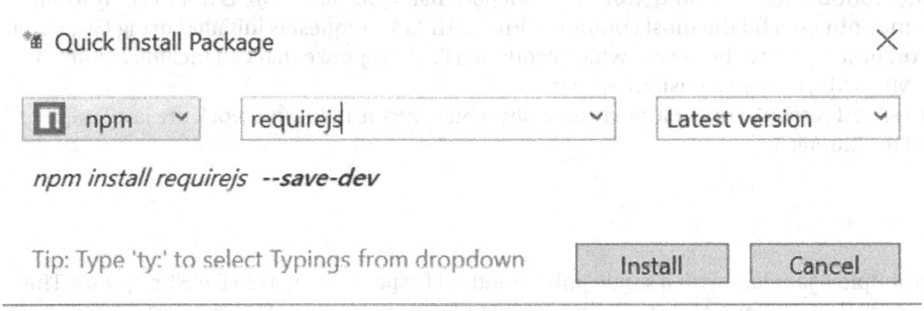

Figure 6-3. Installing libraries in Visual Studio with the Package Manager Extension

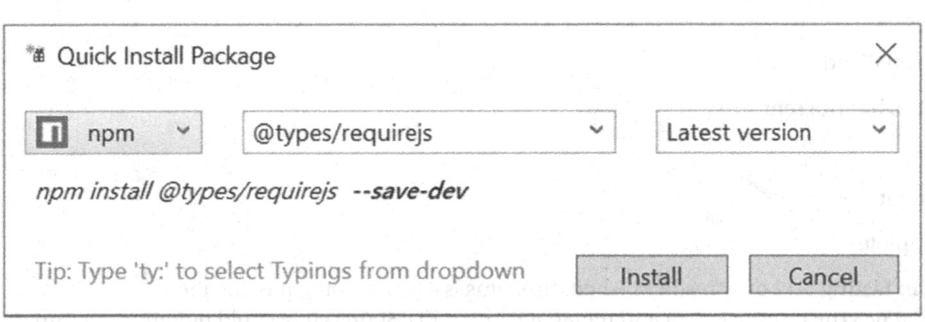

Figure 6-4. Installing type definitions in Visual Studio with the Package Manager Extension

Installing packages and type definitions will result in your package.json file being automatically updated with the dependencies. You can also directly edit the package.json file with additional package names in either the dependencies or development dependencies sections.

If you are not using Visual Studio, you can also install packages on the command line using the command `npm install [library-name] --save`, for dependencies or `npm install [library-name] --save-dev`, for development-only dependencies. Development dependencies are for packages that will not be required by downstream consumers of your code.

Using NPM to obtain both JavaScript libraries and their type definitions is the recommended setup for all TypeScript projects, and it integrates well with Visual Studio as well as other popular editors.

The ability to find and change elements on a web page becomes more powerful when you combine this feature with real-time data from your server. The next section covers making background requests to a web server to save and retrieve information without reloading the entire web page.

Network

Since its invention toward the end of the 1990s, AJAX has dominated the networking requirements for JavaScript in the web browser. Despite its dominance, there have been some newer entrants into the networking space that are useful for browser-based applications. This section introduces the three major techniques for communicating from the browser, allowing you to pick and choose the methods that best serve your program.

AJAX

AJAX stands for asynchronous JavaScript and XML. This is a poor name because XML is not the only format used for data, and it may not even be the most common format. An AJAX request is initiated using JavaScript in the browser. The request is sent to the server, which sends an HTTP response that can include a body in plain text, JSON, HTML, XML, or even a custom format.

The HTTP request and response occur asynchronously, which means it doesn't block the JavaScript event loop described in Chapter 5.

HTTP Get

Listing 6-12 shows a simple `Ajax` class with a single public method for performing HTTP GET requests. The method creates a new `XMLHttpRequest` object, which is the standard way to make AJAX requests. A callback is then attached to the `onreadystatechange` event on the request. This is called for each of the states that a request transitions to, but normally you will be primarily interested in the *completed* state. The potential states are

- 0—Uninitialized

- 1—Set up, but not sent

- 2—Sent

- 3—In flight

- 4—Complete

The `Ajax` class in Listing 6-12 only resolves when the status is 4 (Complete), passing the XMLHttpRequest that has the response data and metadata. The HTTP status code could potentially be any of the codes described in the HTTP specification maintained by the W3C (1999).

The open method accepts the HTTP verb for the request and the URL. The third parameter sets whether the request is asynchronous. Finally, with the state change listener attached and with the request set up with an HTTP verb and URL, the send method can be used to begin the request.

Listing 6-12. HTTP Get method

```
export class Ajax {
    private readonly READY_STATUS_CODE = 4;

    private isCompleted(request: XMLHttpRequest) {
        return request.readyState === this.READY_STATUS_CODE;
    }
    httpGet(url: string) {
        return new Promise<XMLHttpRequest>((resolve, reject) => {
            // Create a request
            const request = new XMLHttpRequest();

            // Attach an event listener
            request.onreadystatechange = () => {
                if (this.isCompleted(request)) {
                    resolve(request);
                }
            };

            // Specify the HTTP verb and URL
            request.open('GET', url, true);

            // Send the request
            request.send();
        });
    }
}
```

■ **Note**   You should always make your AJAX requests asynchronous and use a callback to execute dependent code. Although making a request synchronous appears convenient, you will tie up the event loop for a long period of time and your application will appear unresponsive. The Ajax class in these examples wraps the native XMLHttpRequest in a promise-like interface. The Fetch API introduces a promise-based API for asynchronous HTTP requests, as described in Chapter 5.

HTTP Post

The example code in Listing 6-13 is an httpPost method that can be added to the Ajax class from Listing 6-12. As well as changing the HTTP verb to 'POST', the content type request header is added and the data are sent in the request body. The data in this example must formatted as key/value pairs, for example, 'type=5&size=4'. To send a JSON string containing the data, you would have to set the content type to 'application/json'.

Listing 6-13. HTTP Post method

```
httpPost(url: string, data: string) {
    return new Promise<XMLHttpRequest>((resolve, reject) => {
        const request = new XMLHttpRequest();
```

```
        request.onreadystatechange = () => {
            if (this.isCompleted(request)) {
                resolve(request);
            }
        };

        request.open('POST', url, true);
        request.setRequestHeader('Content-type', 'application/x-www-form-urlencoded');
        request.send(data);
    });
}
```

You can send different data formats by specifying the appropriate Content-type, for example, application/json or application/xml, and by passing the data in the appropriate serialized format. You are only limited by what your server-side program accepts.

You can call the Ajax class whenever you need to make an HTTP request, and an example call is shown in Listing 6-14. You could also extend the Ajax class to handle other HTTP requests, such as PUT and DELETE.

Listing 6-14. Using the Ajax class

```
import { Ajax } from './Listing-6-013';

var ajax = new Ajax();

// Making a GET request
ajax.httpGet('data.html')
    .then((request) => {
        document.getElementById('content').innerHTML = request.responseText;
    });
```

If you attempt to make an AJAX request to a different domain, you will find that the request is blocked by a cross-origin security feature in modern browsers. You will encounter this even across subdomains on the same website, or between HTTP and HTTPS pages. In cases where you want to enable cross-origin request sharing (CORS), and if the server supports it, you can add an additional header to your AJAX request, as shown in Listing 6-15. This header causes a preflight OPTIONS request to be sent to ask if the server will accept the actual request, which follows if the server confirms that it will accept the cross-origin communication.

Listing 6-15. Allowing CORS, client side

```
const request = new XMLHttpRequest();
request.setRequestHeader('X-Requested-With', 'XMLHttpRequest');
// ...
```

Although server configuration is beyond the scope of this chapter, for a server to support CORS, it must accept and respond to the preflight OPTIONS request that is issued before the actual cross-origin request with an Access-Control-Allow-Origin response header. This header indicates the domains that the server is willing to communicate with. This acts as a handshake between the client and server to verify that the cross-domain communication can proceed.

WebSockets

One of the most common uses of AJAX has been to poll a server to check for updates. One particular implementation of this is long polling; the AJAX request is made, but the server delays responding to the request until it has an update to send. Long-polling implementations must deal with timeout issues and concurrent request limits. Long polling can also cause problems on some servers where the number of clients waiting for a response can tie up a large number of request threads.

The WebSocket specification solves this problem by establishing a persistent two-way communication channel between the server and client that can be used to send messages in either direction. This means you can send messages at any time without having to reestablish a connection and you can receive messages in the same way. Listing 6-16 is a simple example of establishing communication with a server using the ws:// protocol, listening for messages, and sending a message to the server.

Listing 6-16. Establishing a WebSocket connection

```typescript
const webSocket = new WebSocket('ws://localhost:8080/WS');

webSocket.onmessage = (message: MessageEvent) => {
    // Log message from server
    console.log(message.data);
}

webSocket.send('Message To Server');
```

When you are finished with a WebSocket connection, you can end the communication by calling webSocket.close(). If you want to learn more about web sockets, you can read *The Definitive Guide to HTML5 WebSockets* by Wang, Salim, and Moskovits (Apress, 2013).

Real-Time Communications

The next evolution in network communications is real-time peer-to-peer audio and video streaming. The WebRTC specification being drafted by the W3C (2013) allows streaming between browsers without the need for browser plugins or additional installed software. Although the specification currently has limited support, the potential for the technology is incredible. Video and audio calls would be possible between browsers without the need for a communication provider in the middle.

WebRTC is supported in several browsers in an experimental state, with most browsers offering the feature using a prefixed version that is subject to change. To use WebRTC in TypeScript you will need to extend the library definitions to include these transitional browser implementations.

A full implementation of WebRTC is outside of the scope of this book, but Listing 6-17 shows how to capture a media stream with video and audio, playing the stream back into a video element on the HTML page.

Listing 6-17. Display a video stream

```typescript
const constraints = {
    audio: true,
    video: {
        width: 1280,
        height: 720
    }
};
```

```
const videoElement = document.createElement('video');
videoElement.setAttribute('width', Math.floor(constraints.video.width / 2).toString());
videoElement.setAttribute('height', Math.floor(constraints.video.height / 2).toString());
document.body.appendChild(videoElement);

navigator.mediaDevices.getUserMedia(constraints)
    .then(function (mediaStream) {
        const video = document.querySelector('video');
        video.srcObject = mediaStream;
        video.onloadedmetadata = function (e) {
            video.play();
        };
    })
    .catch(function (error) {
        console.log(error.name, error.message);
    });
```

The getUserMedia method accepts constraints, which allow you to specify the features of the stream you would like to capture. The result of this script is usually the pleased face of a programmer being shown back to them on the web page.

Obtaining video and audio is the first step toward establishing a peer-to-peer stream, and if you are interested in this technology there are entire books dedicated to this fascinating subject. Despite being a part of the WebRTC specification, the getUserMedia API has other potential uses outside of peer-to-peer communication. You may want to grab an image from the video stream to use in your program, or even use the stream in a more traditional manner to send to a server.

Networking provides the tools you need to communicate from the local browser to a server or remote peer. The next section covers storing data locally, which can allow your program to continue to work even when the network is unavailable.

Storage

Storage on the user's machine has come a long way since cookies, with their size limitations and terrible API. Depending on what you need, there are several available storage options with different life spans, soft limits, and APIs that you can use to keep hold of data locally.

Both session storage and local storage have an identical API, but they offer different life spans. However, IndexedDB offers a more advanced data storage mechanism. All three of these storage APIs are described in the following.

Session Storage

Session storage is attached to a page session. A page session starts when a page is opened and continues even if the page is reloaded or restored within a browser tab. Opening the same page in a separate tab or browser window results in a new page session.

Listing 6-18 shows how simple the session storage API is, allowing a simple key/value pair to be stored with the setItem method. Both the key and the value must be strings, so objects would need to be serialized to a string to be stored.

Listing 6-18. Session storage

```
const storageKey = 'Example';

// null the first time, 'Stored value' each subsequent time
console.log(sessionStorage.getItem(storageKey));

sessionStorage.setItem(storageKey, 'Stored value');
```

To demonstrate the life span of this storage mechanism, the getItem method is called before the item is set; when the page first loads, the null value is logged, but on subsequent refreshes the stored value is logged. If you open the page in a new tab, once again the null value will be logged. If you view the page, visit an entirely separate page in the same tab, then load the original page once again, you'll see that the value has been retained. The session remains as long as the tab is open, even if other pages are loaded in the tab — the browser may even support the resumption of the session after a restart.

Listing 6-19. Removing and clearing session storage

```
// Remove an item using a key
sessionStorage.removeItem(storageKey);

// Clear all items
sessionStorage.clear();
```

Listing 6-19 shows the methods for removing an item based on its key and for clearing all items from the session storage for the page. These methods follow the same scope and life cycle as the other session storage methods described earlier.

Local Storage

The local storage API is identical to the session storage API, but the storage persists until it is deleted by the user or cleared for privacy reasons. Local storage can also be accessed from multiple pages on the same domain as well as in multiple browsers and tabs.

Because local storage items are shared across pages, tabs, and browsers it can be used to store a cache of data to reduce network traffic. It also can be used to store user-entered data while there is no connection or to store data that never needs to be transmitted, such as a temporary application state.

Listing 6-20 contains a script that stores a value including the current date and time in local storage. An event listener is attached to the storage event, which should fire whenever a change is made in another tab or window.

Listing 6-20. Local storage and events

```
import { addEvent } from './Listing-6-011';

const storageKey = 'Example';

localStorage.setItem(storageKey, 'Stored value ' + Date.now());

addEvent(window, 'storage', (event: StorageEvent) => {
    console.log(`${event.key} "${event.oldValue}" changed to "${event.newValue}"`);
});
```

If you run this script in multiple browser tabs, each tab will log the change in local storage except for the tab that initiated the change. This allows you to keep all tabs updated with changes in data made in any other tab.

Storage Restrictions

For both session storage and local storage, browsers are likely to follow a series of restrictions and configurations described in the Web Storage specification, once again maintained by the W3C (2014).

Browsers are likely to limit the amount of storage available to a page initially to prevent malicious attempts to exhaust the user's disk space. The limit applies across subdomains and, when reached, will cause a prompt to be shown to the user asking for permission to increase the allocated storage space. The recommended limit for storage is five megabytes before the user is prompted for permission.

To protect user privacy, browsers are likely to prevent third-party access to storage. This means that you will only be able to access storage on the same domain as it was stored. Browsers can clear out storage based on user preferences (e.g., every time the browser is closed or when it reaches a certain age) and there will also be options available to the user to view and clear storage as well as white list or blacklist sites. It may even be possible for blacklisted sites to be shared across a community, allowing automatic blocking of storage for a domain based on a number of users blacklisting it.

For security reasons, you should consider whether it is appropriate for a particular piece of information to be stored, and you should avoid using storage when working on a shared domain as storage would be available to other pages on the shared domain. You cannot restrict access to storage by path. For example, the same storage could be accessed by both of the following paths:

- `www.shared.com/your-site/`

- `www.shared.com/third-party-site/`

IndexedDB

Although session storage and local storage are simple and convenient ways to store small amounts of data in a key/value store, IndexedDB allows much larger volumes of data to be stored in a structured way that allows fast searches using indexes.

IndexedDB is designed to work asynchronously, which means you supply a callback to each method on the API that executes when the operation has completed. A synchronous version of IndexedDB has a specification, but currently no browsers implement this style of the API. It is generally preferable to use asynchronous APIs to avoid blocking the event loop from running on the main thread, so learning to use the asynchronous version of IndexedDB is worth the additional effort.

The IndexedDB API is demonstrated using the `Product` class shown in Listing 6-21. The `Product` class has two public properties for `productId` and `name`. The `productId` will be used as the key for items stored in the database.

Listing 6-21. Product.ts

```
export class Product {
    constructor(public productId: number, public name: string) {

    }
}
```

Listing 6-22 shows an empty `ProductDatabase` class. This will be expanded to perform database operations such as storing, retrieving, and deleting products. This class will also reduce the dependency on the IndexedDB API in the program code.

Listing 6-22. Empty ProductDatabase.ts

```
import { Product } from './Listing-6-021';

export class ProductDatabase {
    constructor(private name: string, private version: number) {
    }
}
```

The `ProductDatabase` constructor takes the database name and the version number. The version number is used to detect if the database stored locally needs to be upgraded to a new version. Each time you change the schema, you should increment the version number. The version number must be an integer, even though there is no native integer type in JavaScript or TypeScript.

Upgrade Required

A database upgrade is determined by comparing the local version number with the version number in your program. If the program version number is larger than the local version number, an onupgradeneeded event is triggered. The event is also fired if there is no local database. You can specify a method to be executed in the event of an upgrade that handles the schema changes and adds any required data.

Listing 6-23 contains an updated constructor for the `ProductDatabase` class that issues a request to open the database and adds a listener to the onupgradeneeded event. If an upgrade is needed, the update method is called.

Listing 6-23. ProductDatabase supporting upgrades

```
import { Product } from './Listing-6-021';

export class ProductDatabase {

    constructor(private name: string, private version: number) {
        const openDatabaseRequest = indexedDB.open(this.name, this.version);
        openDatabaseRequest.onupgradeneeded = this.upgrade;
    }

    upgrade(event: any) {
        const db = event.target.result;

        // The keyPath specifies the property that contains the id
        const objectStore = db.createObjectStore("products", { keyPath: 'productId' });

        objectStore.createIndex('name', 'name', { unique: false });

        objectStore.transaction.oncomplete = () => {
            // Example static data
            const products = [
                new Product(1, 'My first product'),
                new Product(2, 'My second product'),
                new Product(3, 'My third product')
            ];
```

```
        // Add records
        const productStore = db.transaction('products', 'readwrite').
        objectStore('products');
        for (let product of products) {
            productStore.add(product);
        }
      }
    }
  }
}
```

The update method in this example uses createObjectStore to create a products table. The options argument specifies a keyPath, which tells the database that the objects stored will have a productId property that should be used as the unique key. You can opt to have a key automatically created for you by passing the autoIncrement option with a value of true instead of passing the keyPath property.

The createIndex method adds an index to the name property to make searches by name faster. It is possible to make an index unique, although in the example duplicates have been allowed by setting unique to false. Attempting to create a unique index will fail if the database already contains duplicates.

Finally, a transaction is created on the products object store and used to add products to the database. This step is useful if you need to seed the database with static data.

Listing 6-24. Instantiating a ProductDatabase

```
import { ProductDatabase } from './Listing-6-023';

const versionNumber = 1;

const db = new ProductDatabase('ExampleDatabase', versionNumber);
```

Listing 6-24 shows the code that instantiates an instance of the ProductDatabase class. Although the constructor assigns the event handler for the onupgradeneeded event, the constructor will complete before the event fires.

Querying the Database

Because IndexedDB is designed to work asynchronously, some operations seem to require more effort than you might expect. Despite this, it is worth taking advantage of asynchrony — even if the synchronous versions of these operations eventually get implemented by a browser. If the callback chains offend you, you can use a library such as Dexie, or ZangoDB to wrap IndexedDB in a promise-based interface, which is much cleaner. You can read about the benefits of a promise-based interface in Chapter 5. The full callback chain version is demonstrated in this chapter as this is the native browser API.

Listing 6-25 shows a getProduct method for the ProductDatabase class, which handles the database opening request, transactions, and queries. This allows calling code to simply pass the productId and a callback to process the result.

Listing 6-25. getProduct method

```
getProduct(productId: number, callback: (result: Product) => void) {
    // Open the database
    const openDatabaseRequest = indexedDB.open(this.name, this.version);

    openDatabaseRequest.onsuccess = () => {
```

```
        // The database is open
        const db = openDatabaseRequest.result;

        // Start a transaction on the products store
        const productStore = db.transaction(['products']).objectStore('products');

        // Request the query
        const query = productStore.get(productId);
        query.onsuccess = () => {
            callback(query.result);
        };
    };
}
```

The getProduct method creates a request to open the database, supplies a callback to create a transaction, and runs the query when the connection has opened successfully. You can also supply a callback to be executed on error, which will be called if the database could not be opened. The query request is also supplied with a callback that is passed to the result of the query.

To use the product database, Listing 6-26 contains a simple HTML page for the user to enter a product ID and view the result obtained from the database.

Listing 6-26. HTML page

```
<!DOCTYPE html>
<html lang="en">
<head>
    <meta charset="utf-8" />
    <title>IndexedDB</title>
    <link rel="stylesheet" href="app.css" type="text/css" />
</head>
<body>
    <h1>IndexedDB</h1>
    <div>
        <label>Product Id: <input type="number" id="productId" /></label>
    </div>
    <div id="content"></div>
    <script data-main="app" src="/Scripts/require.js"></script>
</body>
</html>
```

The code to collect the data entered by the user and call the ProductDatabase class is shown in Listing 6-27. The product ID entered into the input is collected using the keyup event and is passed to the getProduct method, along with a callback that displays the result on the web page if there is a matching record.

Listing 6-27. Calling getProduct

```
import { addEvent } from './Listing-6-011';
import { Product } from './Listing-6-021';
import { ProductDatabase } from './Listing-6-025';

const db = new ProductDatabase('ExampleDatabase', 1);
```

179

```
// Wait for entry in the productId input
addEvent(document.getElementById('productId'), 'keyup', function () {
    // Get the id entered by the user, convert to number
    const productId = +this.value;

    // Search the database with the id
    db.getProduct(productId, (product) => {
        document.getElementById('content').innerHTML = product ?
            `The result for product id: ${product.productId} is: ${product.name}` :
            'No result';
    });
});
```

Running this example will confirm that despite some of the code appearing a little complex, the retrieval of records is blisteringly fast because no network round trip is required. The data is also available offline, which means your program can continue to work without a connection.

Adding a New Record

Adding a new record to the database is slightly simpler than obtaining a record with a query, as shown in the previous section, because adding a record requires one less callback. The general pattern is the same, as shown in Listing 6-28, requesting a connection and starting a transaction inside the success callback.

The product is then stored using the add method, which takes in the product object and automatically finds the productId property to use as the unique key as per the database configuration in Listing 6-23.

Listing 6-28. addProduct method

```
addProduct(product: Product) {
    // Open the database
    const openDatabaseRequest = indexedDB.open(this.name, this.version);

    openDatabaseRequest.onsuccess = () => {
        // The database is open
        const db = openDatabaseRequest.result;

        // Start a transaction on the products store
        const productStore = db.transaction('products', 'readwrite').
objectStore('products');

        // Add the product
        productStore.add(product);
    };
}
```

The code to call the addProduct method is shown in Listing 6-29. Because the ProductDatabase class has handled the connection request, all the calling code needs to do is supply the new product that is to be stored.

Listing 6-29. Calling addProduct

```
import { Product } from './Listing-6-021';
import { ProductDatabase } from './Listing-6-028';

const db = new ProductDatabase('ExampleDatabase', 1);

const newProduct = new Product(4, 'Newly added product');

db.addProduct(newProduct);
```

Because the database is available offline, it is possible to store records without a network connection and then later synchronize them to the server when a connection is available. You could use a holding table for the records to synchronize, or flag records to show whether they are synchronized.

Deleting a Record

The method for deleting a record from the database is shown in Listing 6-30. The unique key is used to identify the record to be removed. Once again there is the need to open the database and open a transaction on the product store.

Listing 6-30. deleteProduct method

```
deleteProduct(productId: number) {
    // Open the database
    const openDatabaseRequest = indexedDB.open(this.name, this.version);

    openDatabaseRequest.onsuccess = (event: any) => {
        // The database is open
        const db = openDatabaseRequest.result;

        // Start a transaction on the products store
        const productStore = db.transaction('products', 'readwrite').
objectStore('products');

        // Add the product
        const deleteRequest = productStore.delete(productId);
    };
}
```

The calling code to delete a product is shown in Listing 6-31, which is as simple as calling deleteProduct with the unique key for the product.

Listing 6-31. Calling deleteProduct

```
import { Product } from './Listing-6-021';
import { ProductDatabase } from './Listing-6-030';

const db = new ProductDatabase('ExampleDatabase', 1);

db.deleteProduct(4);
```

IDBRequest Interface

The IDBRequest is prevalent in the IndexedDB model. Any request you create against the database supports this interface whether it is indexedDB.open, objectStore.get, objectStore.add, or objectStore.delete.

The beauty of this convention is that you can add a listener to any of these operations to handle both success and error events. Within the event handler you can access the original request object, which contains the following information:

- result—the result of the request, if available.

- error—the error message, if available.

- source—the index or object store, if applicable to the request.

- transaction—the transaction for the request, if the request is within a transaction; you can undo the changes in the transaction by calling transaction.abort().

- readyState—either pending or done.

In all of these examples, event handlers could have been supplied as shown in Listing 6-32. If you are writing a robust program that uses IndexedDB you should use these events to ensure that database operations are successful and to detect any errors.

Listing 6-32. IDBRequest convention

```
deleteProduct(productId: number) {
    // Open the database
    const openDatabaseRequest = indexedDB.open(this.name, this.version);

    openDatabaseRequest.onsuccess = (event: any) => {
        // The database is open
        const db = openDatabaseRequest.result;

        // Start a transaction on the products store
        const productStore = db.transaction('products', 'readwrite').
objectStore('products');

        // Add the product
        const deleteRequest = productStore.delete(productId);

        deleteRequest.onsuccess = () => {
            console.log('Deleted OK');
        }

        deleteRequest.onerror = () => {
            console.log('Failed to delete: ' + deleteRequest.error.name);
        }
    };
}
```

The examples in this section have all used the TypeScript arrow function syntax. This is not to preserve the meaning of the this keyword, but to reduce the noise of the many nested function declarations that would otherwise be present in the code.

Storage Roundup

This section introduced several options for storage within the browser. Although this has involved a great many examples, it really only described the most common aspects of the storage mechanisms that you may use.

Whatever storage mechanism you use, you cannot guarantee that the data you store will persist long term. All the storage specifications describe instances where the data may be deleted, including when the user opts to clear it manually. For this reason, any storage supplied by the browser should be treated as potentially volatile.

Another consideration when using browser storage is that many users have different devices that they may use to access your browser-based application. Therefore, synchronization with your server will be required if you want their experience to persist across these devices.

Geolocation

The geolocation API provides a single mechanism for obtaining the user's location no matter whether the user's device supports location using the global position system or network-based inference to determine the actual location.

You can only obtain the user's location if they grant your application permission to access the information, so you will need to supply a fallback mechanism to handle denied requests as well as older browsers and failed lookups. The usual mechanism for obtaining a location when geolocation fails is to allow the user to enter a search term to find their location.

■ **Note**   Most web browsers will only allow the Geolocation API to be called in a secure context, and the user will not even be prompted for their permission when the page is not secure.

Listing 6-33 shows a one-off location lookup using the getCurrentPosition method. If the request is approved and succeeds the success callback will be called, with an argument containing the position information. The position object contains latitude and longitude and can also contain additional data about altitude, direction, and speed, if available. The output of Listing 6-33 assumes the user is located at the foot of the London Eye.

Listing 6-33. Geolocation getCurrentPosition

```
function success(pos: Position) {
    console.log('You are here: Lat=' + pos.coords.latitude +
        ' Long=' + pos.coords.longitude +
        ' Altitude=' + pos.coords.altitude +
        ' (Accuracy=' + pos.coords.altitudeAccuracy + ')' +
        ' Heading=' + pos.coords.heading +
        ' Speed=' + pos.coords.speed);
}

navigator.geolocation.getCurrentPosition(success);

// You are here: Lat = 51.5033 Long = 0.1197
// Altitude = 15 (Accuracy = 0)
// Heading = 0 Speed = 0
```

As well as obtaining a single reading of the user's position, you can watch the position for changes using the watchPosition method. Listing 6-34 reuses the success callback function from the previous example to listen to changes in the user's location. The output from this example assumes the user has traveled quickly between the top of the London Eye and the top of The Gherkin in one second, causing a speed of 3,379 meters per second to be registered. The heading is represented by degrees with north being 0, east being 90, south 180, and west 270 degrees.

Listing 6-34. Geolocation watchPosition

```
function success(pos: Position) {
    console.log('You are here: Lat=' + pos.coords.latitude +
        ' Long=' + pos.coords.longitude +
        ' Altitude=' + pos.coords.altitude +
        ' (Accuracy=' + pos.coords.altitudeAccuracy + ')' +
        ' Heading=' + pos.coords.heading +
        ' Speed=' + pos.coords.speed);
}

const watch = navigator.geolocation.watchPosition(success);

// You are here: Lat = 51.5033 Long = 0.1197
// Altitude = 135 (Accuracy = 15)
// Heading = 0 Speed = 0

// You are here: Lat = 51.5144 Long = 0.0803
// Altitude = 180 (Accuracy = 15)
// Heading = 60 Speed = 3379
```

If you want to stop tracking the user's location, you can call the clearWatch method, passing in a reference to the original watchPosition request to end listening to changes in location. The code in Listing 6-35 ends the watch from the previous example.

Listing 6-35. Clearing a watch

```
navigator.geolocation.clearWatch(watch);
```

In cases where you need to know that the request for the user's location has been denied or failed, you can pass an additional callback to be called if the request fails. Listing 6-36 shows an updated call to watchPosition that passes the additional error function. You can call getCurrentPosition with an error callback too.

Listing 6-36. Failing to obtain the location

```
function success() {
    console.log('Okay');
}

function error() {
    console.log('Position information not available.');
}

const watch = navigator.geolocation.watchPosition(success, error);
```

Geolocation is commonly used to customize a page based on the user's current location or to store the location as metadata when the user performs an action such as posting a message. Once the user has granted permission for your website, the browser may store this to avoid prompting the user every time they use the web application. The default behavior in most browsers is to remember the permission for pages served over a secure connection but not for unsecure pages.

Sensors

There are several APIs already published for working with sensors from within a browser. This is thanks, in part, to organizations such as Mozilla and Nokia (among others) pushing for features for smartphones, and the traction HTML, CSS, and JavaScript have on mobile platforms.

Despite being influenced by mobile devices, the standards for these APIs are being published via the World Wide Web Consortium (W3C), which means they live alongside the existing web standards and can be implemented in browsers regardless of whether the device is considered portable. There are likely to be more APIs published than the selection covered in this section, but you will notice from the examples given that there is a distinct pattern to the implementation of sensor APIs.

Many of the APIs featured in this section were originally part of a general System Information API that was proposed by the W3C (2014), but the editors decided to work on individual specifications for each API to speed up the process of writing the standards. For example, a disagreement on the Vibration API could have delayed the Battery Status API if both were part of the same specification.

■ **Note**   You can try out the device sensor events and APIs on a device that has the appropriate sensors, and a browser that has implemented the standard. For example, you can try motion and orientation, light, and proximity on a Google Pixel running the Firefox browser.

Battery Status

To get autocompletion and type checking for the battery status API, you will need to supply a type definition containing two interfaces. These interfaces are shown in Listing 6-37. The BatteryManager interface contains the properties and events that make up the battery status API. The Navigator interface extends the existing interface in the TypeScript library to add the battery property.

Listing 6-37. Type definitions for battery status

```
interface BatteryManager {
    charging: boolean;
    chargingTime: number;
    dischargingTime: number;
    level: number;
    onchargingchange: () => any;
    onchargingtimechange: () => any;
    ondischargingtimechange: () => any;
    onlevelchange: () => any;
}

interface Navigator {
    battery: BatteryManager;
    mozBattery: BatteryManager;
    webkitBattery: BatteryManager;
}
```

To obtain information from the battery API, you first need to detect the presence of the feature before calling the properties on the battery manager. Listing 6-38 is a complete example using the battery manager to display information on a web page.

The battery level is supplied as a value between 0 and 1.0, so you can obtain the percentage charge by multiplying this value by 100. All the times given in the battery information are supplied in seconds, which you can convert into minutes or hours as required. The charging flag indicates whether the battery is currently connected to a power source.

Listing 6-38. Battery status

```typescript
const battery: BatteryManager = (<any>navigator).battery
    || (<any>navigator).mozBattery
    || (<any>navigator).webkitBattery;

if (battery) {
    const output = document.getElementById('content');

    function updateBatteryStatus() {
        // Gets the battery charge level
        const charge = Math.floor(battery.level * 100) + '%';

        // Detects whether the battery is charging
        const charging = battery.charging ? ' charging' : ' discharging';

        // Gets the time remaining based on charging or discharging
        const timeLeft = battery.charging ?
            `Time until charged (${Math.floor(battery.chargingTime / 60)} mins)` :
            `Time umtil empty (${Math.floor(battery.dischargingTime / 60)} mins)`;

        output.innerHTML = charge + timeLeft + charging;
    }

    // Update the display when plugged in or unplugged
    battery.onchargingchange = updateBatteryStatus;

    // Update the display when the charging time changes
    battery.onchargingtimechange = updateBatteryStatus;

    // Update the display when the discharging time changes
    battery.ondischargingtimechange = updateBatteryStatus;

    // Update the display when the battery level changes
    battery.onlevelchange = updateBatteryStatus;
}
```

There are four events that you can subscribe to that allow you to detect a change in battery status. You may be interested in just one or a combination. For example, although the most likely case for using this API is to display the information obtained as shown in the example, you could use the onchargingchange event to sound an alarm if a device is taken off charge, either to warn the user or as a rudimentary security mechanism that detects the device is being stolen. You could also use the battery information to be sensitive to low-battery situations — perhaps by throttling your application when the battery is below 20%.

■ **Note**   The battery sensor API is on a sabbatical while some privacy wrinkles get ironed out.

Proximity Sensor

The proximity sensor is a very simple API that determines whether the user is very close to the device. Typically, the sensor is located at the top of a mobile phone, near the phone speaker. When the user holds the phone to their ear, the API detects that something is close to the speaker. When the phone is moved away, the device detects that the user is no longer near.

The primary purpose of this sensor is to hide the screen and disable touch when the user is speaking on the phone and then redisplay the screen when the user moves the phone away from their ear. Despite the humble purpose of the proximity sensor, you may determine a more innovative purpose for it in your program.

The proximity API allows for two different kinds of event: a user proximity event that supplies a property to state whether the user is near, and a device proximity event that supplies a measurement within a range. The device proximity event information will differ based on the specific implementation.

Listing 6-39. Proximity events

```
import { addEvent } from './Listing-6-011';

interface ProximityEvent {
    min: number;
    max: number;
    value: number;
    near: boolean;
}

const output = document.getElementById('content');

function sensorChange(proximity: ProximityEvent) {
    const distance =
        (proximity.value ? proximity.value + ' ' : '') +
        (proximity.near ? 'near' : 'far');

    output.innerHTML = distance;
}

// Near or far
addEvent(window, 'userproximity', sensorChange);

// Measurement within a range
addEvent(window, 'deviceproximity', sensorChange);
```

Unlike the battery sensor, which supplies a manager with properties that can be tested at any time, the proximity API is based on the userproximity and deviceproximity events, which pass an event argument containing the data. If the sensor is not available or the API is not supported on the device, these events will never fire; otherwise the event handler will be called whenever there is a change in the proximity status.

Light Sensor

The ambient light sensor supplies a single reading that represents the current ambient light as measured in lux units. Lux units represent one lumen per square meter, which is a reasonable representation of light intensity as seen by the human eye. A full moon on a clear night can supply up to one lux of light. Office lighting typically ranges from 300 to 500 lux, while a television studio might use 1,000 lux. Direct sunlight can achieve a range from 32,000 to 100,000 lux.

The light sensor API has a devicelight event, which supplies a single value as shown in Listing 6-40.

Listing 6-40. Ambient light sensor

```
import { addEvent } from './Listing-6-011';

const output = document.getElementById('content');

function sensorChange(data: DeviceLightEvent) {
    output.innerHTML = 'Ambient light reading: ' + data.value;
}

addEvent(window, 'devicelight', sensorChange);
```

Although the devicelight event in the example supplies the greatest level of granularity, there is also a lightlevel event that returns the more abstract enum values dim, normal, or bright depending on the ambient light.

Motion and Orientation

The motion and orientation API is already contained within the TypeScript standard library, so no additional types need to be declared on top of the existing DeviceMotionEvent type.

The example in Listing 6-41 obtains the motion, measured as the acceleration in meters per second squared and the rotation measured in degrees.

Listing 6-41. Motion and orientation

```
import { addEvent } from './Listing-6-011';

const output = document.getElementById('content');

function sensorChange(event: DeviceMotionEvent) {
    var motion = event.acceleration;
    var rotation = event.rotationRate;

    output.innerHTML = '<p>Motion :<br />' +
        motion.x + '<br />' +
        motion.y + '<br />' +
        motion.z + '</p>' +
        '<p>Rotation:<br />' +
        rotation.alpha + '<br />' +
        rotation.beta + '<br />' +
        rotation.gamma + '</p>';
}

addEvent(window, 'devicemotion', sensorChange);
```

The acceleration property is normalized to remove the effects of gravity. This normalization can only take place on devices that have a gyroscope. In the absence of a gyroscope, an additional property named accelerationIncludingGravity is available, which includes an additional measurement of 9.81 on the axis currently facing up/down (or spread between multiple axes if the device is at an angle where no single axis is pointing directly up/down). For example, if the device was flat on its back with the screen facing up, you would get the following values:

- acceleration: { x: 0, y: 0, z: 0 }
- accelerationIncludingGravity: { x: 0, y: 0, z: 9.81 }

Other Device Sensors

As you may have noticed in the previous examples, where the sensor supplies a single value, there is a distinct pattern to the way you use the API. In particular, you can update the code in Listing 6-42 to work for light, temperature, noise, or humidity sensor APIs simply by changing the sensorApiName variable.

Listing 6-42. The device API pattern

```
import { addEvent } from './Listing-6-011';

const sensorApiName = 'devicetemperature';

const output = document.getElementById('content');

addEvent(window, sensorApiName, (data) => {
    output.innerHTML = sensorApiName + ' ' + data.value;
});
```

The sensorApiName in this example can be changed to any of the following event names and any future event names that follow this implementation pattern.

- devicehumidity—the value will be the percentage humidity.
- devicelight—the value is the ambient light in lux.
- devicenoise—the value is the noise level in dBA.
- devicetemperature—the value is the temperature in degrees Celsius.

Sensor Roundup

The device sensor APIs show how the lines between web page, web application, and native device are gradually eroding. The experimental nature of this set of device APIs has made the progress very slow, especially since Mozilla ditched their Firefox OS project, which was a native HTML and JavaScript-based operating system.

The pattern used throughout the APIs — listening for a specific event triggered on the window object — means that you don't even need to test the feature before using it. If the API is not available, the event will simply never fire.

Simply put, sensors can be used to supply measurements to the user, but with a little creativity they could be used to provide interesting user interactions, adaptive interfaces, or inventive games. Perhaps you'll choose to change the theme of the page based on the ambient light, control page elements using motion or rotation, or even log the quality of the user's sleep using a combination of light, motion, and noise sensors.

Web Workers

JavaScript was designed to run an event loop on a single thread, and this is the model you should typically embrace. If you come across a situation that calls for additional threads, you can use web workers. Web workers allow scripts to run on a background thread, which has a separate global context and can communicate back to the task that spawned the thread using events.

To create a new worker, the code to run on a background thread must be contained in a separate JavaScript file. The code in Listing 6-43 shows the code in `worker.ts`, which will be compiled into the `worker.js` file that will be spawned on a background thread.

Listing 6-43. worker.ts

```
declare function postMessage(message: any): void;

let id = 0;

self.setInterval(() => {
    id++;
    var message = {
        'id': id,
        'message': 'Message sent at ' + Date.now()
    };

    postMessage(message);
}, 1000);
```

The `setInterval` method in this example is not called on `window` but on `self`. This reflects the fact that the worker runs in a separate context with its own scope. The `postMessage` event is the mechanism for sending information back to the main thread from the worker, and any object passed to or from a worker is copied not shared.

The code to create the worker and listen for messages is shown in Listing 6-44. The worker is instantiated with the path to the JavaScript file that contains the worker code. The `workerMessageReceived` function is attached to the `message` event and is called whenever the worker posts a message.

Listing 6-44. Creating and using a web worker

```
const worker = new Worker('/Listing-6-043.js');

function workerMessageReceived(event) {
    const response = event.data;

    console.log(response.id, response.message);
};

worker.addEventListener('message', workerMessageReceived);
```

If you run this example enough times, you will encounter a frailty in this implementation: the worker starts to run immediately in the background, which means it may start posting messages before the message event handler has been added. This problem would never occur normally in JavaScript as the main thread is not available to process other items in the event loop until a function completes.

If you need to avoid the race condition that can occur when setting up a worker, you can wrap the code inside of the worker in a function and post a message to tell the worker that you have set up the event listener and are ready for it to begin processing. The updated worker code is shown in Listing 6-45. The original setInterval call is wrapped in a function, which is called when the worker receives a start message.

Listing 6-45. Worker that waits for a start signal

```
declare function postMessage(message: any): void;

let id = 0;

function start() {
    self.setInterval(() => {
        id++;
        const message = {
            'id': id,
            'message': 'Message sent at ' + Date.now()
        };

        postMessage(message);
    }, 1000);
}

self.onmessage = (event) => {
    if (event.data === 'Start') {
        start();
    } else {
        console.log(event.data);
    }
}
```

When the worker is created, it will no longer run the messaging code until it receives the 'Start' message. Passing the start message to the worker uses the same postMessage mechanism that the worker uses to communicate back to the main thread. By placing the start message after adding the event handler, the race condition is prevented.

Listing 6-46. Signaling the worker to start

```
const worker = new Worker('/Listing-6-045.js');

function workerMessageReceived(event) {
    const response = event.data;

    console.log(response.id, response.message);
};

worker.addEventListener('message', workerMessageReceived);

worker.postMessage('Start');
```

Web workers provide a simple mechanism for processing code on a background thread along with a pattern for safely passing messages between threads. Despite the simplicity, if you find yourself routinely spinning up web workers, you may be using them for the wrong reasons, especially given that long-running operations typically follow either the callback pattern, or use promises, without requiring web workers.

If you do find yourself performing a long-running process or calculation, a web worker can allow the event loop to continue processing on the main thread while the number crunching happens in the background.

Packaging Your Program

This section takes a break from the practical examples of interesting APIs to discuss how to package your TypeScript program.

When you switch to TypeScript from JavaScript, it is tempting to transfer your existing packaging strategy to your TypeScript program. It is common to see people switching to TypeScript, using namespaces to organize their program, and adding a build step to combine the code into a single file and minify it before it is included in the final program. This strategy works for programs up to a certain size, but if your program continues to grow, this method of packaging your program cannot scale indefinitely. This is why TypeScript has first-class support for module loading.

If you organize your program using modules rather than namespaces, you can use a module loader to fetch dependencies as they are needed, loading just the part of the program that you need. This on-demand loading means that, although your program may be hundreds of thousands of lines of code, you can load just the components you need to perform the current operation and load additional modules if (and when) needed.

When you are certain your program will remain small, the bundling and minification strategy may be the right choice, but you can still write your program using modules and use a tool such as the RequireJS optimizer to combine the output without limiting your future options.

There is more information on module loading and packaging in Chapter 2.

Summary

This chapter has been an epic dash through some diverse but interesting web browser features, from the browser itself to the many APIs that allow you to create interesting and inventive applications. Although there is a lot of information about many features, you can always return to this chapter later to refresh your memory.

Key Points

- By avoiding unnecessary reflows, your program will appear more responsive.

- There are multiple methods for finding elements on a web page. Each of them returns different types, although you can use a type assertion to change that type.

- Constructing a nested set of elements before adding them to the page can be more efficient than adding each in turn.

- AJAX allows asynchronous calls to the server and allows data in many different formats.

- WebSockets offer persistent connections with two-way communication and WebRTC allows real-time audio and video streams.

- You can store data on the local computer using session storage, local storage, or IndexedDB. However, there is no guarantee the data will persist.

- You can get the user's location with their permission, and the browser will use the most accurate available method of finding the location.

- There are a number of sensors that you can access, and they all have a similar implementation pattern.

- Web Workers run in a separate thread, with messages being posted between the main thread and the worker thread, and vice versa.

■ ■ ■

CHAPTER 7

Running TypeScript on a Server

If it seems strange to you that Node achieves parallelism by running only one piece of code at a time, that's because it is. It's an example of something I call a backwardism.

—Jim R. Wilson

Running JavaScript on a server is not a new concept — Netscape Enterprise Server offered this feature as long ago as 1994. There are currently a whole host of server-side implementations of JavaScript running on more than six different script engines. In addition to these pure JavaScript implementations, JavaScript can also be run within any platform that has a script host.

Although the JavaScript language is common to all these implementations, each one will supply different APIs, frameworks, modules, or base-class libraries for performing operations that are not usually available within a browser-based JavaScript program. The range of available modules within a server-side implementation is paramount, which is why Node has become such a great success (and why it has been selected for this chapter).

Not only does Node have over 475,000 modules available, from simple helpers to entire database servers, it is possible to add them to your program with one simple command, thanks to the Node Package Manager (NPM). This means you can add a database module such as MongoDB simply by typing npm install MongoDB into a command window. Node is cross-platform and offers installers for Windows, Mac OSX, Linux, Docker, and SunOS.

To demonstrate the use of Node within TypeScript, this chapter gradually evolves a simple application into one that uses several modules. This demonstrates the code as well as the process of adding packages and type definitions. Although the examples show screenshots from Visual Studio and Windows Command Prompt, you can easily transfer everything you learn to other development tools and operating systems, for example, Sublime Text 2 and Terminal on OSX or WebStorm and the terminal on Linux. The combinations are many and varied and several integrated development environments are cross-platform if you want a similar experience on different machines (Visual Studio Code, Cloud9, Eclipse, Sublime Text 2, Vim, and WebStorm all run on Windows, OSX, and Linux).

Install Node

You can download the installer for your chosen platform from the NodeJS website

https://nodejs.org/en/download/

Creating a New Project

The example program will start from a completely empty project. Figure 7-1 shows the starting state of the example project and solution, which contains a single empty server.ts file.

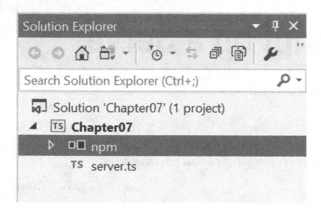

Figure 7-1. *Empty TypeScript project*

If you are using Visual Studio 2017, you can replicate this by creating a new Blank Node.js Application, with the TypeScript language. If you are using a different development environment, you can simply start a new project or folder and add an empty server.ts file.

To get autocompletion and type checking for Node, you will need a type definition that describes the standard Node API. The quickest way to do this is with NPM.

NPM

You can use NPM to handle both production and development dependencies. Production dependencies are modules that must be present for your application to run. Development dependencies include tooling and type definitions that you only need while coding and that you don't need when running the application.

Before you add packages, you'll need a special file called package.json, which is shown in Listing 7-1. This file describes your program, including any dependencies it has. Whenever you add a production or development dependency, this file will be updated.

Listing 7-1. The empty package.json file

```
{
  "name": "NodeApp"
}
```

■ **Note**   This isn't yet a valid package.json file, but a valid version is shown a little later in this chapter. This super-terse version will make the NPM examples easier to understand.

Once you have the package.json file, the only thing you need to know to add a dependency is its name. For all the examples below we are using Express, which is a lightweight web framework for Node.

The first mechanism for installing packages is the Visual Studio package search, which is available by right-clicking on the "npm" branch of Solution Explorer. The left-hand side of the package explorer UI allows you to search for packages, and you can install selected packages using the form at the bottom of the right-hand side. The standard options will add the latest version of the package to the project.

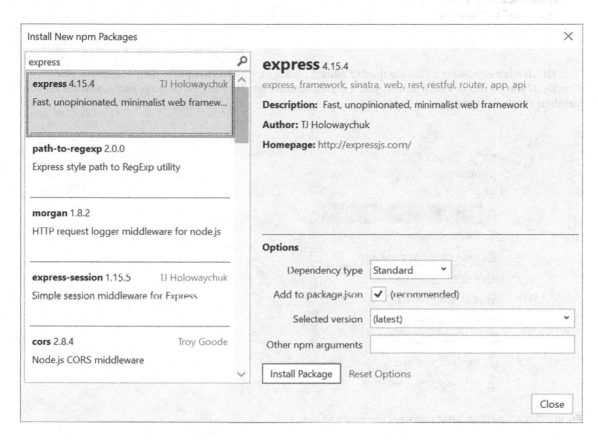

Figure 7-2. Installing NPM packages via Visual Studio

You can achieve an identical result by running the command shown in Listing 7-2. This happens to be the raw command issued by the UI. Both NPM and NodeJS are simple to use from your preferred command window.

Listing 7-2. Installing NPM packages via a command

```
npm install express --save
```

Whether you use the UI, or directly type the command, the save flag in the install command results in the package.json file being updated to show the dependency, as shown in Listing 7-3.

Listing 7-3. Updated package.json

```
{
  "name": "NodeApp",
  "dependencies": {
    "express": "^4.15.4"
  }
}
```

This leads neatly onto a third method of adding packages, which is to update the package.json file directly. If you do this in Visual Studio, you'll get autocompletion for both the package name, and the version number; this is demonstrated in Figure 7-3.

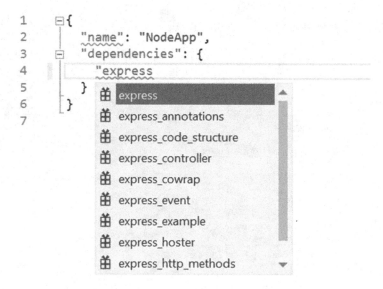

Figure 7-3. *Installing NPM packages via package.json*

For type definitions, the dependency is only needed while developing and not in production. You can mark a package as a development dependency either by selecting the "Development" dependency type in the package explorer UI, or by using the --save-dev variation of the save flag when running the install command. When adding the development dependency via the package.json file, it should go into the separate devDependencies dictionary.

Listing 7-4. Updated package.json with node type definition

```
{
  "name": "NodeApp",
  "dependencies": {
    "express": "^4.15.4"
  },
  "devDependencies": {
    "@types/node": "^8.0.26"
  }
}
```

Now you're an NPM pro, you'll be able to add any dependencies that are required to create a working NodeJS web application, which is the topic of this chapter.

Simple Node Program

Now that the project is set up, it is possible to demonstrate Node using a simple program that runs a web server and responds to requests. The HTTP server simply passes all requests to a callback function that you supply. There is no built-in facility to handle different requests or routes or to help formatting a response (if you want these, they are available in middleware, such as Express, which is covered later in this chapter).

Listing 7-5 shows the complete program, which creates an http server listening on port 8080. All requests are passed to the requestListener function, which gives a standard text response to all requests. The requestListener function is passed to two arguments representing the request and the response. Information can be obtained from the request parameter, such as the method, headers, and body of the request. You can add content to the head and body of the response parameter. You must indicate that you are finished by calling response.end(); otherwise the HTTP server sends no response to the client leaving the client waiting for a response until it times out.

A reference comment is used to indicate the location of the Node type definitions. This allows the import statement to reference the http module, which is not present as an external module in the project — the http module will be supplied by Node at runtime.

Listing 7-5. A simple Node server

```
/// <reference path="./node_modules/@types/node/index.d.ts" />

import * as http from 'http';

const portNumber = 8080;

function requestListener(request: http.ServerRequest, response: http.ServerResponse) {
    response.writeHead(200, { 'Content-Type': 'text/plain' });
    response.write('Response Text Here');
    response.end();
}

http.createServer(requestListener).listen(portNumber);

console.log('Listening on localhost:' + portNumber);
```

If you place this example code in a file named app.ts, you can run the http server from this listing by running the command node app.js from the folder containing the source code (note that you pass the compiled JavaScript file in this command, not the TypeScript file). You should see the message "Listening on localhost:8080" in the command window as shown in Figure 7-4. The server runs for as long as the command window remains open.

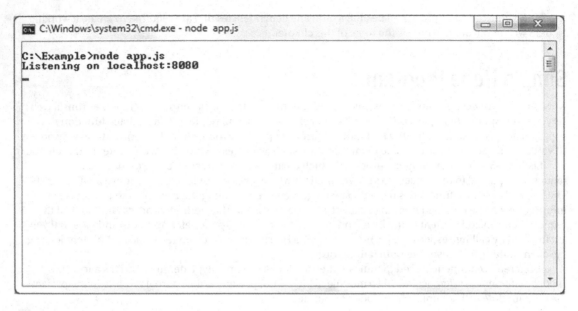

Figure 7-4. *Running the program*

To make a request to the server, open a web browser and enter localhost:8080 in the address bar. You should receive the "Response Text Here" message shown in Figure 7-5. Because all requests to the server are sent to the same requestListener method, you can enter any address at localhost:8080 and receive the same message, for example localhost:8080/Some/Path/Here/ or localhost:8080/?some=query&string=here.

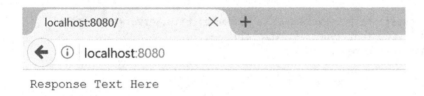

Figure 7-5. *Calling the program from a browser*

Request Information

Being able to start a web server so easily is great, but it is almost certain that you will want to obtain information from the request to provide a response that matches the requested information. Listing 7-6 shows how to obtain the request method and information about the requested URL, which could be used for routing a request or obtaining data to be used to find data matching the request.

Listing 7-6. Getting more information from the request

```
/// <reference path="./node_modules/@types/node/index.d.ts" />

import * as http from 'http';

const portNumber = 8080;
```

```
function requestListener(request: http.ServerRequest, response: http.ServerResponse) {
    response.writeHead(200, { 'Content-Type': 'text/plain' });
    response.write('Method: ' + request.method + '\n');
    response.write('Url: ' + request.url + '\n');
    response.write('Response Text Here');
    response.end();
}

http.createServer(requestListener).listen(portNumber);

console.log('Listening on localhost:' + portNumber);
```

In this example, the information obtained from the request is simply appended to the response to show you the information in the browser when the request is made. The response is shown in Figure 7-6 based on entering http://localhost:8080/Customers/Smith/John into the address bar. You can use the properties of the request to decide how to handle the request.

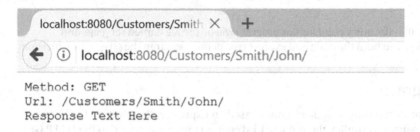

Figure 7-6. *Displaying information about the request*

Although you could use this information to write your own framework for servicing the requests made to your Node server, the work of routing requests and obtaining information from the request has been done elegantly already and is available as a module that you can install with NPM. Unless you want to use the request information to do something unusual, you may find that using an existing module that provides a framework for your program will save time and effort as well as covering scenarios you have not planned for.

The next section describes how to build an application using the Express module, a lightweight web framework for Node that doesn't dictate the details of authorization, persistence, or templating.

Using Express to Write Applications

Working with the raw request and response in Node allows access to the low-level details of HTTP communication; but in most cases, you won't be interested in dealing with all the details yourself. The Express module provides a lightweight framework that allows you to concentrate on your application rather than on routing and HTTP communication. Express is both a quick way to get started and a robust framework for bringing together your program.

To use Express, you'll need both the Express dependency, and the Express type definition development dependency. A more complete version of the package.json file for the application is shown in Listing 7-7, which includes these two dependencies.

Listing 7-7. Example package.json

```json
{
  "name": "node-app",
  "version": "0.0.1",
  "description": "NodeApp",
  "main": "server.js",
  "author": {
    "name": "Steve Fenton"
  },
  "dependencies": {
    "express": "4.15.4"
  },
  "devDependencies": {
    "@types/node": "8.0.26",
    "@types/express": "4.0.37"
  }
}
```

The package.json file notes that the entry point for our program will be the file named server.js, and contains the Express dependency, and both the node and express type definitions from the @types organization.

Simple Express Program

Listing 7-8 is an updated version of the simple Node program based on Express, rather than on the http module. Although the general pattern is similar, the requestListener is specifically added to the HTTP GET method at the root address of the application.

This means that the requestListener function will only be called for requests to http://localhost:8080/. Unlike the earlier examples, requests that don't match the route will fail, for example, a request to http://localhost:8080/Customers would receive a 404 response with the message "Cannot GET /Customers/Smith/John".

Listing 7-8. Using Express

```typescript
import * as express from 'express';

const portNumber = 8080;
const app = express();

app.get('/', (request, response) => {
    response.send('You requested ' + request.query.firstname + ' ' + request.query.
lastname);
})

app.listen(portNumber, 'localhost', () => {
    console.log('Listening on localhost:' + portNumber);
});
```

A correct request to this example should include firstName and lastName query string arguments. Express maps the query string to the request.query property. The full example request address of http://localhost:8080/?firstname=John&lastname=Smith will result in the message "You requested John Smith" being returned in the response, as shown in Figure 7-7.

You requested John Smith

Figure 7-7. *Calling the Express program*

Multiple Routes

You can provide different handlers for different routes in your program, for example, the code in Listing 7-9 provides one handler for `http://localhost:8080/One/` and another for `http://localhost:8080/Two/`. Express handles all the routing for you and ensures the correct function handles each request.

Listing 7-9. Using multiple routes

```
import * as express from 'express';

const portNumber = 8080;
const app = express();

app.get('/', (request, response) => {
    response.send('You requested ' + request.query.firstname + ' ' + request.query.
lastname);
})

app.get('/One/', (request, response) => {
    response.send('You got handler One');
});

app.get('/Two/', (request, response) => {
    response.send('You got handler Two');
});

app.listen(portNumber, 'localhost', () => {
    console.log('Listening on localhost:' + portNumber);
});
```

You can test these routes in a browser, just as before, and get the appropriate responses

- `http://localhost:8080/One/` -> "You got handler One"

- `http://localhost:8080/Two/` -> "You got handler Two"

Requests to routes that have not been registered will result in a 404 *not found* response.

Handling Errors

You can supply a general error handler for your application by supplying a function that accepts four arguments to the `app.use` method. In Listing 7-10 the `handler` function has been changed to throw a deliberate error. The error handler is set using the `app.use` method and logs errors to the console before returning a 500 response code.

Listing 7-10. General error handler

```typescript
import * as express from 'express';

const portNumber = 8080;
const app = express();

app.get('/', (request, response) => {
    throw new Error('Deliberate Error!');
})

app.listen(portNumber, 'localhost', () => {
    console.log('Listening on localhost:' + portNumber);
});

app.use(function (error, request, response, next) {
    console.error(error.message);
    response.status(500).send('An error has occurred.');
});
```

When you make a request to this version of the application, the full error stack will be displayed in the command window, but the web browser will display the general error message, as shown in Figure 7-8. This neatly allows you to perform logging actions with the full error information without disclosing anything publicly.

An error has occurred.

Figure 7-8. *General error in the browser*

The error handler in this example is a good demonstration of middleware in Express, which is a set of functions that are organized into a chain of responsibility. Each middleware can operate over the request and response, allowing you to separate your cross-cutting concerns. In practice, this means that you can avoid a handler that is responsible for logging, authorization, and error handling and instead supply separate middleware for each of these responsibilities.

You can add middleware by calling app.use, where app is the name of your Express application. The function you pass to be used as middleware must follow one of the two signatures below:

- Request Handler (request: Request, response: Response, next: NextFunction) => void;

- Error Request Handler: (error: any, request: Request, response: Response, next: NextFunction) => void;

Each middleware is called in turn and must either call the next middleware using the next() function, or end the response. If no middleware ends the response, the result is a 404 error.

Express Book Project

Now we have covered the basic concepts of Node and Express, we will use a small example application to put it all together. To follow along, you'll need to install some free software and some NPM packages. The application will contain multiple routes, collect user-entered data, and store information in a database.

- MongoDB Community Server from www.mongodb.com/download-center;

- The NPM packages shown in Listing 7-11.

To create the application, you will use a few additional packages from NPM, which will make things faster and easier. Install the dependencies listing the package.json file in Listing 7-11. The additional packages help to parse forms that are posted back to the server, talk to the MongoDB database, and parse our views, which are written using Pug – a simple HTML templating language.

Listing 7-11. Additional dependencies

```
{
  "name": "pro-typescript-book-app",
  "version": "0.0.1",
  "description": "An example book application",
  "main": "server.js",
  "types": "server.d.ts",
  "author": {
    "name": "Steve.Fenton"
  },
  "dependencies": {
    "body-parser": "1.17.2",
    "express": "4.15.4",
    "method-override": "2.3.9",
    "mongoose": "4.11.9",
    "pug": "2.0.0-rc.3"
  },
  "devDependencies": {
    "@types/body-parser": "1.16.5",
    "@types/express": "4.0.37",
    "@types/method-override": "0.0.30",
    "@types/mongoose": "4.7.21",
    "@types/node": "8.0.26",
    "@types/pug": "2.0.4"
  }
}
```

The main entry point for application will be the server file, which is shown in Listing 7-12. This file contains all the dependencies needed to run the full application, and has a single root to capture requests to the home page. The view engine is also set to use Pug, with templates being located in the "views" folder.

Listing 7-12. Server.ts

```
import * as express from 'express';
import * as http from 'http';
import * as path from 'path';
import * as bodyParser from 'body-parser';
import * as methodOverride from 'method-override';
```

```typescript
import * as routes from './routes/index';

const portNumber = 8080;
const app = express();

app.set('port', portNumber);

// Configure view templates
app.set('views', path.join(__dirname, 'views'));
app.set('view engine', 'pug');

http.createServer(app).listen(app.get('port'), () => {
    console.log('Express server listening on port ' + app.get('port'));
});

app.use(bodyParser.json());
app.use(bodyParser.urlencoded({ extended: true }));
app.use(methodOverride());

// routes
app.get('/', routes.index);

// static files, such as .css files
app.use(express.static('.'));
```

Rather than directly placing the function to handle the home page in the server file, the code has been placed in a module located within a folder that will contain all the route handlers. As your application grows, organizing your code in this way will keep each file small and maintainable. The contents of the home page route handler is shown in Listing 7-13, which has a single exported function that renders the response with a small data model.

Listing 7-13. /routes/index.ts

```typescript
import * as express from 'express';

/* GET home page. */
export function index(request: express.Request, response: express.Response) {
    response.render('index', { title: 'Express' });
};
```

Because we have set up Pug as our view engine, we need to supply a template file to be used for the home page. The name of the file should match the name used in Listing 7-13 when we call response.render. The Pug view for the home page is shown in Listing 7-14. The template extends a shared layout, which can be used to provide a consistent HTML layout for all your pages, or for groups of pages. The template for the home page inserts a heading, paragraph, and anchor tag into the "content" zone of the shared layout.

Listing 7-14. Pug template for the home page

```
extends layout

block content
  h1= title
  p Welcome to #{title}
  a(href='/book') Books
```

The shared layout template is shown in Listing 7-15, and it is a simple HTML document with a title and style sheet, and a content block that can be populated by child templates.

Listing 7-15. Shared layout for Pug templates

```
doctype html
html
  head
    title= title
    link(rel='stylesheet', href='/style.css')
  body
    block content
```

The CSS for a simple style sheet is shown in Listing 7-16. This can be placed in a file in the root folder named style.css. Because we set up the Express server to handle static files using `app.use(express.static('.'))`; the request to for the style sheet will be handled by the static file middleware. Without this middleware, the request for the style sheet would result in a 404 error, even though the file does exist on the server.

Listing 7-16. Style Sheet

```
body {
        padding: 50px;
        font: 14px "Lucida Grande", Helvetica, Arial, sans-serif;
}

a {
        color: #00B7FF;
}
```

You can run the Express server using the command shown in Listing 7-17. When the server is running, you can view it in your browser by navigating to `localhost:8080`.

Listing 7-17. Run the Express server

```
node server.js
```

You should see the output shown in Figure 7-9, which means the route, route handler, view templates, and style sheet are all loading successfully. If you click on the books link, you will receive an error because there is not yet a handler for this route.

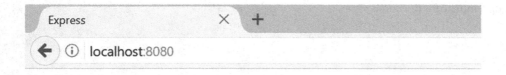

Express

Welcome to Express

Books

Figure 7-9. *Home Page*

The example so far demonstrates how to separate the route handler into a separate module, how to use Pug templates for the views, and how to enable static files with middleware. Next we'll look at connecting to a database to store and retrieve data.

Adding the Book Route

To manage a list of books, the application needs to support a /book route. To support a typical route you need to add a route handler module, a Pug template, and reference the route handler in your Express application.

Listing 7-18 shows the starting point for the book.ts file that will handle requests to the /book address. Like all request handlers, the list function has request and response parameters. The handler calls the response.render method on the result, passing in the view name and the model object that represents the data to be displayed.

Listing 7-18. The routes/book.ts file

```
import * as express from 'express';
declare var next: (error: any) => void;

/* GET /book */
export function list(request: express.Request, response: express.Response) {
    response.render('book', { 'title': 'Books', 'books': [] });
};
```

For this handler to work there must be a view with the specified name in the views folder. Listing 7-19 shows the book.pug template that will render the data supplied by the request handler. The template reuses the layout.pug file, which is the default layout for the application and renders the title from the model object.

Listing 7-19. The views/book.pug file

```
extends layout

block content
  h1= title
  p Welcome to the #{title} page.
  p #{message}
```

To register this route in your application, you need to amend the server.ts file to add the import statement to reference the book.ts file and to add the route registration. Listing 7-20 shows the two additional lines needed to link the /book address to the book.ts file containing the request handler.

Listing 7-20. The additions to the server.ts file

```
import * as book from './routes/book';

// ...

// routes
app.get('/', routes.index);
app.get('/book', book.list);
```

When you run your application and visit the /book address in a web browser, you should see a page displaying the message "Welcome to the Books page." If you don't get to the new page, check the command window to view any errors. The most common error is a misspelling, for example, accidentally entering 'books' as the view name when it should be 'book'.

Collecting Data

The first step toward storing some data is to supply a form that allows the user to enter information. Listing 7-21 shows the updated book.pug template, which now has a form accepting a title and author as well as an optional ISBN identifier for the book.

The HTML attributes are added to elements by appending them in parentheses to the element name. Each input's type and name attributes are added in this way. The notable attribute in the listing is the pattern attribute on the ISBN input. The ISBN isn't required, but if it is supplied it must match the pattern supplied in this attribute.

Listing 7-21. Adding a form to the Pug view

```
extends layout

block content
  h1= title
  p Welcome to the #{title} page.
  p #{message}
  form(method='post')
    fieldset
        legend Add a Book
        div
            label Title *
                br
```

```
                input(type='text', name='book_title', required)
        div
            label Author *
                br
                input(type='text', name='author', required)
        div
            label ISBN
                br
                input(type='text', name='book_isbn', pattern='(?:(?=.{17}$)97[89][ -](?:[0-
                9]+[ -]){2}[0-9]+[ -][0-9]|97[89][0-9]{10}|(?=.{13}$)(?:[0-9]+[ -]){2}[0-
                9]+[ -][0-9Xx]|[0-9]{9}[0-9Xx])')
        div
            button Save
```

If you are worried about having to write patterns such as the monstrous one above that accepts the various formats of an ISBN, don't worry as this one and many others can be found in the HTML5 Pattern Library at http://html5pattern.com/. When you add a pattern attribute to an input element, the text entered will be validated to match the expression.

To process the form when it is submitted, a function that handles the form post must be added to the book.ts file in the routes directory. Listing 7-22 shows the updated file with the submit function. At this stage the function simply provides a message to the view to confirm that nothing has been saved because there is no database yet. The database will be added in the next section.

Listing 7-22. Adding a handler to the book.ts file

```
import * as express from 'express';
declare var next: (error: any) => void;

/* GET /book */
export function list(request: express.Request, response: express.Response) {
    response.render('book', { 'title': 'Books', 'books': [] });
};

/* POST /book */
export function submit(request: express.Request, response: express.Response) {
    const newBook = new Book({
        title: request.body.book_title,
        author: request.body.author,
        isbn: request.body.book_isbn
    });

    response.render('book', { title: 'Books', 'books': [newBook] });
}
```

To send the form post to the submit function, the route must be registered in the app.ts file. Listing 7-23 shows the updated routes, which has the new post route that will forward matching requests to be handled by the book.submit function.

Listing 7-23. The updated routes in the app.ts file

```
// routes
app.get('/', routes.index);
app.get('/book', book.list);
app.post('/book', book.submit);
```

If you compile and run the updated application and visit the /book address, you should see the form that allows books to be added. You will only be able to submit the form if you supply both a title and an author. If you enter any value into the optional ISBN input, it must be a valid format, for example the 10-digit 0-932633-42-0 or the 13-digit 9780932633422.

Books

Welcome to the Books page.

```
┌─Add a Book────────────────────────────────────────────────┐
│                                                             │
│  Title *                                                    │
│  ┌──────────────────────────────┐                          │
│  │                           [▣] │                          │
│  └──────────────────────────────┘                          │
│  Author *                                                   │
│  ┌──────────────────────────────┐                          │
│  │                              │                          │
│  └──────────────────────────────┘                          │
│  ISBN                                                       │
│  ┌──────────────────────────────┐                          │
│  │                              │                          │
│  └──────────────────────────────┘                          │
│  ┌────────┐                                                 │
│  │  Save  │                                                 │
│  └────────┘                                                 │
│                                                             │
└─────────────────────────────────────────────────────────────┘
```

Figure 7-10. Book Page

When you successfully submit the form, the result is not yet saved in a database. The next step in developing this application is to persist the data so it can be reliably retrieved later.

Installing Mongoose

There are many options for storing data in your Node application. You can use the file system, a relational database such as MySQL, or a NOSQL database like MongoDB. In this example MongoDB will be wrapped with Mongoose to supply the data access for the application. Mongoose can simplify the handling of validation, queries, and type casting among other things.

Before you can follow the code in this section, you will need to set up your database. To download MongoDB for your platform visit https://www.mongodb.com/download-center. The download is a simple installer for your selected platform.

MongoDB stores your data on the file system, so you need to set up a folder to be used for storage. By default, MongoDB looks for a c:\data\db directory, so you should add this directory before you proceed. If you don't add this folder, the MongoDB server will stop immediately when you try to start it. You can place the data in a different directory if you want to. You will also need to supply the path to MongoDB when you start the database server. For now, just add the default directory.

To start the MongoDB database server, run the code shown in Listing 7-24 in a command window. This command was written for version 3.4 of MongoDB, so you will need to change the path if you have a different version.

Listing 7-24. Running the database server

```
C:\Program Files\MongoDB\Server\3.4\bin\mongod.exe
```

You should get a message saying that the server is "waiting for connection on port [number]". The number shown in this message (usually 27017) will be needed when you connect to the database from your application. If you get any errors, double-check that you have set up the c:\data\db directory.

The Mongoose module and type definitions should already be available as it was added to the package. json early in this chapter. You should now have everything you need ready to start saving your data. The next section is a walkthrough of the changes to the Express Book Project to store and retrieve the books entered by the user.

Storing Data

To store the data received when the user submits a new book, the book.ts file in the routes directory must be changed to call the newly installed database.

Listing 7-25 shows the updated handlers, the list handler that displays the books from the database, and the submit handler that saves new submissions. The code to connect to the database is outside of the functions and is shared between them. A more detailed walkthrough of all the changes is shown below.

Listing 7-25. The updated routes/book.ts file

```
import * as express from 'express';
import * as mongoose from 'mongoose';
declare var next: (error: any) => void;

// MongoDB typically runs on port 27017
mongoose.connect('mongodb://localhost:27017/books', { useMongoClient: true });

// Defines a book
interface Book extends mongoose.Document {
    title: string;
    author: string;
    isbn: string;
}

// Defines the book database schema
const bookSchema = new mongoose.Schema({
    title: String, author: String, isbn: String
});

const Book = mongoose.model<Book>('Book', bookSchema);

/* GET /book */
export function list(request: express.Request, response: express.Response) {
    Book.find({})
        .then((res) => {
```

```
        response.render('book', { 'title': 'Books', 'books': res });
    })
    .catch((err) => {
        return next(err);
    });
};

/* POST /book */
export function submit(request: express.Request, response: express.Response) {
    const newBook = new Book({
        title: request.body.book_title,
        author: request.body.author,
        isbn: request.body.book_isbn
    });

    newBook.save()
        .then((res) => {
            response.redirect('/book');
        })
        .catch((err) => {
            return next(err);
        });
}
```

The database connection is made using the mongoose.connect call. The connection string in the example uses port 27017; you should use the port number that was shown when you started the MongoDB server. When your application connects to the database, each connection will be logged to the MongoDB command window.

The bookSchema variable is assigned a new Mongoose schema. This schema defines the shape of the documents to be stored in a collection. Mongoose sets up the MongoDB collection for you and can handle default values and validation. The schema for books is set using title, author, and ISBN properties, which are all assigned the type String. The definition of schemas is strikingly similar to TypeScript type annotations. Because of the context of the statement, the TypeScript compiler is intelligent enough to realize that they are not type annotations; therefore, it doesn't use type erasure to remove them from the compiled output. The String type in question is not the String interface that backs the string type annotation in TypeScript but a mongoose.Schema.Types.String. If you accidentally use the lowercase string type, the compiler will give you a warning about your mistake.

The Book variable is assigned a model object that Mongoose creates. This saves you having to write your own implementation of a Book class. You can use this model to create new instances of books whenever you need one, just as if you had written your own class.

Although this has taken a few paragraphs of text to explain, it is worth revisiting the code listing to confirm that it is possible to connect to a database and set up the schema for the book data in three lines of code. This setup is used in both functions that handle requests.

The list function calls the Book.find method supplied by Mongoose for retrieving records. You can supply an object to the find method to be used to filter the results. The object can be a partial match for the book schema. For example, you could use { author: 'Robert C. Martin' } to retrieve all the books by Uncle Bob. In the example, the empty object indicates that you want all documents in the collection.

Because the query is executed asynchronously, the code that depends on the result goes in the appropriate then block. If you forget to place your code inside the then block, the response will be sent before the query is finished. Errors are handled using the catch block. The books collection is added to the model object passed to the view.

■ **Note**   Although the example uses an empty object to query the collection and retrieve all books, this query will get slower over time as more and more books are added to the database. You can paginate your results using the skip and limit query methods.

The submit function instantiates a new Book object with the data submitted by the user and then calls the save method that Mongoose provides. Once again the database call is asynchronous and promises are used to continue once the query is resolved. In the code listing, when the record is saved successfully the response is simply a redirection to the list action. Redirecting the request after a submission prevents the user from accidentally resubmitting the same data by refreshing their browser. The pattern of redirecting after a successful submission is named the Post Redirect Get pattern.

Now that the route handler is passing the book data to the view, the view can be updated to show the data. The additional markup to add a table is shown in Listing 7-26.

Listing 7-26. The Pug table template

```
table
    thead
        tr
            th Title
            th Author
            th ISBN
    tbody
        if books
            each book in books
                tr
                    td= book.title
                    td= book.author
                    td= book.isbn
```

The each loop in the Pug template repeats the nested output for each item in the books collection. The table cells are declared using the shorthand syntax (the element name followed by an =). This means that the data variables do not need to be enclosed in the usual #{} delimiters as they are for the title, for example.

Pug's each loop will handle an empty array but not an undefined value. The if statement before the each loop in the example prevents undefined values reaching the each loop.

You now have a fully functioning application that will save and display books. You can enter a book into the form, as shown in Figure 7-11.

Books

Welcome to the Books page.

```
┌─Add a Book────────────────────────────────────────┐
│ Title *                                            │
│ ┌────────────────────────┐                         │
│ │Start With Why       ▣  │                         │
│ └────────────────────────┘                         │
│ Author *                                           │
│ ┌────────────────────────┐                         │
│ │Simon Sinek             │                         │
│ └────────────────────────┘                         │
│ ISBN                                               │
│ ┌────────────────────────┐                         │
│ │0241958229              │                         │
│ └────────────────────────┘                         │
│ ┌──────┐                                           │
│ │ Save │                                           │
│ └──────┘                                           │
└────────────────────────────────────────────────────┘
```

Title Author ISBN

Figure 7-11. *Completed Book Form*

When you click the save button, your book will be stored and you'll see the page in Figure 7-12. You can return to your application at any time and the stored books will still be available.

Books

Welcome to the Books page.

```
┌─Add a Book────────────────────────────────────────┐
│ Title *                                            │
│ ┌────────────────────────┐                         │
│ │                     ▣  │                         │
│ └────────────────────────┘                         │
│ Author *                                           │
│ ┌────────────────────────┐                         │
│ │                        │                         │
│ └────────────────────────┘                         │
│ ISBN                                               │
│ ┌────────────────────────┐                         │
│ │                        │                         │
│ └────────────────────────┘                         │
│ ┌──────┐                                           │
│ │ Save │                                           │
│ └──────┘                                           │
└────────────────────────────────────────────────────┘
```

Title	Author	ISBN
Start With Why	Simon Sinek	0241958229

Figure 7-12. *Stored Book*

The data stored in MongoDB is persistent, which means you can restart the machine and the data will still be stored. This gives you a permanent store, with the exception of a total machine meltdown, in which case you may want to consider an appropriate backup strategy for your data. You can find out more about MongoDB backup methods at https://docs.mongodb.com/manual/core/backups/.

215

Summary

JavaScript is no stranger to web servers and has gained huge traction, thanks to Node and the many thousands of modules available via the Node Package Manager. As larger programs are written to run on Node, the language features and tooling provided by TypeScript increase quickly in value. A great deal of time can be wasted on simple mistakes such as placing code dependent on an asynchronous call outside of the callback function or using `string` when you mean to use `String`, and TypeScript can help you to avoid these common errors.

The Express framework is a fast way to get started on Node and will provide some familiarity to programmers that have worked with Sinatra (or Nancy in .NET). Even for those not familiar with this exact style of implementation, the separation of the route handlers and views is likely to be recognizable. Using Express will boost your productivity compared to handling the low-level HTTP requests and responses in Node.

Mongoose fulfils a similar role for the database, providing many shortcuts that will boost your productivity. MongoDB is not particularly tricky if you want to drop down a level and handle the models and validation yourself by calling MongoDB directly to store and retrieve data.

Although this chapter has happily stuck with many of the defaults that ship with Express, you are not limited to using these defaults. It is trivial to replace template engines and middleware with a single line of code.

Key Points

- JavaScript has been running on web servers for over 20 years.

- Node will happily run on any platform.

- You can get type information for Node and many of the Node modules from the @ types organization in NPM.

- Express supplies a lightweight and flexible application framework that is easier to use than the lower-level Node HTTP request and response.

- Mongoose and MongoDB supply simple persistence with an asynchronous API.

CHAPTER 8

Exceptions, Memory, and Performance

The primary duty of an exception handler is to get the error out of the lap of the programmer and into the surprised face of the user. Provided you keep this cardinal rule in mind, you can't go far wrong.

—Verity Stob

Despite lacking the appeal of language features or runtime environments, understanding exceptions and memory management will help you to write better TypeScript programs. Exceptions in JavaScript and TypeScript may look familiar to programmers who have used C#, Java, PHP, or many other languages, but there are some subtle yet important differences. The topics of exception handling and memory management are inextricably linked because they share a language feature, which is described later in this chapter.

The subject of memory management is often dominated by folklore, falsehoods, and blindly applied best practices. This chapter deals with the facts of memory management and garbage collection and explains how you can take measurements to test your optimization ideas, rather than applying a practice that may make little or no difference (or even perform worse than the original code). This will lead briefly to the subject of performance.

Exceptions

Exceptions are used to indicate that a program or module is unable to continue processing. By their very nature, they should only be raised in truly exceptional circumstances. Hence the name! Often, exceptions are used to indicate that the state of the program is invalid or that it is not safe to continue processing.

Although it can be tempting to start issuing exceptions every time a routine passes a disagreeable value as an argument, it can often be more graceful to handle input that you can anticipate without raising an exception.

When your program encounters an exception, it will be shown in the console unless it is handled in code. The console allows programmers to write messages, and it will automatically log any exceptions that occur while running the program.

You can inspect the console for exceptions in all modern web browsers. The shortcut key differs from browser to browser and varies by platform, but if CTRL + SHIFT + I fails to work on your Windows or Linux machine or CMD + OPT + I fails on your Mac, you can try the F12 key, or find the tools in the browser's menu listed under "Developer Tools, Browser Console" or a similar name. For Node, the error and warning output will appear in the console window you use to run the HTTP server.

S. Fenton, *Pro TypeScript*, https://doi.org/10.1007/978-1-4842-3249-1_8

Throwing Exceptions

To raise an exception in your TypeScript program you use the throw keyword. Although you can follow this keyword with any object, it is best to provide either a string containing an error message, or an instance of the Error object wrapping the error message.

Listing 8-1 shows a typical exception being thrown to prevent an unacceptable input value. When the errorsOnThree function is called with a number, it returns the number, unless it is called with the number three, in which case the exception is raised.

Listing 8-1. Using the throw keyword

```
function errorsOnThree(input: number) {
    if (input === 3) {
        throw new Error('Three is not allowed');
    }

    return input;
}

const result = errorsOnThree(3);
```

The general Error type in this example can be replaced with a custom exception. You can create a custom exception using a class that implements the Error interface as shown in Listing 8-2. The Error interface ensures that your class has a name and message property.

The toString method in Listing 8-2 is not required by the Error interface, but is used in many cases to obtain a string representation of the error. Without this method, the default implementation of toString from Object would be called, which would write "[object Object]" to the console. By adding the toString method to the ApplicationError class you can ensure that an appropriate message is shown when the exception is thrown and logged.

Listing 8-2. Custom error

```
class ApplicationError implements Error {

    public name = 'ApplicationError';

    constructor(public message: string) {
        if (typeof console !== 'undefined') {
            console.log(`Creating ${this.name} "${message}"`);
        }
    }

    toString() {
        return `${this.name}: {this.message}`;
    }
}
```

You can use custom exceptions in a throw statement to classify the kind of error that has occurred. It is a common exception pattern to create a general ApplicationError class and inherit from it to create more specific kinds of errors. Any code that handles exceptions is then able to take different actions based on the type of error that has been thrown, as demonstrated in the later section on exception handling.

Listing 8-3 shows a specific `InputError` class that inherits from the `ApplicationError` class. The `errorsOnThree` function uses the `InputError` exception type to highlight that the error has been raised in response to bad input data.

Listing 8-3. Using inheritance to create special exception types

```
class ApplicationError implements Error {

    public name = 'ApplicationError';

    constructor(public message: string) {
        if (typeof console !== 'undefined') {
            console.log(`Creating ${this.name} "${message}"`);
        }
    }

    toString() {
        return `${this.name}: {this.message}`;
    }
}

class InputError extends ApplicationError {
}

function errorsOnThree(input: number) {
    if (input === 3) {
        throw new InputError('Three is not allowed');
    }

    return input;
}
```

The `InputError` in the example simply extends the `ApplicationError`; it doesn't need to implement any of the properties or methods as it only exists to provide a category of exceptions to use within your program. You can create exception classes to extend `ApplicationError`, or to further specialize a subclass of `ApplicationError`.

■ **Note**   You should treat the native `Error` type as sacred and never throw an exception of this kind. By creating custom exceptions as subclasses of the `ApplicationError` class, you can ensure that the `Error` type is reserved for use outside of your code in truly exceptional cases.

Exception Handling

When an exception is thrown, the program will be terminated unless the exception is handled. To handle an exception you can use a try-catch block, a try-finally block, or even a try-catch-finally block. In any of these cases, the code that may result in an exception being thrown is wrapped within the try block.

Listing 8-4 shows a try-catch block that handles the error from the errorsOnThree function in the previous section. The parameter accepted by the catch block represents the thrown object, for example, the Error instance or the custom ApplicationError object, depending on which one you used in the throw statement.

Listing 8-4. Unconditional catch block

```
try {
    const result = errorsOnThree(3);
} catch (err) {
    console.log('Error caught, no action taken');
}
```

The err parameter is scoped to the catch block, making it equivalent to a variable declared with the let keyword, rather than the var keyword, as described in Chapter 4.

It is common in languages that support try-catch blocks to allow specific exception types to be caught. This allows the catch block to only apply to specific types of exceptions and for other types of exceptions to behave as if there were no try-catch block. This technique is recommended to ensure that you only handle exceptions that you know you can recover from, leaving truly unexpected exceptions to terminate the program and prevent further corruption of the state.

There is currently no standards-compliant method of conditionally catching exceptions, which means you catch all or none. If you only wish to handle a specific type of exception, you can check the type within the catch statement and re-throw any errors that do not match the type.

Listing 8-5 shows an exception handling routine that handles ApplicationError custom exceptions, but re-throws any other type. Within the if-statement, the type of the err variable is narrowed to the ApplicationError type.

Listing 8-5. Checking the type of error

```
try {
    const result = errorsOnThree(3);
} catch (err) {
    if (err instanceof ApplicationError) {
        console.log('Error caught, no action taken');
    }

    throw err;
}
```

■ **Note**   By handling only custom exceptions, you can ensure that you are only handling the types of exceptions that you know you can recover from. If you use the default catch block with no instanceof check, you are taking responsibility for every type of exception that may occur within your program.

This example will allow the catch block to handle an ApplicationError, or a subclass of ApplicationError such as the InputError described earlier in this chapter. To illustrate the effect of handling exceptions at different levels in the class hierarchy, Figure 8-1 shows a more complex hierarchy that extends the ApplicationError and InputError classes.

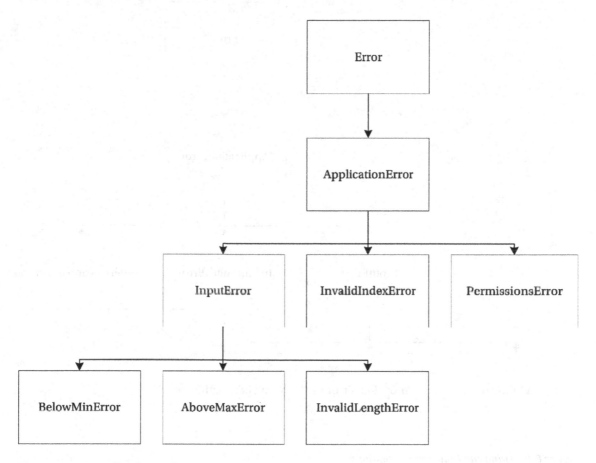

Figure 8-1. *Error class hierarchy*

When you choose to handle the InputError category of exceptions, you will be handling four kinds of exceptions as shown in Figure 8-2: InputError, BelowMinError, AboveMaxError, and InvalidLengthError. All other exceptions will be passed up the call stack as if they were unhandled.

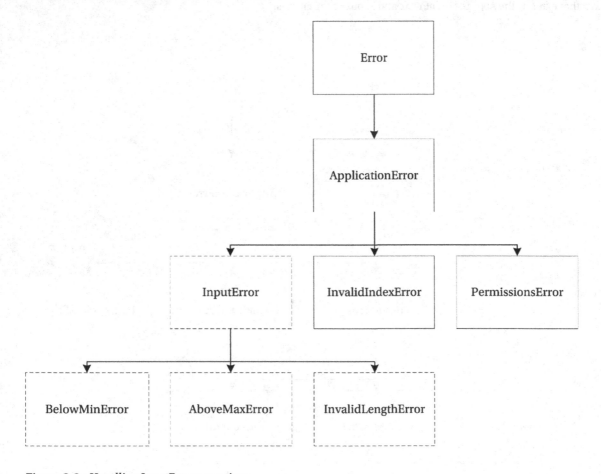

Figure 8-2. *Handling InputError exceptions*

If you were to handle the ApplicationError category of exceptions, you would be handling all seven custom exceptions in the hierarchy as shown in Figure 8-3.

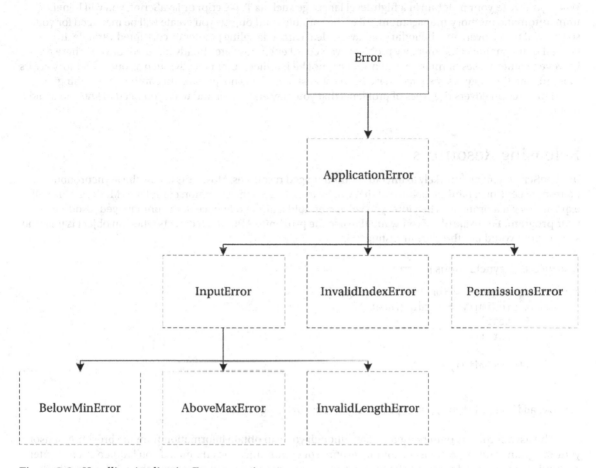

Figure 8-3. *Handling ApplicationError exceptions*

Generally speaking, the exceptions that you handle should be more specific the deeper you are into your program. If you were working near low-level code, you would handle very specific types of exceptions. When you are working closer to the user interface, you would handle more general kinds of exceptions.

Exceptions will crop up again shortly with the discussion on performance because there is a performance cost associated with creating and handling exceptions in your program. Despite this, if you are using them only to signal when the routine cannot continue, you shouldn't worry about their runtime cost.

Memory

When you write your program in a high-level language such as TypeScript or JavaScript, you will benefit from automatic memory management. All of the variables and objects you create will be managed for you, so you will never overrun a boundary or have to deal with a dangling pointer or corrupted variable. In fact, all of the manageable memory problems you could encounter are already handled for you. There are, however, some classes of memory safety that cannot be handled automatically, such as out of memory errors that indicate the system's resources have been exhausted and it is not possible to continue processing.

This section covers the types of problems that you may encounter and what you need to know to avoid them.

Releasing Resources

In TypeScript, you are unlikely to encounter unmanaged resources. Most APIs follow the asynchronous pattern, accepting a method argument that will be called when the operation completes. Modern APIs will expose this via a promise. Therefore, you will never hold a direct reference to the unmanaged resource in your program. For example, if you wanted to use the proximity API, which detects when an object is near the sensor, you would use the code in Listing 8-6.

Listing 8-6. Asynchronous pattern

```
const sensorChange = function (reading) {
    const proximity = reading.near
        ? 'Near'
        : 'Far';

    alert(proximity);
}

window.addEventListener('userproximity', sensorChange, true);
```

The asynchronous pattern means that although you can obtain information from the proximity sensor, your program is never responsible for the resource or communication channel. If you happen to encounter a situation where you do hold a reference to a resource that you must manage, you should use a try-finally block to ensure that the resource is released, even if an error occurs.

The example in Listing 8-7 assumes that it is possible to work directly with the proximity sensor to obtain a reading.

Listing 8-7. Imaginary unmanaged proximity sensor

```
const sensorChange = function (reading) {
    var proximity = reading.near ?
        'Near' : 'Far';
    alert(proximity);
}

const readProximity = function () {
    const sensor = new ProximitySensor();
    try {
        sensor.open();
```

```
        const reading = sensor.read();

        sensorChange(reading);
    } finally {
        sensor.close();
    }
}

window.setInterval(readProximity, 500);
```

The `finally` block will ensure the sensor's `close` method is called, which performs the cleanup and releases any resources. The `finally` block executes even if there is an error calling the `read` method or the `sensorChange` function.

The equivalent example for a promise-like interface is shown in Listing 8-8. When working with promises, usually either the "then" block is executed, or if there is an error the "catch" block is executed. The finally block is called in all cases.

Listing 8-8. Umanaged proximity sensor with promise-like interface

```
const sensorChange = function (reading) {
    var proximity = reading.near ?
        'Near' : 'Far';
    alert(proximity);
}

const readProximity = function () {
    const sensor = new ProximitySensor();

    sensor.open()
        .then(() => {
            return sensor.read();
        })
        .then((reading) => {
            sensorChange(reading);
        })
        .finally(() => {
            sensor.close();
        });
}

window.setInterval(readProximity, 500);
```

In the previous two sections, I have covered exception handling with "catch" and resource management with "finally." In all cases, you can combine the two to perform both exception and memory management.

Garbage Collection

When memory is no longer needed, it needs to be freed for it to be allocated to other objects in your program. The process used to determine whether memory can be freed is called garbage collection. There are several styles of garbage collection that you will encounter depending on the runtime environment.

Older web browsers may use a reference-counting garbage collector, freeing memory when the number of references to an object reaches zero. This is illustrated in Table 8-1. This is a very fast way to collect garbage as the memory can be freed as soon as the reference count reaches zero. However, if a circular reference is created between two or more objects, none of these objects will ever be garbage collected because their count will never reach zero.

Modern web browsers solve this problem with a mark-and-sweep algorithm that detects all objects reachable from the root and garbage collects the objects that cannot be reached. Although this style of garbage collection can take longer, it is less likely to result in memory leaks. To prevent freezes in the browser UI, some JavaScript engines sneak garbage collection into idle time, which means it has less impact on the browsing experience.

Table 8-1. *Reference counting garbage collection*

Object	Reference Count	Memory De-Allocated
Object A	1	No
Object B	1	No
Object C	1	No
Object D	1	No
Object E	*0*	*Yes*

The same objects from Table 8-1 are shown in Figure 8-4. Using the reference-counting algorithm both Object A and Object B remain in memory because they reference each other. These circular references are the source of memory leaks in older browsers, but this problem is solved by the mark-and-sweep algorithm. The circular reference between Object A and Object B is not sufficient for the objects to survive garbage collection as only objects that are accessible from the root remain.

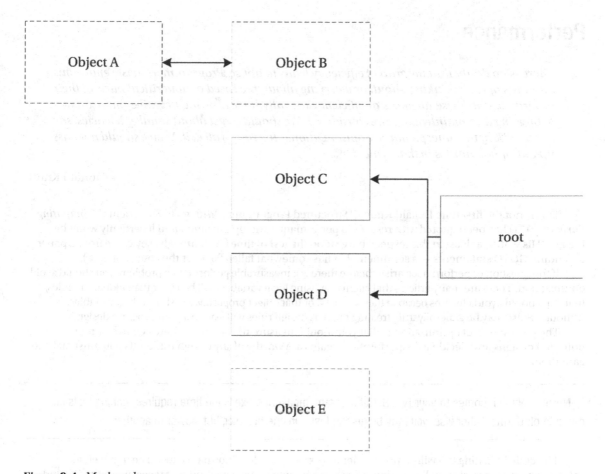

Figure 8-4. *Mark and sweep*

Most modern garbage collectors promote objects through several generations, with the most frequent and most efficient collections being made over short-lived objects. As objects live longer, they are usually checked less often, and collection may be slower. A full garbage collection may also include a compacting step to optimize the memory usage.

The use of mark-and-sweep garbage collection algorithms means that you rarely need to worry about garbage collection or memory leaks in your TypeScript program.

Performance

> *There is no doubt that the grail of efficiency leads to abuse. Programmers waste enormous amounts of time thinking about, or worrying about, the speed of noncritical parts of their programs, and these attempts at efficiency actually have a strong negative impact when debugging and maintenance are considered. We should forget about small efficiencies, say about 97% of the time: premature optimization is the root of all evil. Yet we should not pass up our opportunities in that critical 3%.*

> —Donald Knuth

This is not the first time Donald Knuth ("Structured Programming With go to Statements," *Computing Surveys*, 1974) has been quoted with respect to performance and optimization and it certainly won't be the last. His words, at least in this respect, have stood the test of time (even though they came from a paper defending GOTO statements — a sentiment that has somewhat fallen flat over the course of time).

If the question of performance arises before there is a measurable performance problem, you should avoid optimization. There are many articles that claim that using local variables will be faster than global variables, that you should avoid closures because they are slow, or that object properties are slower than variables. Although these may be generally true, treating them as design rules will lead to a poor program design.

The golden rule of optimization is that you should measure the difference between two or more potential designs and decide if the performance gains are worthy of any design trade-offs you must make to gain them.

■ **Note**   When it comes to your TypeScript program, measuring execution time requires running tests on multiple platforms. Otherwise, you may be getting faster in one browser, but slower in another.

The code in Listing 8-9 will be used to demonstrate a simple performance test. The lightweight CommunicationLines class will be tested. The class contains a single method that takes in a teamSize and calculates the number of lines of communication between team members using the famous $n(n-1)/2$ algorithm. The function named testCommunicationLines instantiates the class and successfully tests two cases for team sizes of 4 and 10, which have 6 and 45 lines of communication respectively.

Listing 8-9. Calculating lines of communication

```
class CommunicationLines {
    calculate(teamSize: number) {
        return (teamSize * (teamSize - 1)) / 2
    }
}

function testCommunicationLines() {
    const communicationLines = new CommunicationLines();

    let result = communicationLines.calculate(4);

    if (result !== 6) {
        throw new Error('Test failed for team size of 4.');
    }
```

```
        result = communicationLines.calculate(10);

        if (result !== 45) {
            throw new Error('Test failed for team size of 10.');
        }
    }
}

testCommunicationLines();
```

The Performance class in Listing 8-10 wraps a callback function in a method that uses the performance.
now method to time the operation using the high-fidelity timer discussed in Chapter 4. To get a fair
measurement, the Performance class runs the code 10,000 times by default, although this number can be
overridden when the run method is called.

The output from the Performance class includes the total time taken to execute the code 10,000 times as
well as the average time per iteration.

Listing 8-10. Performance.ts runner

```
export class Performance {
    constructor(private func: Function, private iterations: number) {

    }

    private runTest() {
        if (!performance) {
            throw new Error('The performance.now() standard is not supported in this
runtime.');
        }

        const errors: number[] = [];

        const testStart = performance.now();

        for (let i = 0; i < this.iterations; i++) {
            try {
                this.func();
            } catch (err) {
                // Limit the number of errors logged
                if (errors.length < 10) {
                    errors.push(i);
                }
            }
        }

        const testTime = performance.now() - testStart;

        return {
            errors: errors,
            totalRunTime: testTime,
            iterationAverageTime: (testTime / this.iterations)
        };
    }
```

```
    static run(func: Function, iterations = 10000) {
        const tester = new Performance(func, iterations);
        return tester.runTest();
    }
}
```

To use the Performance class to measure the program, the code must be imported and the call to the testCommunicationLines function replaced by passing the function into the run method of the Performance class, as shown in Listing 8-11.

Listing 8-11. Running the performance test

```
import { Performance } from './Listing-8-010';

class CommunicationLines {
    calculate(teamSize: number) {
        return (teamSize * (teamSize - 1)) / 2
    }
}

function testCommunicationLines() {
    const communicationLines = new CommunicationLines();

    let result = communicationLines.calculate(4);

    if (result !== 6) {
        throw new Error('Test failed for team size of 4.');
    }

    result = communicationLines.calculate(10);

    if (result !== 45) {
        throw new Error('Test failed for team size of 10.');
    }
}

const result = Performance.run(testCommunicationLines);

console.log(result.totalRunTime + ' ms');
```

The result of this code is that a total run time of 2.73 ms is logged to the console. This means that the entire run of 10,000 iterations (which is 20,000 calls to the communication lines algorithm) takes less than 3 ms. In most cases, a result such as this is a good indication that you are looking in the wrong place for optimization opportunities.

It is possible to get a very different result by adjusting the code as shown in Listing 8-12. The only change made to the code is to check the call to communicationLines.calculate with a team size of four results in seven communication lines. This test will fail and an exception will be raised.

Listing 8-12. Running the performance test with exceptions

```
import { Performance } from './Listing-8-010';

class CommunicationLines {
    calculate(teamSize: number) {
        return (teamSize * (teamSize - 1)) / 2
    }
}

function testCommunicationLines() {
    const communicationLines = new CommunicationLines();

    let result = communicationLines.calculate(4);

    if (result !== 7) {
        throw new Error('Test failed for team size of 4.');
    }

    result = communicationLines.calculate(10);

    if (result !== 45) {
        throw new Error('Test failed for team size of 10.');
    }
}

const result = Performance.run(testCommunicationLines);

console.log(result.totalRunTime + ' ms');
```

Running the code with the failing test and the creation and handling of an exception results in a total run of 214.45 ms — this is 78 times slower than the first test. It is possible to use this data to guide your design decisions. You may want to repeat the tests multiple times or try different iteration sizes to ensure you get consistent results.

Here are some numbers collected using the `Performance` class from Listing 8-10 to evidence the claims made in respect of optimization at the start of this section. Using a simple, but limited test with a baseline time of 0.74 ms per iteration, the results were as follows (where higher numbers indicate slower execution times):

- Global variables: 0.80 ms (0.06 ms slower per iteration)

- Closures: 1.13 ms (0.39 ms slower per iteration)

- Properties: 1.48 ms (0.74 ms slower per iteration)

Over 10,000 executions you can see small differences in the execution times, but it is important to remember that your program will return different results due to differences such as object complexity, nesting depth, number of object created, and many other factors. Before you make any optimizations, make sure you have taken measurements so you can compare the performance before and after any changes to decide whether they have made a positive impact.

Summary

This chapter has covered three important topics that are likely to be fundamental to any large application written in TypeScript. In most cases, these three areas are likely to be cross-cutting concerns that may be easier to consider before you write a large amount of code that needs to be changed.

Using exceptions to handle truly exceptional states in your program prevents further corruption of the program data. You should create custom exceptions to help manage different kinds of errors and test the types in your catch blocks to only handle errors that you know you can recover from.

Modern runtimes all handle memory using the reliable mark-and-sweep algorithm, which does not fall victim to the circular reference memory leak that older reference-counting garbage collectors suffer from. It is generally accepted that programmers don't need to code with garbage collection in mind, but if you can measure a performance problem and discover that garbage collection is the issue, you may decide to help the garbage collector by creating less objects for it to manage.

Whenever you are working on optimization, you should first measure the performance of your program to prove whether your assumption about optimization is correct when making a change. You should measure your changes in multiple environments to ensure you improve the speed in all of them.

Key Points

- You can use the throw keyword with any object, but it is best to use subclasses of a custom error.

- You can handle exceptions with try-catch-finally blocks, where you must specify either a catch or finally block, or both if you wish.

- When working with promises, you can use catch blocks, finally blocks, or both.

- You can't reliably catch only custom exceptions, but you can test the exception type within the catch block.

- Most APIs you encounter will follow the asynchronous or promise-like pattern, but if you find you must manage a resource, use a try-finally block to clean up.

- When it comes to performance, you need before and after measurements to back up any code you change in the name of optimization.

CHAPTER 9

■ ■ ■

Using JavaScript Libraries

I'm not saying that using existing software or libraries is bad. I'm saying that it's always a tradeoff between minimizing effort on one side and minimizing redundant code on the other side. I'm saying that you should consider writing your own code when the percentage of features you need from existing libraries is tiny (let's say less than 20%). It might not be worth carrying the extra 80% forever.

—Lea Verou

The JavaScript community has been one of the busiest when it comes to writing frameworks, toolkits, helpful functions, and useful snippets. If you search for just about any kind of framework or toolkit, you are likely to find a great many options. In fact, the number of options is both a blessing and a curse, although you'll have no problem finding behavior-driven testing frameworks, unit testing frameworks, model view controller (MVC) frameworks, model view viewmodel (MVVM) frameworks, networking toolkits, browser polyfills, and more. Selecting one out of the myriad options to use is no easy task.

Once you have weighed your choices, you can start using the framework in your TypeScript program right away. At runtime, both your program and the framework will be plain JavaScript, but at design time and compile time you'll be mixing your TypeScript code with the plain JavaScript library. Because the TypeScript compiler has no knowledge of the operations supplied in the JavaScript file, you will need to provide hints in the form of *type definitions* to get the same level of tooling support, as you would get for a TypeScript library.

Type definitions are used by the compiler to check your program and by the language service to provide autocompletion in your development tools. All of the type definitions are erased by the compiler, which means they don't add any weight to your production code. This chapter includes an example application that demonstrates how you can create type definitions for third-party JavaScript code, when you need to include it within your TypeScript program.

To illustrate the benefits of type definitions for existing code, let's visit the typical development workflow for working with jQuery in plain JavaScript.

- Type out a selector and method, such as $('#elem').on(
- Search the jQuery documentation for the signature of the on method
- Flip between your code and the documentation to complete your line of code

This is a typical representation of all but the most common operations in jQuery, and I've been generous by not mentioning any copying and pasting of examples (we have all done it). If our developer workflow for even the most common libraries involves flipping between the documentation and our code, there must be a better way. Type definitions are that better way.

© Steve Fenton 2018
S. Fenton, *Pro TypeScript*, https://doi.org/10.1007/978-1-4842-3249-1_9

By including the type definitions for jQuery, you will get intelligent autocompletion for jQuery's members, saving you the tabbing between the editor and the documentation. There is an official repository of type definitions on GitHub (Definitely Typed). All of these definitions can be installed from the Types organization on NPM, as shown in Figure 9-1, or by running the command in Listing 9-1.

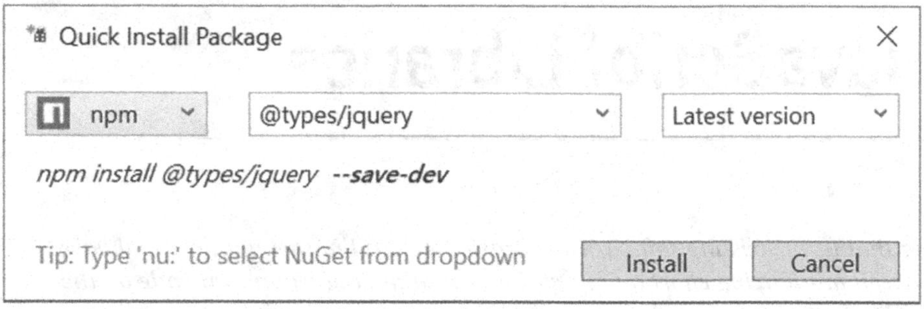

Figure 9-1. *Adding the jQuery type definition*

Note that in both cases, the type definitions are saved as a development dependency, as they are not required at runtime.

Listing 9-1. NPM install command for type definitions

```
npm install @types/jquery --save-dev
```

But before we get too far ahead by retrieving an existing type definition, let's start from scratch and cover scenarios where you may not have a definition available. This will mean you can handle your own JavaScript code, or a niche library that hasn't yet had a community contribution, just as easily as popular frameworks.

Creating Type Definitions

To illustrate the creation of type definitions, this chapter uses Knockout as an example of a JavaScript library. Knockout is an MVVM framework that simplifies dynamic user interfaces by mapping a model to a view, keeping the two in sync as changes occur. Although Knockout is used to illustrate the process of creating a type definition from scratch, this technique can be used to describe any JavaScript code in a way that TypeScript will understand – even your own legacy libraries.

Of course, if you are adding a popular library such as Knockout to your program, the chances are that someone has already undertaken the work of creating a type definition. Therefore, before you spend time making one of your own, check the listings on the Definitely Typed project or via NPM (where you'll find @types/knockout).

```
http://definitelytyped.org/
```

If you are using an open-source library that isn't listed, after you have created a type definition you can submit it to the Definitely Typed project to help other programmers in the future.

A sample of the running application is shown in Figure 9-2. The application allows you to reserve seats and select from a range of food options.

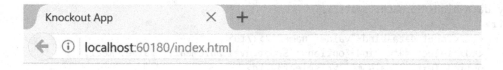

Your seat reservations (2)

Passenger name	Meal	Surcharge	
Steve	Standard (sandwich) ⌄	None	Remove
Bert	Standard (sandwich) ⌄	None	Remove

Reserve another seat

Figure 9-2. Knockout application

Creating a TypeScript Application with Knockout

The application in this chapter allows passengers to reserve seats on an airline along with an in-flight meal. The application consists of an HTML page and an app.ts file containing the Knockout code that binds the data to the view. The HTML page shown in Listing 9-2 provides the view for the application and comes from one of the Knockout tutorials available at

```
http://learn.knockoutjs.com/
```

The interesting parts of this example are the data-bind attributes used by Knockout to bind the view model to your HTML page. Each data-bind attribute takes an expression that describes where on the element the data should be bound, for example, the value attribute or the inner text, and which data should be displayed.

Listing 9-2. The HTML page

```html
<!DOCTYPE html>
<html lang="en">
<head>
    <meta charset="utf-8" />
    <title>Knockout App</title>
    <link rel="stylesheet" href="app.css" type="text/css" />
</head>
<body>
    <h1>Your seat reservations (<span data-bind="text: seats().length"></span>)</h1>

    <table>
        <thead>
            <tr>
                <th>Passenger name</th>
                <th>Meal</th>
                <th>Surcharge</th>
                <th></th>
            </tr>
        </thead>
```

235

```
        <tbody data-bind="foreach: seats">
            <tr>
                <td><input data-bind="value: name" /></td>
                <td><select data-bind="options: $root.availableMeals, value: meal,
                optionsText: 'mealName'"></select></td>
                <td data-bind="text: formattedPrice"></td>
                <td><a href="#" data-bind="click: $root.removeSeat">Remove</a></td>
            </tr>
        </tbody>
    </table>

    <button data-bind="click: addSeat, enable: seats().length < 5">Reserve another
    seat</button>

    <h2 data-bind="visible: totalSurcharge() > 0">
        Total surcharge: $<span data-bind="text: totalSurcharge().toFixed(2)"></span>
    </h2>
    <script src="knockout.js"></script>
    <script src="app.js"></script>
</body>
</html>
```

The app.ts file contains the code that binds the data to the view using Knockout, as shown in Listing 9-3. This file will not be changed throughout this section, but it will instead be used to drive out the type definitions that are needed to get past the compiler errors and provide quality autocompletion and type checking for Knockout.

Listing 9-3. The program in app.ts

```
// Class to represent a row in the seat reservations grid
function SeatReservation(name, initialMeal) {
    var self = this;
    self.name = name;
    self.meal = ko.observable(initialMeal);

    self.formattedPrice = ko.computed(function () {
        var price = self.meal().price;
        return price ? "$" + price.toFixed(2) : "None";
    });
}

// Overall viewmodel for this screen, along with initial state
function ReservationsViewModel() {
    var self = this;

    // Non-editable catalog data - would come from the server
    self.availableMeals = [
        { mealName: "Standard (sandwich)", price: 0 },
        { mealName: "Premium (lobster)", price: 34.95 },
        { mealName: "Ultimate (whole zebra)", price: 290 }
    ];
```

```
    // Editable data
    self.seats = ko.observableArray([
        new SeatReservation("Steve", self.availableMeals[0]),
        new SeatReservation("Bert", self.availableMeals[0])
    ]);

    // Computed data
    self.totalSurcharge = ko.computed(function () {
        var total = 0;
        for (var i = 0; i < self.seats().length; i++)
            total += self.seats()[i].meal().price;
        return total;
    });

    // Operations
    self.addSeat = function () {
        self.seats.push(new SeatReservation("", self.availableMeals[0]));
    }
    self.removeSeat = function (seat) { self.seats.remove(seat) }
}

ko.applyBindings(new ReservationsViewModel(), document.body);
```

If you place these files into your development environment, you will receive a number of errors from the TypeScript compiler due to Knockout's ko variable being unknown. An example of these errors is shown in Figure 9-3.

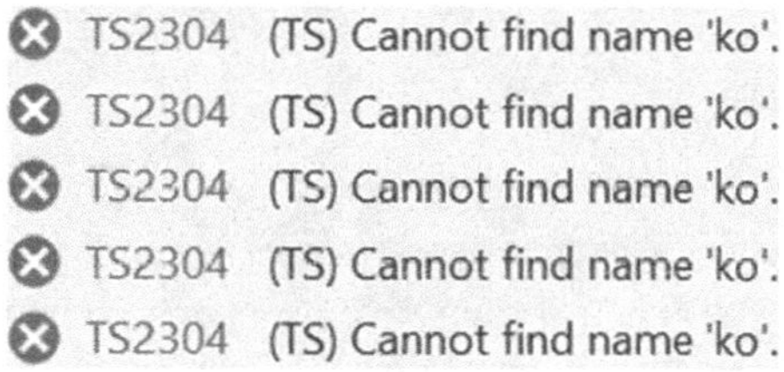

❌ TS2304   (TS) Cannot find name 'ko'.
❌ TS2304   (TS) Cannot find name 'ko'.
❌ TS2304   (TS) Cannot find name 'ko'.
❌ TS2304   (TS) Cannot find name 'ko'.
❌ TS2304   (TS) Cannot find name 'ko'.

Figure 9-3. *The compiler errors*

Silencing the Compiler

If you are just interested in silencing the compiler, you simply need to provide a quick hint that tells the compiler you will take responsibility for all of the code that uses the ko variable causing all of the errors. The type definition that provides this hint is shown in Listing 9-4.

The type definition would normally be placed in a file named knockout.d.ts and referenced in your app.ts using a reference comment or import statement.

Listing 9-4. The quick type definition fix

```
declare var ko: any;
```

When you use this kind of type definition, you turn down the compiler's offer of checking your program and you will not get autocompletion. Although this is a simple quick fix, it is likely that you will want to write a more comprehensive type definition.

Figure 9-4 shows that the type information in the editor is not yet useful, but all of the errors have gone away.

```
self.formattedPrice = ko.computed(function () {
    var price = self.m         [@] var ko: any
    return price ? "$"                    ed(2) : "None";
});
```

Figure 9-4. *The first iteration*

Iteratively Improving Type Definitions

One of the great things about writing type definitions is that you can write them in small increments. This means you can decide how much effort you want to invest in the type definition in return for the benefits of type checking and autocompletion that each increment provides.

Listing 9-5 shows a small incremental improvement in the type definition for Knockout. The Knockout interface supplies type information for all of the first-level properties that are used in the application: applyBindings, computed, observable, and observableArray. The specific details of these four properties are not given; they are simply assigned the any type.

The declared ko variable is updated to use the new Knockout interface, rather than the any type that was used to silence the compiler.

Listing 9-5. First-level type definition

```
interface Knockout {
    applyBindings: any;
    computed: any;
    observable: any;
    observableArray: any;
}

declare var ko: Knockout;
```

Despite the simplicity of this updated definition, it can prevent many common errors that would otherwise go undetected until the incorrect behavior was noticed in the application. Listing 9-6 shows two example errors that would be caught by the compiler based on this first-level type definition.

Listing 9-6. Compiler errors for incorrect code

```
// Spelling error caught by the compiler
self.meal = ko.observabel(initialMeal);

// Non-existent method caught by compiler
ko.apply(new ReservationsViewModel(), document.body);
```

The misspelling of `observabel` where `observable` should have been used and the nonexistent `apply` call where `applyBindings` should have been used will both result in compiler errors. This is as far as the compiler can go because only the names have been specified in the interface, not the method signatures.

Figure 9-5 shows the improved autocompletion with the updated definition. Although members are listed, their type information is not yet provided.

```
self.formattedPrice = ko.computed(function () {
    var price = self.meal
    return price ? "$" +            applyBindings
});                                 computed         (property) Knockout.computed: any
                                    observable
```

Figure 9-5. The second iteration

To increase the detail in the type definition, it is worth referring to the official documentation for the library. By referring to it once when creating a definition, you can save yourself having to do it every time you write code. In the case of `applyBindings`, the documentation states that the method can accept one or two of the following arguments:

- `viewModel`—the view model object you want to use with the declarative bindings it activates.

- `rootNode` (optional)—the part of the document you want to search in for data-bind attributes.

In other words, the `viewModel` is an object and must be supplied, whereas the `rootNode` is an `HTMLElement` and is optional. The updated Knockout interface with this additional type information is shown in Listing 9-7.

Listing 9-7. 'applyBindings' definition

```
interface Knockout {
    applyBindings(viewModel: {}, rootNode?: HTMLElement): void;
    computed: any;
    observable: any;
    observableArray: any;
}

declare var ko: Knockout;
```

■ **Note** Even if you don't yet know the exact signature of a function or object in a library, restricting the type to a general `Function` or `Object` type will prevent a number of possible errors, such as the passing of a simple type.

This updated type definition provides more comprehensive type checking, ensuring that at least one argument is passed to `applyBindings` and that all arguments passed are the correct type. It also allows development tools to provide useful type hints and autocompletion as shown in Figure 9-6.

```
ko.applyBindings()
```

    applyBindings(**viewModel: {}**, [rootNode?: HTMLElement]): void

Figure 9-6. *Autocompletion for the applyBindings method*

Another technique for expanding type information is to supply a signature that you infer from your own usage of the library. Both instances of ko.computed in the application are passed a function that performs the computation. You can update the type definition to show that the computed method expects a function to be supplied as shown in Listing 9-8.

If the return type of the evaluator was fixed, you could specify this in the type definition inside the parentheses. Likewise, if you need to use the value returned from the computed method, you could update the return type outside the parentheses to supply details of the return type.

Listing 9-8. 'computed' definition

```
interface Knockout {
    applyBindings(viewModel: any, rootNode?: any): void;
    computed: (evaluator: () => any) => any;
    observable: any;
    observableArray: any;
}

declare var ko: Knockout;
```

You can continue expanding the definition using the official documentation or by inferring the types based on examples to create the Knockout interface shown in Listing 9-9. This has both first- and second-level type information.

Listing 9-9. Complete second-level definition

```
interface Knockout {
    applyBindings(viewModel: {}, rootNode?: HTMLElement): void;
    computed: (evaluator: () => any) => any;
    observable: (value: any) => any;
    observableArray: (value: any[]) => any;
}

declare var ko: Knockout;
```

To complete the type definition, you repeat the process of transforming each use of any into a more detailed type until you no longer rely on hiding details with dynamic types. Each time a definition expands to an unmanageable size, you can divide it using an additional interface to help limit the complexity of any particular part of your definition.

Listing 9-10 demonstrates the "divide and conquer" technique by moving the details of the applyBindings method into a separate KnockoutApplyBindings interface. This is then used in the Knockout interface to bind the type information to the method.

Listing 9-10. Dividing type definitions into interfaces

```
interface KnockoutApplyBindings {
    (viewModel: {}, rootNode?: HTMLElement): void;
}

interface Knockout {
    applyBindings: KnockoutApplyBindings;
    computed: (evaluator: () => any) => any;
    observable: (value: any) => any;
    observableArray: (value: any[]) => any;
}

declare var ko: Knockout;
```

Although this type definition for Knockout is far from complete, it covers all of the features of Knockout needed to run the example application. You can add more type information as needed, investing only when you get a reasonable payback.

Converting a JavaScript Application

If you have an existing JavaScript application and are switching to TypeScript, there are three potential strategies for handling your old code:

- Write a type definition
- Add your JavaScript files into the compilation
- Add your JavaScript code to a TypeScript file

Writing a type definition for your own JavaScript code is the least desirable solution, as you'll be duplicating or wasting a huge amount of effort. Allowing the compiler to include your JavaScript code allows you to start the process of migrating your code to TypeScript; and moving it into a TypeScript file completes this process.

To illustrate the process of migrating your JavaScript code, we'll use the very basic JavaScript file shown in Listing 9-11. This file contains some arbitrary old processing code that we want to use in our new TypeScript program.

Listing 9-11. An old JavaScript file

```
function old_process(name) {
    return name + ' processed';
}
```

The new code calling the old JavaScript is shown in Listing 9-12.

Listing 9-12. The new code

```
class NewProcessor {
    process(name: string) {
        return old_process(name);
    }
}
```

When you attempt to compile the TypeScript file, you will see the error "mynewlib.ts(3,16): error TS2304: Cannot find name 'old_process'." This is because the old code is not visible to the compiler.

Listing 9-13. Compilation of just the new code

```
tsc mynewlib.ts --outDir ./dist
```

Before writing a type definition, or attempting to upgrade the old library to TypeScript, you can re-compile with JavaScript included. When including JavaScript files in compilation, it is best to redirect your output to a separate folder as the JavaScript input files cannot be overwritten. Listing 9-14 shows the compiler command that allows JavaScript files in the compilation, and includes both the old JavaScript file and the new TypeScript file in the compilation.

Listing 9-14. Compilation including JavaScript

```
tsc myoldlib.js mynewlib.ts --allowJs --outDir ./dist
```

By including the JavaScript file in the compilation, the compiler can infer type information in many cases, and the compiler error is now gone.

You can further improve this as shown in Listing 9-15, where the JavaScript dependency is made explicit in the TypeScript file.

Listing 9-15. JavaScript dependency

```
///<reference path="myoldlib.js" />

class NewProcessor {
    process(name: string) {
        return old_process(name);
    }
}
```

With the reference comment in place, you no longer need to specify the JavaScript file in your compilation. Additionally, your editor will now supply the inferred type information as autocompletion hints.

Listing 9-16. TypeScript and JavaScript compilation with reference comment

```
tsc mynewlib.ts --allowJs --outDir ./dist
```

To improve the developer experience further, you can start to move your JavaScript into TypeScript files, which allows you to add type annotations to improve the type information and assist the compiler where it is unable to understand a type. If your JavaScript code is particularly arcane, the compiler may not be able to infer many types.

If you have a large number of JavaScript files to upgrade, you can upgrade low-level dependencies to TypeScript first, while the other JavaScript files that depend on them continue to reference the compiled output from your TypeScript files. At runtime, it makes no difference whether the file was originally written in TypeScript or JavaScript as long as you add only type annotations and don't restructure the program.

It is best to save any restructuring work until your entire program is written in TypeScript as the refactoring support for TypeScript is more intelligent.

Summary

Almost every popular JavaScript library will already have a type definition listed on Definitely Typed and published via the Types organization on NPM, but if you do come across a more exotic library or a brand new one that isn't listed you can create your own type definitions. Using an iterative/incremental approach to writing type definitions allows you to get the best payback for the amount of time and effort you invest, and you can use the library's documentation to find the type information or infer it by reading examples.

You can reuse your own JavaScript code using the same technique of creating type definitions, but it is likely to be less time consuming to simply move your JavaScript into a TypeScript file and adding any type annotations that the compiler is unable to infer for you.

Whether you are writing type definitions or upgrading your JavaScript to TypeScript, the compiler may find mistakes that you never knew existed — you may be surprised what had been missed before.

Key Points

- Type definitions are usually placed inside a file with a .d.ts file extension.

- You can create new type definitions incrementally—you don't need to invest the time in generating type information for an entire library in one go.

- You can include JavaScript files in your TypeScript compilation.

- It is usually easier to upgrade a file from JavaScript to TypeScript than it is to create a type definition file.

- Because JavaScript is entirely dynamic, you will probably discover and fix bugs that you didn't know existed when you upgrade to TypeScript.

■ ■ ■

CHAPTER 10

Automated Testing

> *My definition of an expert in any field is a person who knows enough about what's really going on to be scared.*
>
> —P. J. Plauger

Automated testing is an essential topic for anyone writing the kind of large-scale applications TypeScript was invented for. By automating the testing of the program, developers can spend more time on new features and less time fixing defects. Automated tests are also essential to refactoring. No single method of testing provides a high-enough defect detection rate on its own. That means a combination of several kinds of testing is needed to detect a reasonable number of problems before the software is released.

It may be surprising, but the empirical evidence suggests that you will achieve the following defect detection rates for different kinds of testing, as documented by Steve McConnell in *Code Complete* (Microsoft Press, 2004):

- Unit testing detects up to 50% of defects.

- Integration testing detects up to 40% of defects.

- Regression testing detects up to 30% of defects.

These numbers suggest that as testing is performed later in the software development life cycle, more defects escape through the net. It is also well known that defects cost more when they are detected later. With this in mind, perhaps test-first programming provides one of the most effective methods of reducing bugs (along with pair programming, as collaborative working methods have been found to detect even more defects than any kind of testing). Proponents of test-driven design (TDD) will also be quick to point out that tests are a bonus, not the primary purpose of TDD, a tool that aids the design of cohesive units of code. They may be right, but the tests are good too!

The purpose of this chapter isn't to convert you to test-driven design. The information in this chapter will be useful whether you choose to write tests before you code, write tests after you have written part of a program, or wish to automate tests rather than perform them manually.

■ **Note**   The acronym TDD was originally coined for test-driven development, but the revised description of test-driven design pays tribute to the role this practice plays in helping to shape the design of your program.

Framework Choices

There are many high-quality testing frameworks written in JavaScript that you can use to test your program. Three of the most popular are listed here, but there are many more not listed and you don't even need to use a framework, as testing is possible in plain TypeScript code too.

- Jasmine

- Mocha

- Jest

The examples in this chapter are written using Jest, which is an easy-to-set-up testing framework that has gained some traction thanks to its close ties to the React framework.

The code shown in the examples covers the first few steps of the FizzBuzz coding kata. A coding kata is a method of practice that involves solving a simple problem that gradually adapts to challenge your design. Coding katas are explained in Appendix 4. The FizzBuzz kata is based on a children's game consisting of a series of counting rules. As you perform the kata, your aim is to pass only the next rule in the game; avoiding the temptation to think ahead. As you write more code, the design will emerge and you can refactor your program (safe in the knowledge that if your tests pass, you haven't accidentally changed the behavior).

Testing with Jest

Jest was written to complement the React framework, but it can be used to test any TypeScript or JavaScript program. The most common way to run Jest is via Node. The syntax is minimal and easy to learn and will be familiar to anyone who has used Jasmine in the past.

Installing Jest

The simplest way to add Jest to your project is to grab the package and type definition from NPM. You can do this by adding the packages to your development dependencies, as shown in Listing 10-1. You'll also notice that we are using the package.json file to tell Node what framework will handle our test run.

Listing 10-1. Package dependencies

```
{
  "name": "fizzbuzz",
  "version": "1.0.0",
  "devDependencies": {
    "@types/jest": "^21.1.0",
    "jest": "^21.1.0"
  },
  "scripts": {
    "test": "jest"
  }
}
```

Once you have downloaded these packages, you are ready to start writing code.

The First Specification

A simple implementation of the FizzBuzz class that will be tested is shown in Listing 10-2. The purpose of the class is to provide a correct answer when given a number played in the FizzBuzz game. The full implementation would respond by returning the played number or by substituting the number with a game word such as "Fizz," "Buzz," or "FizzBuzz" depending on whether the number is divisible by three, five, or both three and five

---

■ **Note**   The FizzBuzz game is usually played in a group. Each person takes a turn to speak the next number in a sequence starting at one. If the number is divisible by three, the player should say "Fizz" instead of the number. If the number is divisible by five the player should say "Buzz," and if the number is divisible by both three and five they should say "FizzBuzz."

Rather than implement all of this logic at once, specifications are used to drive the task of programming. Therefore, the class awaits the Jest specifications before implementing any behavior above and beyond the initial implementation that always returns the number one.

Listing 10-2. FizzBuzz code in FizzBuzz.ts

```
export class FizzBuzz {
    generate(input: number) {
        return 1;
    }
}
```

The Jest test that matches this behavior is shown in Listing 10-3. The test represents the first sentence in a conversation you may have with someone to whom you were explaining the rules of FizzBuzz for the first time. For example, "You should say '1' when the number 1 is played."

Listing 10-3. Jest test in FizzBuzz.test.ts

```
import { FizzBuzz } from './FizzBuzz';

describe('A FizzBuzz generator', () => {
    it('should return the number 1 when 1 is played', () => {
        const fizzBuzz = new FizzBuzz();

        const result = fizzBuzz.generate(1);

        expect(result).toBe(1);
    });
});
```

The describe method accepts the name for a suite of specifications and a function that will test each one. The it method represents a single specification. The language used in the suite and the specification is intended to be human readable. In this case, combining the suite description with the specification text reads,

A FizzBuzz generator should return the number 1 when 1 is played.

By choosing the language in your specification carefully, you can obtain free documentation from your test suite. You may even think of a better way of phrasing this description that describes the behavior in even more human terms. If that is the case, you should change the description to match your improved phrasing. It is worth agonizing a little over these details as it makes the specifications more valuable in the long run.

The function passed into the specification matches this claim by instantiating the FizzBuzz class, playing the number one and checking that the result is one.

Jest looks for tests in files named *.test.js, excluding the files in the node_modules folder, so the naming is important. If you forget this, no tests will be found when you run Jest.

To run Jest, simply run the following command shown in Listing 10-4 in your project folder.

Listing 10-4. Running Jest

```
npm test
```

The output from this command is shown in Figure 10-1.

```
PASS   .\FizzBuzz.test.js
  A FizzBuzz generator
    √ should return the number 1 when 1 is played

Test Suites: 1 passed, 1 total
Tests:       1 passed, 1 total
Snapshots:   0 total
Time:        1.554s
Ran all test suites.
```

Figure 10-1. *The Jest test result*

You now have everything set up and ready to start you testing. Next, you'll use additional tests to drive the implementation of your FizzBuzz program.

Driving the Implementation

Now the test automation is in place, it is possible to drive the implementation using new specifications. Listing 10-5 shows a second specification for the behavior that is expected when the number two is played in a game of FizzBuzz.

Listing 10-5. Extending the specification

```
import { FizzBuzz } from './FizzBuzz';

describe('A FizzBuzz generator', () => {
    it('should return the number 1 when 1 is played', () => {
        const fizzBuzz = new FizzBuzz();

        const result = fizzBuzz.generate(1);

        expect(result).toBe(1);
    });
```

```
    it('should return the number 2 when 2 is played', () => {
        const fizzBuzz = new FizzBuzz();

        const result = fizzBuzz.generate(2);

        expect(result).toBe(2);
    });
});
```

The second specification will fail because the FizzBuzz class is hard-coded to return a "1" no matter which value is played. The result of running the test is shown in Figure 10-2.

```
FAIL  .\FizzBuzz.test.js
  ● A FizzBuzz generator › should return the number 2 when 2 is played

    expect(received).toBe(expected)

    Expected value to be (using ===):
      2
    Received:
      1

      at Object.it (FizzBuzz.test.js:22:28)
      at process._tickCallback (internal/process/next_tick.js:109:7)

  A FizzBuzz generator
    √ should return the number 1 when 1 is played (22ms)
    × should return the number 2 when 2 is played

Test Suites: 1 failed, 1 total
Tests:       1 failed, 1 passed, 2 total
Snapshots:   0 total
Time:        1.631s
Ran all test suites.
npm ERR! Test failed.  See above for more details.
```

Figure 10-2. *The failing test result*

The failure message states that the test "Expected value to be: 2, Received: 1," this means that Jest failed the test because a "1" was returned, when a "2" was anticipated.

To pass the test, the FizzBuzz class must be updated as shown in Listing 10-6. Returning whichever number is input will pass both existing specifications. Although you may know that you will soon be adding more specifications that will not be covered by this implementation, waiting for a failing test before writing the code ensures that tests for each variation are written and fail before you write the code that causes them to pass. Knowing your tests will fail if the behavior is incorrect will give you confidence when you later refactor your program.

Listing 10-6. Updated FizzBuzz class

```
export class FizzBuzz {
    generate(input: number) {
        return input;
    }
}
```

When you rerun the specifications after this change, all specifications will now pass. The results are shown in Figure 10-3.

```
 PASS  .\FizzBuzz.test.js
  A FizzBuzz generator
    √ should return the number 1 when 1 is played
    √ should return the number 2 when 2 is played

Test Suites: 1 passed, 1 total
Tests:       2 passed, 2 total
Snapshots:   0 total
Time:        1.387s
Ran all test suites.
```

Figure 10-3. *The passing test suite*

Listing 10-7 shows the next specification that drives the implementation of the FizzBuzz class. This specification requires that when the number three is played, it should be substituted for the word "Fizz".

Listing 10-7. The Fizz specification

```
it('should return "Fizz" when 3 is played', () => {
    const fizzBuzz = new FizzBuzz();

    const result = fizzBuzz.generate(3);

    expect(result).toBe('Fizz');
});
```

After checking first that the specification fails, you can update the implementation shown in Listing 10-8. This update again is the simplest code that will pass the test.

Listing 10-8. The updated FizzBuzz class

```
class FizzBuzz {
    generate(input: number) : string | number {
        if (input === 3) {
            return 'Fizz';
        }

        return input;
    }
}
```

The results of running the specifications at this stage are shown in Figure 10-4. Read the test output to get a feeling for how the tests can describe the program in the language of the business domain.

```
PASS  .\FizzBuzz.test.js
  A FizzBuzz generator
    √ should return the number 1 when 1 is played
    √ should return the number 2 when 2 is played
    √ should return "Fizz" when 3 is played

Test Suites: 1 passed, 1 total
Tests:       3 passed, 3 total
Snapshots:   0 total
Time:        1.535s
Ran all test suites.
```

Figure 10-4. *The passing test suite of three tests*

Refactoring

Now that a number of specifications have been written and the code to pass them implemented, it is worth refactoring the program. Refactoring code involves changing the structure and design of a program without changing the behavior. The easiest way to know that you really are refactoring (and not inadvertently changing the actual function of the program) is to have automated tests that will highlight any incidental changes.

It also is worth highlighting the fact that your test code deserves to be as well written and maintainable as your production code, but less abstract. For this reason, Listing 10-9 shows the refactored specifications, where the duplicated instantiation of the FizzBuzz class has been moved into a beforeEach method, which Jest will automatically run before every specification.

Listing 10-9. Refactored specifications

```
import { FizzBuzz } from './FizzBuzz';

describe('A FizzBuzz generator', () => {
    let fizzBuzz: FizzBuzz;

    beforeEach(() => {
        fizzBuzz = new FizzBuzz();
    });

    it('should return the number 1 when 1 is played', () => {
        const result = fizzBuzz.generate(1);

        expect(result).toBe(1);
    });

    it('should return the number 2 when 2 is played', () => {
        const result = fizzBuzz.generate(2);

        expect(result).toBe(2);
    });
```

```
    it('should return "Fizz" when 3 is played', () => {
        const result = fizzBuzz.generate(3);

        expect(result).toBe('Fizz');
    });
});
```

Whenever you refactor your code, you should rerun all your tests to ensure that you haven't changed the behavior of your program. If your test suite fails, you can simply undo your change and have another go rather than debugging the program. Each iteration between test runs should be small enough to discard.

Listing 10-10. A working FizzBuzz class using conditional statements

```
export class FizzBuzz {
    generate(input: number): string | number {
        let output = '';

        if (input % 3 === 0) {
            output += 'Fizz';
        }

        if (input % 5 === 0) {
            output += 'Buzz';
        }

        return output === '' ? input : output;
    }
}
```

The code in Listing 10-10 shows a working version of the FizzBuzz class that covers the default rule of returning a number as well as the three variations for Fizz, Buzz, and FizzBuzz. At this point, although the generate method is still quite short, it is possible to see alternate designs emerging from the code. In particular, as new rules are added (perhaps numbers divisible by seven should return 'Bazz'), you may decide to introduce and adapt a design pattern to capture the specific rules.

■ **Note**   The FizzBuzz coding kata is often solved with a design pattern called a *chain of responsibility*, although there are other possible solutions.

The specifications that were created to drive this implementation are shown in Listing 10-11. There are now eight specifications in total to cover the four possible kinds of response.

Listing 10-11. The specifications for the working FizzBuzz class

```
import { FizzBuzz } from './FizzBuzz';

describe('A FizzBuzz generator', () => {
    let fizzBuzz: FizzBuzz;
    const FIZZ = 'Fizz';
    const BUZZ = 'Buzz'
    const FIZZ_BUZZ = 'FizzBuzz';
```

```
    beforeEach(() => {
        fizzBuzz = new FizzBuzz();
    });

    it('should return the number 1 when 1 is played', () => {
        const result = fizzBuzz.generate(1);

        expect(result).toBe(1);
    });

    it('should return the number 2 when 2 is played', () => {
        const result = fizzBuzz.generate(2);

        expect(result).toBe(2);
    });

    it('should return "Fizz" when 3 is played', () => {
        const result = fizzBuzz.generate(3);

        expect(result).toBe(FIZZ);
    });

    it('should return "Fizz" when 6 is played', () => {
        const result = fizzBuzz.generate(6);

        expect(result).toBe(FIZZ);
    });

    it('should return "Buzz" when 5 is played', () => {
        const result = fizzBuzz.generate(5);

        expect(result).toBe(BUZZ);
    });

    it('should return "Buzz" when 10 is played', () => {
        const result = fizzBuzz.generate(10);

        expect(result).toBe(BUZZ);
    });

    it('should return "FizzBuzz" when 15 is played', () => {
        const result = fizzBuzz.generate(15);

        expect(result).toBe(FIZZ_BUZZ);
    });

    it('should return "FizzBuzz" when 30 is played', () => {
        const result = fizzBuzz.generate(30);

        expect(result).toBe(FIZZ_BUZZ);
    });

});
```

As well as testing the FizzBuzz class, these specifications supply accurate documentation for the program. The output is shown in Figure 10-5. You may notice that Jest has marked one of the tests with its time to execute (15 ms), which helps you to identify any tests that are slowing down your test suite.

```
PASS   .\FizzBuzz.test.js
  A FizzBuzz generator
    √ should return the number 1 when 1 is played
    √ should return the number 2 when 2 is played
    √ should return "Fizz" when 3 is played
    √ should return "Fizz" when 6 is played
    √ should return "Buzz" when 5 is played
    √ should return "Buzz" when 10 is played
    √ should return "FizzBuzz" when 15 is played (15ms)
    √ should return "FizzBuzz" when 30 is played

Test Suites: 1 passed, 1 total
Tests:       8 passed, 8 total
Snapshots:   0 total
Time:        1.509s
Ran all test suites.
```

Figure 10-5. *The passing test suite of three tests*

These tests are a form of executable specification — a living form of documentation that also proves your program performs the documented behaviors.

Isolating Dependencies

There may come a time when you need to test a part of your code that depends on a resource, which makes your tests brittle. For example, it may depend on a third-party API or on a database in a particular state. If you need to test code without relying on these dependencies, you can isolate them when testing using the techniques described in this section.

In many programming languages, it has become natural to reach for a mocking framework whenever you need to supply a test double. In TypeScript, though, creation of test doubles is so easy you may never need to search for a framework.

Listing 10-12 shows a modified version of the FizzBuzz class that relies on localStorage, which in TypeScript implements the Storage interface. The constructor takes in the storage object and the generate function uses it to get the display message to be shown in the case of "Fizz".

Listing 10-12. A FizzBuzz class that relies on storage

```
class FizzBuzz {
    constructor(private storage: Storage) {

    }

    generate(input: number): string | number {
        if (input === 3) {
```

```
            return this.storage.getItem('FizzText');
        }

        return input;
    }
}
```

You can satisfy this dependency with a simple object as shown in Listing 10-13. The `storage` variable matches just enough of the `Storage` interface to pass the test. Unlike other programming languages, this solution to the test double issue is so easy; you hardly need to consider using a framework to solve the problem.

Listing 10-13. Using an object

```
describe('A FizzBuzz generator', () => {
    it('should return "FakeFizz" when 3 is played', () => {
        // Create a test double for storage
        var storage: any = {
            getItem: () => 'FakeFizz'
        };

        const fizzBuzz = new FizzBuzz(storage);

        const result = fizzBuzz.generate(3);

        expect(result).toBe('FakeFizz');
    });
});
```

On the whole, you should stick with simple objects as test doubles, and your tests should check outcomes, not specific implementation details. Knowing that you get "Fizz" when you play three is a strong behavioral test, but checking that a `storage` object has been called to supply a value matching a specific key is not a good test at all as this would fail when you change the implementation details.

Summary

Hopefully the value of automated testing has been demonstrated in this chapter. However, if you are still skeptical you can try running coding katas both with and without tests to see if it helps to make up your mind. You can read more in Appendix 4.

Although this chapter has used Jest for all the examples, using Mocha or Jasmine is just as easy, and both provide an equally simple syntax. Whatever you use to run tests, try to craft the output so it presents like human-readable documentation, so if anyone ever asks for documentation you can simply provide the output from your test suite.

I have created an implementation of a Gherkin-language based behavior-driven framework for TypeScript called TypeSpec that you can use to combine business specifications and test automation, but I have used Jest in this chapter as I would prefer programmers to start with more common tools. You can find out more about TypeSpec on GitHub:

https://github.com/Steve-Fenton/TypeSpec

Key Points

- Automated unit tests are more effective than integration testing or regression testing (although a good strategy is to use many kinds of testing to get the best possible defect detection rate).

- There are a lot of frameworks for JavaScript and TypeScript, but you can look at Jest, Jasmine, and Mocha if you want to narrow things down a bit.

- You can use Jest to write specifications that act as tests and documentation.

- Driving the implementation with specifications ensures tests fail if the behavior is not correct. Writing tests after the implementation doesn't guarantee the tests will ever fail.

- You should refactor both production code and test code.

- You can isolate your dependencies using simple objects, and these are preferable to clever tools that may bind your test too tightly to the implementation.

APPENDIX 1

■ ■ ■

JavaScript Quick Reference

If you aren't already familiar with JavaScript, this quick reference is intended to provide an overview of the core features of JavaScript you'll be using within a TypeScript program. Where a feature has been described alongside the TypeScript language, it has been omitted here.

Variables

Variables are used to store the application's state in JavaScript and can contain data of any type from strings to numbers to objects to functions.

Listing A1-1 shows a selection of variables with simple types. Variables can be assigned at the same time as they are declared, in a single statement, or they can be declared and assigned separately. A variable will have the type corresponding to the value that was most recently assigned to it. If no value has been assigned, the value of the variable will be undefined.

There are two keywords you can choose from to declare a variable, let and const. Both declarations are block scoped, just like most other curly-braced languages. When you declare a variable with the let keyword, you can reassign values to the variable later in your code. When you use the const keyword, you are not able to reassign values. The restriction on assigning to a const variable does not make it immutable, it just means the variable itself cannot be overwritten. When choosing between these keywords, start with const and upgrade to let when you decide you need to reassign the variable. Both let and const are preferred over the var keyword, which is function scoped, rather than block scoped.

Listing A1-1. Variables

```
// Variable declaration

let variable;

// Variable assignment

variable = 'A string is assigned';

// Dynamic assignment (changes variable's type to a number)

variable = 10;
```

You can store arrays in a variable. You can use the empty literal [ ] to create a new empty array and add items using array.push. You can also create and fill an array in a single step by placing the value inside the array literal, as shown in Listing A1-2.

S. Fenton, *Pro TypeScript*, https://doi.org/10.1007/978-1-4842-3249-1

Listing A1-2. Arrays

```
// Creating an empty array and adding values

const myArray = [];

myArray.push(1);
myArray.push(3);
myArray.push(5);

// Adding values using an array literal

const myLiteralArray = [1, 3, 5];
```

An *object* can be used to represent data in complex structures. Objects can contain properties that each are like a variable and can contain strings, numbers, arrays, functions, and other objects. Just as with arrays, you can create an empty object using an empty object literal {}, or create and fill an object in a single step by placing the properties within the object literal. Both styles are shown in Listing A1-3.

Listing A1-3. Objects

```
// Objects

const myObject = {};

myObject.title = 'Example Object';
myObject.value = 5;

// Object literals

const myLiteralObject = {
    title: 'Example Object',
    value: 5
};
```

In all the examples, literal assignments have been made, rather than instantiating values using the new keyword. It is possible to create arrays using new Array(), objects using new Object(), and even strings using new String() — but in JavaScript the literal syntax is preferred.

Functions

Functions can be used to create reusable blocks of code in your program. You can create a function using either a function declaration or a function expression as shown in Listing A1-4.

Listing A1-4. Functions

```
// Function declaration

function myFunction(name) {
    return 'Hello ' + name;
}
```

```
// 'Hello Steve'
let greeting = myFunction('Steve');

// Function expression

var myFunctionExpression = function (name) {
    return 'Hi ' + name;
};

// 'Hi Steve'
greeting = myFunctionExpression('Steve');
```

When you declare a function using a function declaration it is created at parse time, which means it is available throughout your program wherever its scope is available. Using a function expression means the function is evaluated at runtime, and it can only be called where both its scope is available and the calling code appears *after* the function expression.

Conditional Statements

Conditional statements can be used to branch logic in your program. You can use conditional statements to execute code only if a certain condition is met.

If statements allow code to be branched based on a custom condition that evaluates to either true or false. The if statements shown in Listing A1-5 execute different code depending on the value in the age variable, for example.

Listing A1-5. If statement

```
// If statements

const age = 21;

if (age > 18) {
    // Code to execute if age is greater than 18
}

if (age > 40) {
    // Code to execute if age is greater than 40
} else if (age > 18) {
    // Code to execute if age is greater than 18
    // but less than 41
} else {
    // Code to execute in all other cases
}
```

A *switch statement* is useful for controlling multiple branches based on a single variable and where only specific values will cause branching. Listing A1-6 shows a typical switch statement that can execute different code based on the value of the style variable. The default condition will execute if no other condition has been executed.

Listing A1-6. Switch statement

```
// Switch statements

const styles = {
    tranditional: 1,
    modern: 2,
    postModern: 3,
    futuristic: 4
};

const style = styles.tranditional;

switch (style) {
    case styles.tranditional:
        // Code to execute for traditional style
        break;
    case styles.modern:
        // Code to execute for modern style
        break;
    case styles.postModern:
        // Code to execute for post modern style
        break;
    case styles.futuristic:
        // Code to execute for futuristic style
        break;
    default:
        throw new Error('Style not known: ' + style);
}
```

■ **Note**   Switch statements work even better with TypeScript enumerations, which are described in Chapter 1.

Loops

Loops are used to repeat a section of code in your program. The most common loop in JavaScript is the *for loop*, which can be used to repeat an action for every item in an array as shown in Listing A1-7.

Listing A1-7. For loop

```
const names = ['Lily', 'Rebecca', 'Debbye', 'Ann'];

for (let i = 0; i < names.length; i++) {
    console.log(names[i]);
}
```

You can simplify the code in Listing A1-7 using a for-of loop. A for-of loop removes the need to track the index number with a variable, and sets the value of each iteration directly in a variable for you to use. Listing A1-8 shows the for-of equivalent of the first example; the result is more expressive and readable.

Listing A1-8. For-of loop

```
const names = ['Lily', 'Rebecca', 'Debbye', 'Ann'];

for (let name in names) {
    console.log(name);
}
```

A *while loop* allows a section of code to be repeated until a condition is met, as shown in listing A1-9. A common use of this would be to add a character to a string and repeat the process until the string matched a certain length.

Listing A1-9. While loop

```
let counter = 10;

while (counter > 0) {
    counter--;
    console.log(counter);
}
```

A *do-while loop* is almost identical to a while loop, except it will run the code at least one time, even if the condition doesn't match.

Listing A1-10. Do-while loop

```
let counter = 0;

do {
    counter--;
    console.log(counter);
} while (counter > 0);
```

Listing A1-10 is like the while loop shown previously, except the counter variable already matches the exit condition because it is not greater than zero. Despite this, the code runs one time before the condition is evaluated, causing the loop to exit.

Strings

Although large volumes of string manipulation can be an indication of a design error, there are some notable developments in how strings are handled in JavaScript that are worth knowing about. Listing A1-11 shows several mechanisms for handling strings.

Listing A1-11. Strings

```
const name = 'Jamie';

// Traditional strings

const classicString = 'Line One\n' +
    'Line Two\n' +
    'Line Three. Hello ' + name + '!';
```

```
// Back-ticked strings

const backtickedString = `Line One
Line Two
Line Three. Hello ${name}!`;

// 'Five plus seven is 12.'
const expressionString = `Five plus seven is ${5 + 7}.`;
```

Traditional strings can use either single or double quotes. Back-ticked strings accept newline characters and allow string interpolation, surrounded by ${}. String interpolation allows variables and expressions to be instated.

Promises

Promises are fast becoming a core feature of JavaScript applications and provide a simple mechanism for coordinating asynchronous actions. Listing A1-12 shows how to program with promises, using the fetch API to retrieve data from a URL.

Listing A1-12. Working with promises

```
fetch('/Your/URL/').then(function (response) {
    // Response received
    if (response.status >= 200 && response.status < 300) {
        // We got a success status code
    }
}).catch(function (error) {
    // Request failed
});
```

There are three parts to a promise: a call to a function that returns a promise, such as the fetch function; a handler for the then result, which is called on success; and a handler for the catch result, which is called when an error occurs.

Listing A1-13. Using your own promises

```
let promise = new Promise(function (resolve, reject) {
    window.setTimeout(function () {
        if (true) {
            resolve('Success');
        } else {
            reject('Failed');
        }
    }, 1000);
});

promise.then(function (message) {
    alert(message);
}).catch(function (error) {
    alert(error);
});
```

When you implement your own promise, using new Promise, your function should accept arguments for handlers that you call in the event of success and failure. These handlers are a loose contract; any arguments that you pass to the resolve and reject functions can be of any type, although conventionally the reject function should be passed as an error message.

Summary

Although this appendix is a fast dash through some very basic features of JavaScript, they are the essential parts that you need to know to get started with TypeScript. Where a feature has substantial relevance to the TypeScript language, I have included it with the TypeScript information rather than in this appendix. There is much more to learn in JavaScript and in the different environments it executes in than I could place here.

Having read this quick start, you should be able to read this book without coming across anything too surprising as all the TypeScript language features are described in detail.

TypeScript Compiler

The TypeScript compiler may well be hidden behind your development tools, but it is worth familiarizing yourself with the various compiler options. Because there are now more than 70 different compiler flags, I have chosen to provide more information on the more common options. The compiler itself is optimized for compiling entire projects, rather than individual files. Running the compiler against the whole project means that you are only loading the standard library once, rather than many times. You may find that running compilation for a single file, including all its dependencies, takes nearly as long as compiling the entire project.

The compiler is called `tsc.exe` and is usually found in the following directory on Windows:

- C:\Program Files (x86)\Microsoft SDKs\TypeScript\[Version]\tsc.exe

To run the compiler, simply call `tsc` from the command line passing in your program's root file name, as demonstrated below. You may need to enter the full address of the `tsc.exe` file. If you get bored of entering the full path, you can add the path to the TypeScript folder to your environment variables.

```
tsc app.ts
```

You can also run the TypeScript compiler using Node on any operating system, as the compiler is written in TypeScript and compiled to JavaScript, as shown here. You will need to enter the full path to the `tsc.js` file (not to the `.ts` file).

```
node tsc.js app.ts
```

Getting Help

If you ever have trouble remembering all the options for the compiler, you can get help using one of the following commands, which will display a list of all the available compiler flags you can set. Each compiler flag exposes a setting that allows you to change how the compiler behaves.

```
tsc --help
node tsc.js
```

Sample File

To illustrate some of the key differences between compiler options, the code in Listing A2-1 has been used to generate output using some of the different compiler options.

Listing A2-1. Sample TypeScript code

```
import * as Dependency from './module';

export class Example extends Dependency.BaseClass {
    exampleMethod(): number {
        return 5;
    }
}

// Comment
let example = new Example();

const val = example.exampleMethod();
```

By examining the JavaScript generated by this listing, you will understand some of the differences in module loading, and down-level compilation, which allows you to use the latest features in TypeScript and have them converted into JavaScript compatible with older versions of the ECMAScript specification. When the output is substantially similar, I have removed the similar lines to make the important differences stand out.

Common Flags

There are a few compiler flags that are so common you are almost certain to use them at some point. These flags are described in the following sections.

Module Kind

The `module` compiler flag is used to generate code that loads external modules using either CommonJS or AMD module patterns. The valid values for the module kind are `commonjs` and `amd`.

```
tsc --module UMD app.ts
```

Universal Module Definition (UMD) creates code that can run in both prevailing module styles, Asynchronous Module Definition (AMD) and CommonJS. For example, this allows you to write code that is loaded by RequireJS in web browsers, or by Node on the server. The output for this mode is more verbose than either AMD or CommonJS because it includes code to feature check to use the correct loading style.

Listing A2-2. UMD modules

```
(function (factory) {
    if (typeof module === "object" && typeof module.exports === "object") {
        var v = factory(require, exports);
        if (v !== undefined) module.exports = v;
    }
    else if (typeof define === "function" && define.amd) {
        define(["require", "exports", "./module"], factory);
    }
})(function (require, exports) {
    "use strict";
```

```
    exports.__esModule = true;
    var Dependency = require("./module");
    // Removed for brevity
    exports.Example = Example;
    // Comment
    var example = new Example();
    var val = example.exampleMethod();
});
```

The AMD module output in Listing A2-3 is shorter as it doesn't need to perform a feature check. This code will be compatible with module loaders such as RequireJS and the Dojo Toolkit.

Listing A2-3. AMD modules

```
define(["require", "exports", "./module"], function (require, exports, Dependency) {
    "use strict";
    exports.__esModule = true;
    // Removed for brevity
    exports.Example = Example;
    // Comment
    var example = new Example();
    var val = example.exampleMethod();
});
```

CommonJS modules are most famously implemented by Node, but they are also found in MongoDB, and CouchDB, among others. Listing A2-4 shows the output using the CommonJS module flag.

Listing A2-4. CommonJS modules

```
"use strict";
exports.__esModule = true;
var Dependency = require("./module");
// Removed for brevity
exports.Example = Example;
// Comment
var example = new Example();
var val = example.exampleMethod();
```

One emerging and notable module style is the ECMAScript module syntax, shown in Listing A2-5. This style of module loading is the most similar to the original TypeScript code.

Listing A2-5. ESNext modules

```
import * as Dependency from './module';
// Removed for brevity
export { Example };
// Comment
var example = new Example();
var val = example.exampleMethod();
```

Both AMD and System module kinds can also be used with the --outFile flag, which combines your program into a single JavaScript file. Before you do this, please read about this flag in the Combined Output section below.

267

ECMAScript Target Version

The `target` flag allows you to set the target ECMAScript version. Currently you can target multiple versions of the ECMAScript specification, including ES3, ES5, ES2015, ES2016, ES2017, or whatever the latest version is using ESNext. For most language features, the compiler will compile the code down to the version you specify, although a small number of features may not be available.

If you are targeting ECMAScript 3, you can't use properties in your TypeScript program as they rely on an ECMAScript 5 feature. When the ECMAScript 6 option is added, it will perform fewer transformations during compilation. This is because ECMAScript 6 supports many of the basic TypeScript features, such as modules, classes, arrow functions, and special parameter types. The ECMAScript 6 support should also allow the new JavaScript features such as `let`, generators, and destructors.

```
tsc --target ES5 app.ts
```

Listing A2-6 shows down-level compilation to the ECMAScript 5 specification. Keywords such as `const` and `let` can't be used, so they are replaced with the `var` keyword. In cases where this would affect the scope of the variable, additional code is generated to enclose the var keyword in a new function scope. Classes are replaced with an immediately invoked function expression (IIFE).

Listing A2-6. ES5 target

```
import * as Dependency from './module';
var Example = (function (_super) {
    __extends(Example, _super);
    function Example() {
        return _super !== null && _super.apply(this, arguments) || this;
    }
    Example.prototype.exampleMethod = function () {
        return 5;
    };
    return Example;
}(Dependency.BaseClass));
export { Example };
// Comment
var example = new Example();
var val = example.exampleMethod();
```

When targeting the latest version of the ECMAScript specification, which supports the module loading, class syntax, and variable declarations that you are using in TypeScript, the JavaScript looks almost identical to your TypeScript as you can see in Listing A2-7.

Listing A2-7. ESNext target

```
import * as Dependency from './module';
export class Example extends Dependency.BaseClass {
    exampleMethod() {
        return 5;
    }
}
// Comment
let example = new Example();
const val = example.exampleMethod();
```

TypeScript tracks the ECMAScript proposal, which means the latest versions of TypeScript and JavaScript will be very similar. The only real difference in the compiled code is type erasure, as there are no plans to add type annotations to JavaScript at this time.

Generate Declarations

The `declaration` flag will generate an additional file with the suffix `.d.ts`, which will contain ambient declarations for your code.

```
tsc --declaration app.ts
```

Listing A2-8 shows the generated declaration file, which you can use as part of your packaging strategy for your program.

Listing A2-8. app.d.ts declaration file

```
import * as Dependency from './module';
export declare class Example extends Dependency.BaseClass {
    exampleMethod(): number;
}
```

This feature is useful if you are packaging you program for use via a package manager such as NPM.

Remove Comments

The `removeComments` flag erases all comments from the output, which will make it smaller if you have a lot of comments in your source code.

```
tsc --removeComments true app.ts
```

Combined Output

You can combine your entire TypeScript program into a single output file using the out compiler flag. When you use the out flag you must also supply a name for the combined file.

```
tsc --out final.js app.ts
```

The concept of squashing an entire program into a single output file runs antithetical to the purpose of TypeScript, which is to write large programs. Even if you are writing a smaller program using TypeScript to learn the habits, module loading is one of the key habits to develop.

Code Quality Flags

The following flags can help you improve the quality of your code and catch loose areas at compile time. If you are writing a new program from scratch, it should be a simple task to switch these on and follow the guidance of the compiler. For an existing program, you may decide to switch these flags on, fix some of the problems the compiler finds, and then switch it back off. This will let you refine your code in many discrete sessions, until you can finally leave them switched on permanently.

Defaults

There are many options that are set to the correct option, in terms of code quality, by default. The values for all the following flags are set to false, and ought to be left that way:

- --allowUnreachableCode
- --allowUnusedLabels
- --noImplicitUseStrict
- --noStrictGenericChecks
- --suppressExcessPropertyErrors
- --suppressImplicitAnyIndexErrors

Strict Switch

On top of the defaults, you can switch on a strict mode to enable the four most common quality flags:

- `--noImplicitAny`: catches cases where a type cannot be inferred, and an annotation is needed
- `--noImplicitThis`: catches expressions where the `this` keyword has an implied any type
- `--alwaysStrict`: parses in strict mode and inserts `"use strict"` statements for each file
- `--strictNullChecks`: catches null and undefined values, preventing accidentally unassigned variables and properties

The strict flag is shown below:

```
tsc --strict true app.ts
```

Catch Accidental Fallthroughs

The `noFallthroughCasesInSwitch` flag warns you about any cases within a switch statement that are not empty, and are missing the `break` keyword.

```
tsc --noFallthroughCasesInSwitch true app.ts
```

The code in listing A2-9 shows a common fallthrough error, which is often accidental. The fallthrough error is only given if the case is not empty, as this represents poorly structured code in terms of readability and maintenance concerns.

Listing A2-9. Accidental fallthrough case

```
// Error: Fallthrough case in switch.
switch (num) {
    case 0:
    case 1:
        // Allowed
        num = num * 2;
        break;
```

```
    case 2:
        // Allowed
        num = num * 4;
        break;

    case 2:
        // Not Allowed
        num = num * 6;
        // No break statement - fallthrough

    case 4:
        // Allowed
        num = num * 8;
        break;
}
```

Catch Missing Return Statements

The noImplicitReturns flag warns you about functions or methods that have a code branch that is missing a return statement.

tsc --noImplicitReturns true app.ts

Listing A2-10 would result in valid JavaScript, as it is allowable to leave out the return statement, resulting in an undefined return value. Anyone who has written JavaScript code for a long time will appreciate the benefits of forcing an explicit return statement for all code branches, as without it you are likely to be surprised by the behavior of your program.

Listing A2-10. Accidental fallthrough case

```
 // Error: Not all code paths return a value
function invert(cond: boolean) {
    if (cond) {
        return false;
    }

    // missing return statement  here
}
```

Unused Local Variables

The noUnusedLocals flag warns you when a variable is never used. This helps to identify redundant code that you can delete.

tsc --noUnusedLocals true app.ts

Unused Parameters

The noUnusedParameters flag highlights function and method parameters that are not used. This flag is trickier than many of the other code quality flags, as there may be cases where you want to ignore a parameter that is passed to a function. You can use this flag until you come across this scenario, and then choose to remove it if causes you problems.

```
tsc --noUnusedParameters true app.ts
```

JavaScript Compilation

If you are making the transition from JavaScript to TypeScript, these compiler options can help you bridge the gap when you have your code divided between the two languages.

Allow JavaScript

The allowJs flag allows JavaScript files to be included in the compilation.

```
tsc --allowJs true app.ts
```

Check JavaScript

The checkJs flag can be used alongside the allowJs flag and causes the compiler to report errors in the JavaScript files.

```
tsc --allowJs true --checkJs true app.ts
```

APPENDIX 3

Bitwise Flags

As described in Chapter 1, you can use an enumeration to define bit flags. Bit flags allow a series of items to be selected or deselected by switching individual bits in a sequence on and off. To ensure that each value in an enumeration relates to a single bit, the numbering must follow the binary sequence whereby each value is a power of two, for example:

```
1, 2, 4, 8, 16, 32, 64, 128, 256, 512, 1024, 2048, 4096, and so on
```

Listing A3-1 is a copy of the example from Chapter 1 and shows bit flags in action. In place of manually assigning powers-of-2, the shift operator is used to switch on the appropriate bit. To add to this enum, you simply increment the right-hand operator by one for each new value. When working with enums, the TypeScript compiler substitutes the expressions with plain numbers, whereas expressions elsewhere are left intact.

- 1 << 0 with 1
- 1 << 1 with 2
- 1 << 2 with 4
- 1 << 3 with 8, and so on.

Listing A3-1. Flags

```
enum DiscFlags {
        None = 0,
        Drive = 1 << 0,
        Influence = 1 << 1,
        Steadiness = 1 << 2,
        Conscientiousness = 1 << 3
}
// Using flags
var personality = DiscFlags.Drive | DiscFlags.Conscientiousness;

// Testing flags

// true
var hasD = (personality & DiscFlags.Drive) == DiscFlags.Drive;

// false
var hasI = (personality & DiscFlags.Influence) == DiscFlags.Influence;
```

© Steve Fenton 2018
S. Fenton, *Pro TypeScript*, https://doi.org/10.1007/978-1-4842-3249-1

```
// false
var hasS = (personality & DiscFlags.Steadiness) == DiscFlags.Steadiness;

// true
var hasC = (personality & DiscFlags.Conscientiousness) == DiscFlags.Conscientiousness;
```

Bit Flags Explained

The flags in Listing A3-1 are illustrated in Table A3-1. Because the bit flags are represented as 32-bit integers in big-endian order, the bit representing the greatest value appears on the left. To show the values in the order they are represented, "Conscientiousness" is shown on the left, because it is represented by the bit with the greatest value in the example: 8.

Table A3-1. *Bit flags illustrated*

Conscientiousness (8)	Steadiness (4)	Influence (2)	Drive (1)	Binary	Decimal
0	0	0	1	0001	1
0	0	1	0	0010	2
0	1	0	0	0100	4
1	0	0	0	1000	8
0	0	1	1	**0011**	**3**
1	1	1	1	**1111**	**15**

If the flag is switched on, the column shows a 1. If the flag is switched off the column shows a 0. The binary value shows that each digit in the binary representation corresponds to a value in the enumeration; whenever "Drive" is switched on, the rightmost column will contain a 1. This is the reason the value of an enumeration being used for flags must use the binary sequence as it is the only sequence that means each flag will only affect a single bit in the set.

Bitwise Operations

Using bit flags also means you can use bitwise operators to manipulate the bits representing the items in the enumeration. Listing A3-2 uses a bitwise AND operator (&) to find matching traits in two sets of flags. Only items that are switched on in both sets of flags are switched on in the result of the bitwise AND operation; this is why a bitwise AND is used to see if an individual value is switched on.

Listing A3-2. Finding matches with a bitwise AND

```
// Both personalityA and personalityB include DiscFlags.Influence
var personalityA = DiscFlags.Drive | DiscFlags.Influence | DiscFlags.Conscientiousness;
var personalityB = DiscFlags.Influence | DiscFlags.Steadiness;

// The result of a bitwise AND contains only matching flags
```

```
// DiscFlags.Influence
var matchingTraits = personalityA & personalityB;

// false
var hasD = (matchingTraits & DiscFlags.Drive) == DiscFlags.Drive;

// true
var hasI = (matchingTraits & DiscFlags.Influence) == DiscFlags.Influence;

// false
var hasS = (matchingTraits & DiscFlags.Steadiness) == DiscFlags.Steadiness;

// false
var hasC = (matchingTraits & DiscFlags.Conscientiousness) == DiscFlags.Conscientiousness;
```

The results of various bitwise operations are illustrated in Table A3-2. They produce the following results:

- AND results in bits being switched on if both sets have the bit switched on.

- OR results in bits being switched on if either, or both, of the sets have the bit switched on.

- XOR results in bits being switched on if one of the sets has the bit switched on. The bit is switched off if neither one of the sources has the bit switched on or if both of the sources has the bit switched on.

- NOT inverts a set, switching off all of the "on" bits and switching on all of the "off" bits.

Table A3-2. *Bitwise operations*

First set	Second set	Bitwise operation	Result
1011	1101	& (AND)	1001
1001	0011	| (OR)	1011
1011	1101	^ (XOR)	0110
1011	n/a	~ (NOT)	0100

APPENDIX 4

■ ■ ■

Coding Katas

Coding katas have become increasingly popular since their invention in 1999. If you want to improve your programming chops, coding katas are like a sharpening block you can use to hone your skills. This appendix will explain what coding katas are and how to get the most out of them. There are some links to coding kata collections and some books that you can use to practice your TypeScript programming.

A coding kata is a method of practicing programming techniques and many katas are designed to exercise your design skills and give you mastery of your tools and workflow. The instructions for a kata describe a problem that simulates real-world coding, sometimes on a very small scale. It is possible to repeat a kata by adding constraints, for example, limiting the language features that can be used, or attempting to complete the kata without using a mouse. Each variation of a kata can allow you to learn or practice different skills.

Because a coding kata is just practice, you can try out ideas safely because you can always delete the code and start from scratch: something you may opt to do several times even if your first attempt goes well. You can even use a kata to try out a new programming language or to try out a new code editor.

You can perform a coding kata individually, but there is even more value in pairing with other programmers to work on a kata. Not only will you be working on your programming skills, you'll be sharing and learning with your partners. Group kata workshops (sometimes called Coding Dojos) supply opportunities to pair with plenty of other programmers. You can even tackle a problem as one big group in a mob-programming session. The more diverse you make your practice, the more experience you bring to your real work. Some of the benefits of coding katas are the following:

- Learning features of your development environment, such as keyboard shortcuts.

- Practicing test-driven development, behavior-driven development, or other test-first techniques.

- Designing object-oriented solutions to the kata problem.

- Refactoring and code design practice.

You can make katas even more interesting by changing the way you approach them. One valuable technique you can employ when undertaking a coding kata with a partner is to play ping-pong. You write a failing test to represent a single behavior and your partner must write the simplest code possible to make the test pass. Then your partner writes a test for you to in the simplest way. You pass the problem back and forth, alternately writing a test or making one pass. You may even find that this practice makes its way into your daily working methods.

Another challenge you can set yourself during a coding kata is to use only the keyboard to complete the task. By discarding all other input devices, you will find interesting and helpful keyboard shortcuts to perform the operations you normally undertake using point, click, and touch.

© Steve Fenton 2018

S. Fenton, *Pro TypeScript*, https://doi.org/10.1007/978-1-4842-3249-1

■ **Note**   The term *coding kata* was coined by "Pragmatic" Dave Thomas. He also maintains a library of kata ideas at `http://codekata.com/`.

Performing a Kata

All you need to perform a coding kata is the following:

- A development environment;

- A test framework or library (see Chapter 9);

- A kata problem.

A coding kata is designed to let you practice the test-driven development cycle of red-green-refactor. This process involves writing a test and ensuring it fails, writing the simplest transformation of your code to pass the test, and refactoring your code once a design becomes obvious. The kata allows you to try ideas in the small that you can later apply to much larger problems. When you come to solve complex real-world problems, the techniques acquired during coding katas will guide you to the right abstraction.

■ **Note**   There are two important terms to remember at this stage. A transformation is a change to the behavior of your code, and a refactoring is a change to your code that doesn't affect the behavior. These are the only two kinds of code change that you'll make in your code.

When you first start working on coding katas, it can help to approach the problem incrementally. Don't read too far ahead; just work through the problem one small step at a time. As you gain confidence, you can practice by undertaking a larger problem and decomposing it to individual tests yourself.

There are several key aspects that you can learn and improve by working on the test-driven design discipline:

- How to break down a complex problem into a single next actionable step.

- The difference between transformations (changing the behavior of your code to pass a test) and refactoring (changing the design of your code without affecting behavior); and how to perform them both.

- Finding the correct level of isolation to ensure your tests do not need to change when you refactor your code.

- How to make tests pass with shameless, simple code; and how to delay the introduction of abstractions until the design becomes obvious.

You can use the same katas to exercise different coding muscles, for example, by focusing specifically on writing the simplest, most readable code to solve the problem on one occasion, and experimenting with different levels of isolation on another. You can also use previously completed katas as the starting point for a kata to refactor the code.

The rules of the kata should reflect the aspirations of the team; this usually means following practices such as test-first programming, pairing, and refactoring. With TypeScript in particular, you should aim to exercise the object-oriented programming practices described in Chapter 3.

Example: The Fizz Buzz Kata

The Fizz Buzz Kata is the canonical example of a coding kata. It originated as a job interview test created by Imran Ghory based on the children's game Fizz Buzz. The original game can be summed up in just a few simple rules, but as the program increases in size to satisfy the rules, it should be just complex enough to give rise to one of many possible design solutions. You can read Imran's original article on his website:

`https://imranontech.com/2007/01/24/using-fizzbuzz-to-find-developers-who-grok-coding/`

There are several key aspects that you can learn and improve by working on the test-driven design discipline:

- Write a program that outputs numbers from 1 to 100.

- For any number that is divisible by three, replace the number in the output with the word Fizz.

- For any number that is divisible by five, replace the number in the output with the word Buzz.

- For any number that is divisible by both three and five, replace the number in the output with the word FizzBuzz.

These requirements are typically enough to stretch your programming muscles. You can use this version, or you can modify and extend it; there is nothing wrong with adapting this kata based on some of the variations of the game or by adding a new rule of your own invention. Known alternative versions of Fizz Buzz include one based on whether the number contains a digit, rather than being divisible by a number, another introduces an additional rule for any prime number in the sequence.

This is a good solid example of a kata, but there are many different ideas to stop you from getting bored. See the references at the end of the appendix for where to find more.

Common Coding Kata Rules

To get as much benefit as possible from the test-driven design process, there are some elements of discipline to follow. These elements are summarized below. You may feel a bit overwhelmed by these rules, principles, and catchphrases, but if this is the case you can start with minimal restrictions and gradually add them as you feel you have mastered your current set.

- We are going to write a test before we write any implementation; this will drive the code to only satisfy known tests, and prompt us to think of test scenarios before we write code.

- We will keep our tests de-coupled from our code. We won't create tests for each function, class, or module – but instead have a set of tests around a set of behaviors. The exact implementation details (i.e., there might be multiple classes and methods satisfying the test) should be invisible in the tests.

- Each individual change we make, no matter how small, should result in working code. When we refactor, the tests should pass every time we stop typing.

There are also a couple of catchy slogans to deal with before we continue.

- Arrange-Act-Assert. Also known as the triple-A, or AAA pattern. This describes the shape of each test you write, which will have code to arrange the program under test, perform an action, and assert the result. Despite this test shape, it is beneficial to start writing your test with the assertion, as it provides focus on the problem at hand.

- Red-Green-Refactor. This is an important concept about using three independent mindsets at different points in the process. When you are writing code to pass a test, speed is more important than design; so you should write whatever is the simplest code that will pass the test. This is important as you should be focussed on passing the test and nothing else. Only when you have iterated the problem for some time, and have only passing tests, should you switch to the refactor mindset – and only when you are refactoring should you think about design.

It can be tempting to start your program with a design pattern, or other solution that you think will provide the correct abstraction for the problem. However, it is better to tolerate duplication in your code rather than anticipate the wrong abstraction. Many of the most time-consuming and complex problems caused in your codebase will be a direct result of choosing the wrong design very early, before the correct design made itself clear. Once you have a working program, the correct abstraction is usually obvious. Additionally, by deferring the refactoring, your tests are less likely to be coupled to your implementation details. In the words of Sandi Metz and Katrina Owen in their book, *99 Bottles of OOP*:

"You should not reach for abstractions, but instead resist them until they absolutely insit upon being created."

If you can't wait to get started, turn back to Chapter 10 for the details of writing tests with the Jest framework. If you are interested in using a behavior-driven development framework for TypeScript that supports the Gherkin syntax for the business specifications, I have written an example using TypeScript that you can learn about on GitHub:

```
https://github.com/Steve-Fenton/TypeSpec
```

Summary

Once you have practiced the Fizz Buzz kata, there are many more available online (for example, `http://codekata.com`). Don't be limited by existing lists of coding katas though; invent your own based on games or problems that you have encountered. The original coding kata was an experiment with different solutions to a real problem in a production system; so, if you are about to add a feature to your program, run a kata to generate and evaluate possible solutions.

You can use the following resources to learn more about katas and test-driven development.

- *Test Driven Development: By Example* (Addison-Wesley, 2002) by Kent Beck

- *The Coding Dojo Handbook* (Emily Bache, 2013) by Emily Bache

- *99 Bottles of OOP* (e-book, 2016) by Sandi Metz and Katrina Owen

- Ian Cooper's NDC presentation: "TDD: Where Did It All Go Wrong?"

  ```
  https://vimeo.com/68375232
  ```

Index

A

Abstract factory pattern, 116–117
Acts function, 125
addEventListener method, 168
allowJs flag, 272
Ambient light sensor, 188
AND (&&) operator, 28, 274–275
ApplicationError class, 219
Application programming interfaces (APIs), 129
Apply method, 135–136
applyBindings method, 239–240
Arrange-Act-Assert (AAA), 280
Aspect-oriented programming (AOP), 77
Asynchronous JavaScript and XML (AJAX)
 HTTP Get, 170–171
 HTTP Post, 171–172
Asynchronous Module Definition (AMD), 266–267
attachEvent method, 167, 168
Automated testing, 245
 frameworks, 246
 Jest (*see* Jest)
 overview, 245

B

BatteryManager interface, 185
Battery status, 185–186
Bit flags, 273–274
Bitwise operator
 AND, 274–275
 NOT, 275
 OR, 275
 XOR, 275
Book project
 adding book routes, 208–209
 CSS, 207
 data collection
  HTML attributes, 209
  submit function, 210
  updated routes, 211

data storage
 Book Form completion, 215
 bookSchema variable, 213
 book variable, 213
 list function, 213
 Pug template, 214
 submit function, 214
 updated handlers, 212–213
home page route handler, 206
MongoDB, 211–212
MongoDB installation, 211
NPM packages, 205
Pug template, 206–207
server output, 207–208
Server.ts, 205
Browser engine, 160

C

CarWashProgram class, 118, 120
Cascading style sheets (CSS), 160
checkJs flag, 272
Classes
 abstract class, 53–54
 access modifiers, 49
 class heritage, 51–53
 constructors, 47–48
 instanceof operator, 56–57
 name property, 57
 in operator, 57
 properties and methods, 49–51
 regular expression, 58
 scope
  callbacks and events, 56
  context, 54
  ECMAScript, 55
  event capturing, 55
  instance methods, 56
  property and arrow
   function, 54
  registerClick method, 55

■ T

Get the eBook for only $5!

Why limit yourself?

With most of our titles available in both PDF and ePUB format, you can access your content wherever and however you wish—on your PC, phone, tablet, or reader.

Since you've purchased this print book, we are happy to offer you the eBook for just $5.

To learn more, go to http://www.apress.com/companion or contact support@apress.com.

Apress®

Printed in the United States
By Bookmasters